SPIRITUAL TRUTHS

for

OVERCOMING ADVERSITY

Life-Changing BIBLICAL INSIGHTS
on Christian Difficulties

SPIRITUAL TRUTHS

for

OVERCOMING ADVERSITY

Life-Changing BIBLICAL INSIGHTS
on Christian Difficulties

GREG HINNANT

CREATION HOUSE
A STRANG COMPANY

Spiritual Truths for Overcoming Adversity by Greg Hinnant
Published by Creation House, A Strang Company
600 Rinehart Road, Lake Mary, Florida 32746
www.strangbookgroup.com

Unless otherwise noted, all Scripture quotations are from the New Scofield Reference Bible, King James Version (New York: Oxford University Press, 1967). The New Scofield Reference Bible contains introductions, annotations, subject chain references, and some word changes in the King James Version that will help the reader.

Scripture quotations marked AMP are from the Amplified Bible. Old Testament copyright © 1965, 1987 by the Zondervan Corporation. The Amplified New Testament copyright © 1954, 1958, 1987 by the Lockman Foundation. Used by permission.

Scripture quotations marked ESV are from the Holy Bible, English Stand Version, copyright © 2001 by Crossway Bibles, a division of Good News Publisher. Used by permission.

Scripture quotations marked GNT are from Good News Translation (Today's English Version, second edition). Copyright © 1992 American Bible Society. All rights reserved.

Scripture quotations marked NAS are from the New American Standard Bible. Copyright © 1960, 1962, 1963, 1968, 1971, 1972, 1973, 1975, 1977, 1995 by the Lockman Foundation. Used by permission (www.Lockman.org).

Scripture quotations marked NCV are from The Holy Bible, New Century Version. Copyright © 1987, 1988, 1991 by Word Publishing, Dallas, Texas 75039. Used by permission.

Scripture quotations marked NIV are from the Holy Bible, New International Version of the Bible. Copyright © 1973, 1978, 1984, International Bible Society. Used by permission.

Scripture quotations marked NKJV are from the New King James Version of the Bible. Copyright © 1979, 1980, 1982 by Thomas Nelson, Inc., publishers. Used by permission.

Scripture quotations marked NLT are from the Holy Bible, New Living Translation, copyright © 1996, 2004. Used by permission of Tyndale House Publishers, Inc., Wheaton, IL 60189. All rights reserved.

Scripture quotations marked THE MESSAGE are from The Message: The Bible in Contemporary English, copyright © 1993, 1994, 1995, 1996, 2000, 2001, 2002. Used by permission of NavPress Publishing Group.

Scripture quotations marked WEY are from Weymouth's New Testament in Modern Speech by Richard Francis Weymouth. Copyright © 1939 by The Pilgrim Press, Cleveland, Ohio.

Scripture quotations marked YLT are from Young's Literal Translations by Robert Young, 1989. Reprinted by Baker Book House, Grand Rapids, Michigan, copyright © 2003.

Author's Note: Some Scripture quotations have specific words and/or phrases that I am emphasizing. I have added italics to these verses to show that emphasis. Also, in some of the Scripture quotations, with the exception of the Amplified Bible, I have inserted in brackets explanatory text to help with the understanding of certain words or phrases.

Design Director: Bill Johnson
Cover design by Rachel Lopez

Visit the author's website: www.greghinnantministries.org

Library of Congress Control Number: 2010940914
International Standard Book Number: 978-1-61638-439-5

First Edition

10 11 12 13 14 — 9 8 7 6 5 4 3 2 1
Printed in Canada

CONTENTS

God forges us
on an anvil of adversity
for a purpose known only to Him.
That is the way He
prepares us for
life.

—J. E. Broyhill

PREFACE

THOUGH WE WOULD prefer to live in continuous success and prosperity, adversity cannot be avoided in the way of true Christianity. In a fallen world, loyalty to God and His Word carries with it a permanently fixed price tag. Jesus taught, "Tribulation or persecution ariseth because of the word" (Matt. 13:21). When the enemy comes in like a flood, our reaction is crucial. It makes or breaks us as disciples of Jesus Christ.

Satan attacks serious Christians with a set purpose in view. He seeks to cause us to become offended with God, to end our fellowship with Him, to halt the development of our Christian character, and to prevent us from bearing further fruit unto God. If we fail to overcome our trials, Satan's objectives are realized.

God, on the other hand, permits Satan's onslaughts for His own equally clear purpose. He is using the enemy and his agents to train us in scriptural thinking and spiritual living and to establish us as full-fledged overcomers. When our season of testing arrives, if we sit down with Jacob and sob, "All these things are against me" (Gen. 42:36), we will never overcome. But if we learn the fundamental secret of accepting every circumstance as being from the hand of God and determine to keep His Word patiently, we will rise above the wiles of the enemy every time. With each new spiritual victory we will grow in knowledge of God, strength of character, discernment, spiritual authority, and Christian compassion. In this way God prepares us to rule eternally with Christ.

But to overcome and thus qualify to rule with Christ, we must have *spiritual understanding*, or God-given insight, concerning our various trials; we must see them from God's viewpoint. Nothing else will hold us steady in the time of trouble: "Understanding shall keep thee" (Prov. 2:11). The Bible is the only source of this precious spiritual understanding, and we must constantly turn to it for help in difficult times.

This book contains spiritual truths mined from the pages of the Bible. These simple yet powerful and timeless truths are capable of sustaining us when the spiritual "winds, rains, and floods" beat vehemently and relentlessly against our "houses" of faith. For frightened Christian pilgrims caught in the storms of adversity, these truths illuminate God's pathway through the darkness and show us what the Lord would have us think, say, and do. If faithfully and tenaciously obeyed, they will bring us safely through to the end of every test.

Born in the study of the Scriptures, proven in the fires of testing, and confirmed in numerous lives, these spiritual truths are offered here to those who seek to overcome every adversity they meet.

—GREG HINNANT

THE ATTITUDE OF ACCEPTANCE

In everything give thanks; for this is the will of God in Christ Jesus concerning you.

—1 Thessalonians 5:18

W E EITHER ACCEPT or reject everything we meet daily. As life acts upon us, we react. However proactive we may be, we nevertheless spend much of our time reacting to life's assaults on our souls. Aware of this, God has dedicated a considerable portion of His Word, the Bible, to teaching us how to react to life.

Untaught, our initial reaction to any adverse thing is...*resist it!* Rebels by nature and stubborn by habit, it doesn't take much to get our neck stiff and our war mode activated: "Ye stiff-necked...ye do always resist the Holy Spirit; as your fathers did, so do ye" (Acts 7:51). "Ye fight and war" (James 4:2). From the womb we strive, argue, rebel, protest, and fight against everything and everyone we dislike. We need no training, no education in the art of resistance. It comes naturally, immediately, instinctively. The "old man," or sin nature, in each of us has an inborn aversion for all forms of change or trouble. When undesirable change confronts us—even that which is clearly helpful—we reach for our sword to combat this unauthorized intruder. And we go all lengths to avoid trouble, dodging, ducking, and denying with the utmost speed and cleverness.

Off-key with resistance as we are, we need to hear the right keynote, or keyword, to sing and live in harmony with God in this life.

An Inspired Keyword

Through redemption, God has undertaken the enormous task of transforming confirmed resisters, such as you and me, into practicing acceptors. To facilitate this wonder He has given us an inspired keyword: 1 Thessalonians 5:18. Consider these renderings of this transformative New Testament verse that encapsulates the attitude of acceptance, which is the prime principle of overcomers:

> In everything give thanks: for this is the will of God in Christ Jesus concerning you.
>
> —KJV

> Give thanks in all circumstances, for this is God's will for you in Christ Jesus.
>
> —NIV

> Give thanks whatever happens. That is what God wants for you in Christ Jesus.
>
> —NCV

> Thank God no matter what happens. This is the way God wants you who belong to Christ Jesus to live.
>
> —The Message

By commanding us to give Him thanks in every situation, God seeks to instill in us that habit of accepting all happenings and events—good, bad, and in between—as coming directly from Him, even if Satan and his servants, including disobedient Christians, are sometimes the errand boys.

The Book of Job, more clearly than any other biblical text, shows that everything that touches God's redeemed ones comes by His personal permission. Satan could not touch Job, or anyone or anything pertaining to him, until God personally reviewed his proposal and "signed off" on it (Job 1:12; 2:6). This text also affords us some excellent examples of an overcomer giving thanks in all situations. When on two separate occasions multiple, mean-spirited adversities of the worst and lowest kind suddenly struck Job, his reaction was stellar: "The LORD gave, and the

L<small>ORD</small> hath taken away" (Job 1:21); "Shall we receive good at the hand of God, and shall we not receive evil?" (Job 2:10). But why give thanks?

W<small>HY</small> A<small>CCEPT</small> E<small>VERY</small> S<small>ITUATION</small>? W<small>HY</small> G<small>IVE</small> T<small>HANKS</small>?

If you are wondering why God asks you to accept and give thanks in "all circumstances," or "no matter what happens," you're not alone. Every thoughtful Christian wonders the same.

The Founder of sound reason as well as the Father of strong faith, God has good reasons for ordering us to "in everything give thanks." Here are some excellent ones.

It's a matter of obedience.

In our quest to discover deeper insights hidden in Bible verses, we sometimes overlook the obvious.

In this context, we should develop the attitude of acceptance, embracing every new change with fresh thanks to God, for one huge reason: God says so! It's a matter of obedience. When men speak, we do well to question first, and then, if reason confirms the order, obey. But when God speaks, the opposite is the mark of supreme wisdom and sublime trust: We should obey first and question later—"Trust in the Lord with all thine heart, and lean not unto thine own understanding" (Prov. 3:5)—knowing God always has His reasons, and they're always wise and good. That God says, "In everything give thanks" is reason enough for the truly child-hearted Christian. The heavenly Father has spoken! We need only obey!

Every such act of obedience honors God, humbles us, and makes us more fit for God's use.

It's God's will.

God is as kind as He is powerful, and His commands are always accompanied by reasonable explanations sufficient to satisfy our need to know why. If we ponder the explanations He gives, they will inspire us to rise and obey the command He issues.

In 1 Thessalonians 5:18, He commands, "Give thanks in all circumstances" (NIV); then He explains, "For this is God's will for you in Christ Jesus." This reveals that God wants us to give thanks every time we meet new situations or changes because:

1. *Thanksgiving is God's will.* He wants us offering thanks and praise, instead of murmuring and complaining, in every situation every day of our lives. This is the New Testament "sacrifice of praise, that is the fruit of our lips giving thanks to his name" (Heb. 13:15). The thankful Christian is God's will incarnate.

2. *Every situation we meet is God's will.* As taught in Job 1–2, everything that touches our life has been divinely approved. Whether sweet or bitter, easy or hard, exciting or monotonous, it will serve a divine purpose in or for us, if we only react with trust and obedience instead of offense. (See Romans 8:28.)

It enables us to access God's wisdom.

By giving thanks to God in every scenario, we acknowledge His sovereignty and wisdom in permitting it. Without this, we can't obtain God's wisdom to help us know how to react properly. Why?

To fail to give thanks is to fail to accept God's will, and to fail to accept His will is to reject it—and Him! When we reject the trouble or undesired changes God wills to send us, we cut ourselves off from His help, especially His wisdom, or good judgment in the spontaneous and fluid situations of life. Rejecting God's will puts us in rebellion, and rebellion severs all communications with heaven. But acceptance reverses this. The instant we accept our problems as from Him, God's wisdom becomes accessible.

James 1:2–5 confirms this. The order of James' instructions is inspired. First he commands, "My brethren, count it all joy when ye fall into various trials" (v. 2). Then he adds, "If any of you lack wisdom, let him ask of God, who giveth to all men liberally...and it shall be given him" (v. 5). This ordering implies if we joyfully accept our problems when we "fall into various trials," we may then "ask of God" for His wisdom and expect Him to give it.

We begin receiving insight from Him and, after prayerfully searching His Word, eventually discover His full mind in the matter. We recognize what He wants changed, how to change it, and what He wants left alone. We distinguish matters needing quick, decisive action from those needing believing, persistent prayer only. We recognize temptations and say no, and we see open doors and say yes. We discern God's initiatives and Satan's impostors. We sense God's appointments and Satan's distractions. We recognize demonic opposition to God's will and how God would have us "resist the devil" (James 4:7)—by speaking God's Word aloud as Jesus did (Luke 4:4–12), prayerfully and patiently reasoning with opponents, or simply maintaining the position to which God has called us. We know when to say little and when to speak freely. Thus we react wisely in our tests.

These good decisions in the free-flowing situations of life are withheld from Christians who consistently resist, but they're freely released to those who acknowledge God's sovereign wisdom in every circumstance with three simple words, spoken from the heart: "Thank You, Lord!"

It enables us to see ways of escape.

When Abraham accepted his severe test and grasped the knife to slay Isaac, his son, the angel of the Lord opened his eyes to see the "ram caught in a thicket" (Gen. 22:13). God had a way of escape already prepared for Abraham, but he couldn't see it until he had fully accepted the painful obedience God asked. Put simply, acceptance showed him the way out. It does the same for us.

The attitude of acceptance opens our eyes to hidden solutions and escapes God has already provided for us. When we embrace our tests, however trying, the Holy Spirit immediately begins illuminating the way out of our maze. Our "ram," or divinely prepared way of escape, is soon clearly visible. God has promised this: "God is faithful, who will not permit you to be tempted above that ye are able, but will, with the temptation, also make the way to escape" (1 Cor. 10:13). His way out will not always be what we wanted or prayed for, but it will always be perfect—the very best solution conceivable under the present circumstances.

Conversely, resistance hides God's solutions from us. It leaves us "carnally minded," or unspiritual in our thinking, seeing life without the Holy Spirit's liberating insight and peaceful guidance. We see only the visible, the natural, the human side of things, not the invisible, the spiritual, the providential. We see only stubborn people and unsolved problems. As with Balaam, the very "angel of the Lord" (Christ) could be standing right in front of us and we wouldn't even realize it (Num. 22:31). We think only of our wants, not God's will; our comfort, not others' needs; our immediate relief, not God's eternal purposes. It is a blindness we cannot afford.

For this reason Paul prayed that "the eyes of your understanding [might be] enlightened" (Eph. 1:18). Meeting every situation with "Thank You, Jesus" enables God to answer Paul's prayer in your soul. Will you accept what you're in so you can see your way out?

Some clarification is needed at this point.

Clarifying: How to Fight, How Not to Fight

The attitude of acceptance is *not* mere passivity. God doesn't want us to lie down and play dead, allowing everyone and everything to simply run over us, no questions asked or prayers raised. The fatalistic mentality—"what will be, will be"—neither pleases God nor accomplishes His will.

In these tumultuous last days, Jesus needs strong vessels, not limp dishrags. He takes no delight in apathetic souls. Rather, He calls us to fight, not naturally but spiritually; not in our ways and strength but in His ways, His wisdom, His power; not to have our way but to insist that He has His way: "*Thy will* be done...in earth" (Luke 11:2). This is the "good fight" of vigorous New Testament faith. As the much-afflicted apostle and chief of overcomers, Paul, wrote his disciple, Timothy, "I have fought a *good fight*...I have kept the faith" (2 Tim. 4:7).

Paradoxically, to fight this good fight and keep our faith, we must not resist—or rebel against our circumstances. When we do, we don't fight in the proper way. When our basic reaction to trouble is to reject it outright, we neither think wisely nor act swiftly in the heat of trial. Instead we become offended, anger simmers, fear and discouragement set in, and we lie down and quit trusting and obeying God. Then the devil and his workers of iniquity promptly trample us under their feet. But when we accept adversity as being allowed by God to train us, we see clearly how He would have us do spiritual battle. Consequently, we stand, pray, hear from heaven, make wise decisions, take bold action, confound our enemies, check the devil's plans, and overcome!

The Christian who rebels against his tests succumbs constantly to Satan's subtle strategies. These "wiles" of the devil are always intended to provoke us to disobey Christ's commands. Jesus said, "But I say unto you that ye *resist not evil*" (Matt. 5:39). In this context "evil" (Greek *ponēros*) means "wicked, evil, hurtful"[1] people and the acts they commit that cause the righteous to experience adversity, injustice, and affliction. By resisting adversity, then, we are disobeying our Lord. That's exactly what the enemy wants. By our disobedience, we put ourselves over onto his ground. Having yielded to the spirit of disobedience, we become temporarily subject to Satan, the arch disobeyer: "Know ye not that to whom ye yield yourselves servants to obey, his servants ye are whom ye obey, whether of sin...or of obedience?" (Rom. 6:16). If we accept and stand, we overcome. But when we rise up to fight, we come under the enemy's influence. To fight in the natural is to lose in the spiritual. If we disobey Jesus, Satan wins.

After being grievously cheated and insulted by Nabal, David hastily gave the order, "Gird ye on every man his sword," and went forth to take vengeance on Nabal—and inevitably slaughter many innocents in the process (1 Sam. 25:13). When Abigail, Nabal's wife, met David, he was headed straight for spiritual failure. Had he not yielded to her wise counsel, he would have played right into the devil's hands, displeased God, and possibly lost His approval for service. Satan's strategy operating through Nabal, aimed at provoking David to commit murder, would have been successful. And the enemy would have had a legitimate reproach to bring against the Lord and His servant.

The Overcomer's Psychological Foundation

The attitude of acceptance is the great psychological foundation of all overcomers. They have a common keyword, key revelation, and key determination imbedded in their souls.

The keyword, or spiritual keynote, which we discussed earlier, is 1 Thessalonians 5:18. As long as they "give thanks whatever happens," overcomers sing in tune with God and rise above "whatever." The key revelation is, "This thing is from me" (1 Kings 12:24). This reminds overcomers that, whoever delivers it, every situational package sent them is *from above*—even if it passed through the lower regions before arriving. As John the Baptist put it, "A man can receive *nothing*, except it be *given him from heaven*" (John 3:27). The overcomer is convinced God controls everything that breaks through the all-encompassing angelic "hedge" surrounding his life (Job 1:10) and turns it, sooner or later, to serve His higher purposes (Rom. 8:28). Gripped and nourished by this keyword and key revelation, overcomers determine to accept every circumstance, no matter how adverse. Why? They realize that to reject their tests is to fail their examinations before they've even begun. So they say to every adversity, "Ye thought evil against me; but *God meant it unto good*" (Gen. 50:20).

This biblical psychological foundation drives a distinctly different behavior pattern and propels overcomers onward and upward over adversities that drive others down into defeat. Overcomers accept what other Christians reject. When they rebel, overcomers yield. When they harden their necks in pride, overcomers bend and submit to Jesus' yoke of meekness. When, offended, they fall, overcomers stand, "approved unto God" (2 Tim. 2:15). When they turn back, overcomers press on, finish their race, and win a full reward—from the Chief Overcomer.

JESUS THE OVERCOMER—AND PETER THE OVERCOME!

We see the attitude of acceptance on display in Jesus and its opposite in Peter when the two were suddenly faced with Judas' treachery in the garden of Gethsemane.

> Judas then, having received a band of men and officers from the chief priests and Pharisees, cometh...
> —JOHN 18:3

> Then Simon Peter, having a sword, drew it, and smote the high priest's servant, and cut off his right ear.... Then said Jesus unto Peter, Put up thy sword into the sheath; the cup which my Father hath given me, shall I not drink it?
> —JOHN 18:10–11

In the garden Peter resisted and Jesus accepted. Peter fell, while Jesus stood. Peter came under, while Jesus came over. Peter was gripped with fear and panic, while Jesus remained calm in faith. Peter rebelled and therefore could not see the hand of God in it all. Jesus accepted the evil as from above—"the cup which my Father hath given me"—and therefore endured as seeing Him who is invisible.

Due to the sorrow Peter was experiencing, he collapsed. For the joy set before Him, Jesus stood and walked steadily forward. Because Peter resisted, he failed in the fiery trial. Because Jesus accepted, He overcame everything and everyone—Judas, Pilate, the chief priests, the blood-thirsty crowd, the Roman executioners, the mocking onlookers, the thief who reviled him, the devil, and death itself. What more could He have overcome?

After the Lord's resurrection, Peter experienced a second conversion. This was not a religious conversion to faith in Christ (he had already experienced that) but an attitude conversion, a distinct change in his basic outlook on life in general and adversity in particular. Peter was transformed from a typically human resister into an unusually spiritual accepter. Then the Lord took him and used him to help other believers learn, among many other doctrines, the attitude of acceptance. We see evidence of this in Peter's epistles:

> For God is pleased with you when you do what you know is right and patiently endure unfair treatment....If you suffer for doing good and endure it patiently, God is pleased with you.
> —1 PETER 2:19–20, NLT

So Jesus' prophecy was fulfilled: "When thou [Peter] art converted, strengthen thy brethren" (Luke 22:32). Peter put away his sword permanently. From that point on he received every "cup" his heavenly Father gave him, even as Jesus had, and grew steadily in the grace of acceptance, being ever more "conformed to the image of his Son" (Rom. 8:29). So complete was his transformation that in the end he quietly accepted martyrdom at the hands of Roman executioners, evil as it was, because this too was part of "the will of God in Christ Jesus" for him. (See John 21:18; 2 Peter 1:14.)

My friend, we must follow in Peter's footsteps and enter into the attitudinal conversion he experienced. When we "fall into various trials" (James 1:2), we must train ourselves to react from the spiritual viewpoint. We must deliberately *think*, "Count it all joy" (v. 2), instead of "I can't take this anymore." We must deliberately *say*, "Thank You, Lord," instead of, "Oh no, look what the devil has done now!" We must consciously *"resist* the devil [his plan]" (James 4:7) by submitting to God's tests rather than submit to the devil's plan by rebelling against our tests. Then we can seek and receive God's wisdom, react according to His

Word, and in time discover our "way to escape." This plan of response will increasingly conform us, as it did Peter, to the image of the Chief Overcomer, Jesus.

From this day forward, let's put away our "swords" of resistance, accept every "cup" our Father sends, and overcome. This will generate amazing spiritual power.

THE POWER TO ENDURE

Be assured that the testing of your faith leads to power of endurance.
—JAMES 1:3, WEY

THE ATTITUDE OF acceptance will see every Christian through every test every day. And the more tests we pass through in obedience, the more spiritual power we gain.

"My brethren, count it all joy when ye fall into *various trials*" (James 1:2). "Various trials" are God's special means of strengthening us in Christ. Oh yes, we gain edification from meditation in God's Word, prayer, worship, and the fellowship of the saints, but this strength can evaporate quickly if we don't learn to pass our tests in the circumstances God arranges for us daily. Permanent strength of character comes only by passing through many tests of faith and patience in a submitted, obedient frame of mind: "Knowing this, that the testing of your faith *worketh patience*" (v. 3); or "develops perseverance (NIV); or "produces endurance" (NAS); or "produces steadfastness" (ESV).

George Mueller, whose orphanages in Bristol, England, eventually cared for 2,100 orphans a day by faith alone,[1] said:

> The only way to learn strong faith is to endure great trials. I have learned my faith by standing firm amid severe testings.[2]

THE POWER TO ENDURE

"Be assured that the testing of your faith leads to *power of endurance*" (James 1:3, WEY). This "power to endure" is the ability to bear stress with ease, to be in distress without distress being in you. It's God's supernatural grace manifested in us. Situations that wear out others beyond recovery don't exhaust our energies or love. We go through spiritual or emotional "fire" but are not burned by hatred; others inquisitively sniff but can't smell the smoke of bitterness on us. (See Daniel 3:1–30.) We walk calmly and steadily through the midst of the most dreadful difficulties conceivable without mental, physical, or emotional damage. In fearful circumstances, we're calm and unafraid. In offensive situations, we're not offended. When faced with deadlines, we work steadily but don't panic. When repeatedly wronged, we neither seek nor desire revenge. (See Genesis 50:15–21.)

Where does this exceptional grace, this power to endure, come from? Not merely from Bible study, prayer, fellowship, or worship, but from personal victories gained in personal tests—lots of them! We "buy," or pay the price to obtain, this power to endure by surrendering our proud will and humbly obeying God's will in the thick of these trying situations. Like the wise virgins of Jesus' parable, wise Christians urge us to "buy" this valuable spiritual commodity: "Go…and *buy* for yourselves…" (Matt. 25:9). Every spiritually awakened Christian will soon be "buying" the power to endure in these challenging last days before Jesus appears to receive us: "…and while they went to *buy*" (v. 10). If we "buy" enough of it, we'll become "rich."

So precious is this overcoming grace, and the faith and knowledge of God it fosters, that Jesus likens it to *gold*: "I counsel thee to buy of me *gold tried in the fire…*" (Rev. 3:18). And He openly urges us to make it our ambition to become "rich" in this spiritual wealth: "…that thou mayest be *rich*" (v. 18). Peter agrees. He urges us to endure our "manifold trials," however heavy and long, so we will be found spiritually rich when Jesus appears: "that the trial of your faith, being *much more precious than of gold* that perisheth, though it be tried with fire, might be found unto praise and honor and glory at the appearing of Jesus Christ" (1 Pet. 1:7).

Are you "rich" in the power to endure? Are you "buying" it? For that you must submit to a spiritual training process.

A MATTER OF SPIRITUAL CONDITIONING

The power to endure is largely a matter of spiritual conditioning, of what level of difficulties we become capable of handling.

Every test we go through successfully conditions or prepares us to go through the next one. The more we take, the more we can take. Every strain we accept and bear in full submission to God enlarges us and creates within us the ability to bear even greater adversities with equal ease. In this way, our tests are constantly taking us from one level of strength to a greater one. Every time we pass through another "valley of Baca," or place of sorrowful, tearful trials, we "go from strength to strength—increasing in victorious power" (Ps. 84:6–7, AMP). Heavenly Olympians, we are growing in spiritual athleticism—thanks to our master Trainer!

A good athletic trainer knows his athlete's endurance level and how much he can take without breaking. He constantly pushes his trainee to the limits of his physical endurance, but never beyond. By repeated workouts at one maximum level of exertion, the trainee gains strength to increase his output. As his strength increases, his endurance level rises. This new strength must then be put to the test by being exercised. Realizing this, the trainer changes his trainee's workout schedule to increase its difficulty. He requires more of him, making him work harder. He pushes him beyond his former limit of endurance, but not beyond his new one. And so, by this discipline, a good athletic trainer increases his athlete's power to endure.

Our heavenly Father is *the* master Trainer. He knows our present personal capabilities perfectly—how much stress we can take, how much work we can turn out, how much confusion we can analyze and reorder, how much sorrow we can rise above, how long we can wait without becoming discouraged, and so forth. With the utmost sensitivity, He orders our personal tests according to our current abilities in Christ, never allowing the strain to be more than we can presently bear in Him: "God is faithful [utterly reliable], who will not permit you to be tempted above that which ye are able, but will, with the temptation, also make the way to escape, that ye may be able to bear it" (1 Cor. 10:13); or, "He will not let you be tempted beyond your ability" (ESV); or, "He will not allow the temptation to be more than you can stand" (NLT). What a deep comfort it is to know that, if our watchful, loving, faithful, heavenly Father "permits" a test, this is proof that "we are able" to endure it in perfect peace, as long as we trust and obey Him. When new challenges come, we can say, "If my Trainer permits it, I can perform it."

As we learn to overcome at one level of Christian experience, our spiritual strength is increasing. As we handle our God-given difficulties by carefully and consistently doing God's Word and will, our inner man is growing firmer and more established. With each new victory, God strengthens and hardens our resolve to endure: "I will strengthen and harden you to difficulties" (Isa. 41:10, AMP). This new spiritual strength calls for new testing. Therefore, our master Trainer increases our "workout schedule." He sends trials of greater severity and length. These new difficulties exercise our souls in new ways. They constrain us to "work out your own salvation" as never before (Phil. 2:12). But, ever faithful, God never pushes us beyond our current limit of endurance.

However, we sometimes think He has overworked us. We feel drained and pressed out of measure. Why? Before we accuse the Lord of poor training, let's examine ourselves. Are we accepting every detail of our circumstances as from the Lord? "In all thy ways *acknowledge him* [His presence, control, benevolent will]" (Prov. 3:6). Are we abiding in close fellowship with Him daily, faithfully walking in His "ways" (spiritual daily life habits), and obeying His biblical commands?

Our Trainer has made the conditions of spiritual success very plain. "*If ye abide in me, and my words abide in you*, ye shall ask what ye will, and it shall be done unto you" (John 15:7). If after God increases His demands on us, we find ourselves "out of it," or burned out, it's probably because we haven't yet fully accepted our circumstances as coming from Him, we haven't been taking enough time alone with Him, or we've not been doing His Word in our new setting. Instead of thanking and praising our Trainer, we're pouting inwardly at Him and, like lazy athletes, refusing to adapt ourselves to our new "workout schedule." As soon as we yield, we'll realize that God never lays upon us anything we cannot endure *abiding in Him.* His control of circumstances is amazing! Precise! Perfect! He gradually increases the severity of our tests, causing them to begin and end at just the right moment, all by His personal orders: "Thus far shalt thou come, but no farther" (Job 38:11).

DISOBEDIENCE REVERSES THE PROCESS

Any consistent disobedience on our part reverses God's spiritual training process.

When we rebel against today's tests, we're less fit to meet tomorrow's. We lose strength in our trials rather than gain it. And the more trials we pass through in disobedience, the more spiritual power we lose. Before long our power to endure is significantly diminished—and we begin recognizing it. One day it dawns on us: we're failing miserably in the same situations we formerly overcame with ease. Why should this matter to us?

Satan takes no timeouts. Mercilessly, methodically, frighteningly, our adversary sends his lethal legions—the adversities of life—marching right at us. This is no sport; it is war. Our adversary is not just fighting to win a match or contest; he's shooting to kill. His vexations are relentless and his onslaughts potentially fatal to faith. Sometimes we find ourselves wanting to signal "timeout" to heaven's referees. But none of us can stand still spiritually. Our daily trials are constantly taking us up or down, into greater strength or weakness of character. From this perpetual process of testing there is no escape.

Have we embraced this fact of spiritual life? If so, we'll fear God and avoid disobedience.

A RELATIVE THING

The power to endure is a relative thing. Our present circumstances seem easy or hard to us as we compare them to what we have become accustomed to in our past experiences.

When God's angels have protected you in a major hurricane, a gale doesn't frighten you. When the Lord has provided for you in a full-scale economic depression, a few months of recession seem easy. When by your God you have endured reproach from your own family and close friends, it's a light thing when strangers disparage you. When you have waited on God for years before seeing the answers to your prayers materialize, it's nothing to wait a few weeks or months for His hand to move. When you have seen God provide even when your income was completely cut off, a reduction in pay causes no panic. "His riches in glory" were sufficient before; they will be sufficient again (Phil. 4:19). Our past victories, therefore, make our current tests less formidable.

The overcomer's logic is simple: "God did it for me in the past; if I just continue abiding closely, He'll do it again." And he says with David, "The LORD who delivered me out of the paw of the *lion*, and out of the paw of the *bear*, he will deliver me out of the hand of *this Philistine*" (1 Sam. 17:37).

So don't complain about that "lion" of an enemy or fear your "bear" of a problem. They are only serving you. They are building into you the power to endure a "Goliath" of a challenge. Keep believing, trusting, and obeying God, so He may fully enlarge your strength of character: "Thou hast enlarged me when I was in distress" (Ps. 4:1). Today, with things just as they are, praise and thank God that "the testing of *your* faith leads to power of endurance" (James 1:3, WEY).

And be comforted—endurance training puts you in good company.

MADE STRONG THROUGH ADVERSITY

The righteous also shall hold on his way, and he that hath clean hands shall be stronger and stronger.

—JOB 17:9

THE COMPANY OF God's empowered endurers includes some of His greatest saints, like Job, Joseph, and Nehemiah.

These three spiritual giants were not born exceptional souls. Nor were they strengthened by exceptional parenting, teaching, or mentoring alone. Or by a sudden dynamic anointing of the Spirit alone. Their characters were each made strong through adversity—methodically forged in the fires of unwanted, undeserved, unfriendly trouble! Apart from it, they could never have become what God intended them to be.

Let's review the cases of these three exceptionally strong characters.

THE CASE OF JOB

In Job 17:1–9, Job describes his tribulation, prophesies the outcome he is expecting, and declares that his adversity will make him stronger. He frankly concedes that at the moment he is:

- **Sick and ready to die:** "My breath is corrupt, my days are extinct, the grave is ready for me" (v. 1).
- **Mocked and provoked continually:** "Are there not mockers with me? And doth not mine eye continue in their provocation?" (v. 2).

- **Trusted by no one:** "Who is he who will strike hands with me?" (v. 3).
- **Misunderstood by even his best friends:** "For thou hast hidden their heart from understanding" (v. 4).
- **A public laughingstock and reviled pitilessly:** "He hath made me also a byword of the people; and I was as one before whom men spit" (v. 6).
- **Oppressed with a sorrowful, hopeless outlook:** "Mine eye also is dim by reason of sorrow" (v. 7).

Yet in spite of all this trouble, Job declares confidently, "The righteous also shall hold on his way, and he that hath clean hands shall be stronger and stronger" (v. 9).

He believes firmly that any sufferer who is truly right with God and innocent of wrongdoing will keep up his good living right in the midst of unjustified affliction: "The righteous also shall *hold on his way*," or "The righteous *keep moving forward*" (NLT). Instead of being crushed by adversity, he will be strengthened by it. He further states that when the full truth is made known, good men, shocked, will rally behind him and rise to condemn the hypocrites who have risen to condemn him: "Upright men shall be astounded ['appalled,' NAS] at this, and the innocent shall stir up himself against the hypocrite" (v. 8).

What a mighty burst of faith! Job begins his speech with one foot in the grave and ends it by declaring that he fully expects to "grow stronger and stronger." Faith lifted him from the grave of despair to the rock of prophecy! (Compare Habakkuk 1:1–4 and 3:17–19 for a similarly dynamic upsurge of faith in a moment of deathly discouragement.)

Did Job's prophecy come true? The last chapter in the Book of Job describes "the end of the Lord" (James 5:11). When this blessed conclusion finally came, Job was purer in heart, humbler in spirit, clearer in spiritual vision, increased in knowledge, confirmed in faith, closer to God, restored in relationships, and richer in blessings. In every way, then, he was stronger for having passed through his divinely arranged adversity in trust and obedience. Then the Lord richly added other enviable human blessings—restored children, friends, possessions, reputation, and longevity (ministry too, I believe; see Job 4:3–4 and Job 42:16)—on top of all Job's rich spiritual growth: "So the LORD blessed the latter end of Job more than his beginning" (Job 42:12).

THE CASE OF JOSEPH

In the Book of Genesis, Joseph's adversity is described memorially in Jacob's prophetic blessing:

> Joseph is a fruitful bough, even a fruitful bough by a well, whose branches run over the wall. The archers have harassed him, and shot at him, and hated him; but his bow abode in strength, and the arms of his hands were made strong by the hands of the mighty God of Jacob.
>
> —GENESIS 49:22–24

Oh, how God immersed Joseph in adversity: "harassed," "shot at," "hated!" But, oh, how he was strengthened by it all! At the time his envious brothers sold him into slavery, he was just the fair-skinned favorite son of Jacob, surely protected and spared from excessive hardships: "Now Israel [Jacob] loved Joseph more than all his children, because he was the son of his old age" (Gen. 37:3).

But after God's ministry of adversity ran its course, this boy became a man. And what a man he was! With God-given wisdom and skill, he counseled kings, administrated great works, handed down judgments, and foretold the future. The psalmist wondered as he wrote: "He made him lord of his house, and ruler of all his substance, to bind his princes at his pleasure, and teach his elders wisdom" (Ps. 105:21–22).

When Joseph's brothers were later reunited with him, they saw no untested youth standing at the right hand of Pharaoh. No, Joseph had become a full-fledged man of God—wise, strong, and spiritual. Pharaoh was deeply impressed with Joseph: "And Pharaoh said...Can we find such an one as this is, a man in whom the Spirit of God is?...There is none so discreet and wise" (Gen. 41:38–39). The murderous persecution Jacob's older sons had instigated against their younger brother was intended to snuff him out. They hoped to terminate the "dreamer" (Gen. 37:19), as they called him, to quench his gift and silence his testimony forever. But God had something else in mind. He caused their very resistance to make Joseph strong and godly. His dreams and interpretations continued, the number of souls he helped increased greatly, and his testimony, not his termination, was established forever in the Holy Scriptures.

THE CASE OF NEHEMIAH

Nehemiah was also forged by the very fires his enemies stoked to incinerate him.

Of the Samaritan's malicious plan to stop his God-given work, the reconstruction of Jerusalem's walls, Nehemiah wrote, "They were all trying to frighten us, thinking, 'Their hands will get too weak for the work, and it will not be completed'" (Neh. 6:9, NIV). Then he added, "But I prayed, 'Now strengthen my hands'" (v. 9). God heard Nehemiah's brave request to strengthen his hands and made this strong man of God even stronger. As Job had predicted, "The righteous also...shall grow stronger and stronger" (Job 17:9). Rebuilding Jerusalem's walls was a tremendous task under even the best of conditions. But Nehemiah's circumstances were far from that. In fact, *they were the worst conditions conceivable.* Consider what he was up against.

His prime enemies, the Samaritans, were strong, outspoken, and very active. Throughout the reconstruction of the walls, they vexed Nehemiah daily, and with each new day came yet another cross for him to bear, courtesy of the Samaritans. Let's pause to ponder their persecutions:

> They tried to discourage him by mocking his and the other faithful Jews' efforts: "What are those feeble Jews doing? Will they restore their wall? Will they offer sacrifices? Will they finish in a day? Can

they bring the stones back to life from those heaps of rubble—burned as they are?" (Neh. 4:2, NIV).

They planned a secret paramilitary assault on the city: "And [they] conspired all of them together to come and to fight against Jerusalem" (Neh. 4:8). They apparently also plotted to ambush the individual Jewish laborers as they returned to their homes in the surrounding villages. The Jews' sympathetic neighbors informed them when they got wind of this plan: "The Jews who dwelt by them... said... From all places where ye shall return unto us they will be upon you" (v. 12).

They tried to waste Nehemiah's time in purposeless conversations aimed, not at finding common ground, but at setting him up for an assassination attempt: "That Sanballat... sent unto me, saying, Come, let us meet together in one of the villages in the plain of Ono. *But they thought to do me mischief*" (Neh. 6:2), or "But I realized they were plotting to harm me" (NLT).

They spread false reports about Nehemiah. One stated that he was planning to declare himself king of Judah and rebel openly against Persian authority: "Then sent Sanballat... an open letter... in which was written, It is reported among the nations, and Gashmu saith it, that thou and the Jews think to rebel [against Persian authority]; for which cause thou buildest the wall, that thou mayest be their king.... Now shall it be reported to the king [of Persia] according to these words" (Neh. 6:5-7).

They even hired false prophets to try to trick Nehemiah into breaking God's law so that they might truthfully accuse him of wrongdoing: "And, lo, I perceived that God had not sent him, but that he pronounced this prophecy against me; for Tobiah and Sanballat had hired him. Therefore was he hired, that I should be afraid, and do so, and sin, and that they might have a matter for an evil report, that they might reproach me" (vv. 12–13).

In addition to these numerous difficulties from outside his own "camp," Nehemiah had much to contend with from within. Consider these difficulties springing from his own people in Jerusalem:

> At first, the scene in Jerusalem was very depressing and the remnant quite discouraged: "The remnant...are in great affliction and reproach; the wall of Jerusalem also is broken down, and its gates are burned with fire" (Neh. 1:3).

> Some of the wealthier citizens refused to lower themselves to do manual labor: "Their nobles put not their necks to the work of their Lord" (Neh. 3:5), or "The leading men of the town refused to do the manual labor assigned to them by the supervisors" (GNT).

> The people who worked willingly suffered physical fatigue due to the sheer amount of work they had to do, and at times their morale dropped sharply: "The strength of the laborers is giving out" (Neh. 4:10, NIV).

> Many of the workers also suffered from lack of food and great indebtedness: "Some also there were who said, We have mortgaged our lands, vineyards, and houses, that we might buy grain" (Neh. 5:3).

> Worst of all, Nehemiah suffered treacherous betrayal. Many of his own people in Jerusalem were secretly informing Tobiah and Sanballat, his chief Samaritan enemies, of all his plans and movements as he made them. Repeatedly we read, "When Sanballat heard" (Neh. 2:10, 19; 4:1, 7, 15; 6:1, 16). How did he hear? Tobiah "was by [beside] him" (Neh. 4:3), passing along information he received in "many letters" disloyal Jewish nobles were sending him throughout the reconstruction period: "Moreover, in those days the nobles of Judah sent many letters unto Tobiah.... for there were many [informants] in Judah sworn unto him...and [they] uttered my words to him" (Neh. 6:17–19).

In the face of such extreme opposition we would expect to read that Nehemiah eventually threw up his hands, quit, and returned to Persia, where his life had presumably been relatively resistance free. But he did not. Held in place by his faith—that God would surely bless the doing of His express will, however fiercely resisted—Nehemiah "[held] on his way" (Job 17:9). And with the help of God's always all-sufficient grace, he grew "stronger and stronger" as the days went by.

Miraculously, he finished rebuilding the walls of Jerusalem in only fifty-two days. As his trial comes to its close, we see Nehemiah fully established in divine wisdom, strength, and authority. Afterward he went on to lead the nation in religious reform, initiating vital scriptural changes that brought spiritual refreshment to the people of God (Neh. 13:1–31).

His enemies, on the other hand, who had worked so feverishly to weaken him, emerged from the ordeal thoroughly undone. They were shaken, silent, and bitterly discouraged: "So the wall was finished... [and] when all our enemies heard of this, and... saw these things, they were much cast down in their own eyes; for they perceived that this work was wrought by our God" (Neh. 6:15–16). All their efforts had been aimed at stopping the wall; but now, there it stood, finished and complete before their very eyes. It could only mean one thing: God was with Nehemiah after all, and they were very wrong and foolish to resist him. Overcome and lifeless, they capitulated.

Having overcome, Nehemiah rose like an eagle on a mighty updraft of encouragement in God. Oswald Chambers writes:

> God does not give us overcoming life: He gives us life as we overcome. The strain is the strength. If there is no strain, there is no strength. Are you asking God to give you life and liberty and joy? He cannot, unless you will accept the strain. Immediately you face the strain, you will get the strength. Overcome your own timidity and take the step, and God will give you to eat of the tree of life and you will get nourishment.[1]

Your character empowerment will in some ways parallel the cases of Job, Joseph, and Nehemiah. God's method of making strong servants has never changed: "I am the LORD, I change not" (Mal. 3:6). He still sends not success, popularity, or ease, but *trouble* to make us "stronger and stronger." The Lord wants iron in our souls so we won't bend with the winds of religious fads. He wants to strengthen our knees so we'll stand strong under heavy responsibilities. He wants to firm up our spiritual backbones so we don't cower or collapse before our enemies' threats. And He wants to make our skin thick so we're not easily offended and turned inward with self-pity. Then we'll be ready for spiritual warfare in life, prayer, and ministry.

The apostle Paul, who walked closely with God, maintained a prolific prayer life, and ministered constantly, wrote, "Be strong in the Lord, and in the power of his might" (Eph. 6:10). He warned that we would encounter spiritual attacks from the "rulers of the darkness of this world" (v. 12). Every Christian who walks closely with God, intercedes effectively, and ministers faithfully arouses fierce opposition from the "prince of the power of the air" (Eph. 2:2). Indeed, Satan will incite sinners, carnal Christians, and false or unfaithful ministers alike to try to stamp out the humblest witness who faithfully holds to and holds forth God's Word. So we must become, spiritually speaking, like David's mighty men, "men of might, and men of war fit for the battle" (1 Chron. 12:8).

In these final, turbulent days of the Church Age, as never before the Lord needs strong Christian leaders—tested, proven souls who have been made strong through adversity. He's searching His church for those who are "fit for the master's use, and prepared unto every good work" (2 Tim. 2:21). Like Job, Joseph, and Nehemiah, they're strong, stable, and reliable. Will *you* be one?

If so, expect repetitive cycles of teaching and testing.

Chapter Four

TEACHING AND TESTING

Therefore, whosoever heareth these sayings of mine, and doeth them,
I will liken him unto a wise man, who built his house upon a rock.
And the rain descended, and the floods came, and the winds blew and
beat upon that house, and it fell not; for it was founded upon a rock.

And every one that heareth these sayings of mine, and doeth them
not, shall be likened unto a foolish man, who built his house upon
the sand. And the rain descended, and the floods came, and the
winds blew and beat upon that house, and it fell; and great was the
fall of it.

—MATTHEW 7:24–27

MOST BELIEVERS LOVE being taught but hate being tested. We
much prefer hearing to doing, listening to living, applauding
to applying. But Jesus insists on testing us on every bit of
spiritual truth we have heard. In the divine mind, teaching and testing
always go together, the two constant companions of the growing disciple
and developing spiritual leader.

In Christ, our lives are one unending cycle of teaching on the
mountain and testing in the valley.

Every time we meditate in or study God's Word, or receive instruction from our teachers, we are, in a sense, on the "mountain" of high,
inspiring revelation. We receive the Lord's instruction through His
Word or His teachers just as surely as His original disciples did from
Him personally during the Sermon on the Mount, probably delivered on
a hillside near Lake Galilee: "*He went up into a mountain*: and when he
was seated, his disciples came unto him. And he opened his mouth, *and*

taught them, saying…" (Matt. 5:1–2). The "mountain," therefore, is the place where we are exposed to eternal truth. It is God's classroom.

The "valley," on the other hand, is the place where we must work out, or exercise, God's truth in practical living. It is God's laboratory. There, in personal experience, we discover the reality of what we have heard on the mountain of instruction. For every truth we receive on the mountain, God creates a corresponding test in the valley. He leads us into these appointed places of testing by the invisible working of His Spirit, exactly as He did His own Son: "And Jesus…was led by the Spirit into the wilderness, being forty days tested by the devil" (Luke 4:1–2). The very layout of the text in Jesus' Sermon on the Mount confirms this.

The main body of the sermon is filled with teaching in which Jesus presents a wide range of spiritual truths that touch all areas of Christian thought and conduct (Matt. 5:1–7:23). Then, in the verses immediately following, He ends His sermon with a solemn prophetic warning of an approaching severe test (7:24–27). Thus, in the arrangement of the text, the Holy Spirit establishes a subtle "teaching-testing" pattern. What is His implied message?

Simply this: as Jesus' warning of testing follows immediately after the main body of His teaching in the Sermon on the Mount (which represents all His teachings), so it is in our lives. *Our God-arranged tests follow soon after our teaching sessions, our personal "sermons on the mount."* God teaches us, then tests us. We listen, then we live. We applaud, then we apply. Every lecture in God's classroom is followed by experimentation in the lab of daily living.

Jesus dealt in this manner with the original twelve disciples. He taught them on the mountain and then tested them in the valley. And their trials were not on random subjects, but always along the lines of what they had been taught. God carefully tailored circumstances to give Jesus' disciples opportunities to put into action the very truths Jesus had been teaching them.

THE SERMON ON THE MOUNT—
AND SITUATIONS IN THE VALLEY

Note carefully the connection between what Jesus taught the twelve disciples in the Sermon on the Mount and these situations that followed in their valley experiences.

Praying and trusting for provision

Jesus taught His disciples to trust their heavenly Father for their daily bread (Matt. 6:11, 25–34). He then tested them by asking Philip where they could find food for the hungry multitude: "When Jesus then lifted up his eyes, and saw a great company come unto him, he saith unto Philip, Where shall we buy bread, that these may eat? And *this he said to test him*; for he himself knew what he would do" (John 6:5–6).

Now it was time to live the lecture. Philip and the others were now to remember Jesus' charge to "take no [anxious] thought for your life" but instead to call on their heavenly Father in secret to supply, or direct them to, the provision they needed, and trust Him praisefully to "add" them. Forgetful of this, Philip fretted out loud: "Philip answered him, Two hundred denarii's worth of bread is not sufficient for them, that every one of them may take a little" (v. 7). Teaching forgotten; test failed.

Dealing with enemies

Jesus instructed the disciples on how to deal with their enemies: "Love your enemies, bless them that curse you, do good to them that hate you" (Matt. 5:44). Later He used their long-standing religious enemies, the Samaritans, to test them.

When some ungracious Samaritans prejudicially refused to receive Jesus because He was on His way to Jerusalem,[1] it was time to graciously practice Jesus' preaching and "love," "bless," or "do good" to these rude Samaritans (Luke 9:51–53). Instead, James and John forgot Jesus' teaching, remembered their prejudices, and, misapplying Elijah's example,[2] promptly called on God to "command fire to come down…and consume them, even as Elijah did" (Luke 9:54). Another teaching forgotten, and another test failed.

Accepting and enduring persecution

Jesus taught His disciples to glorify His Father by accepting and enduring persecution for being right with Him: "Blessed are they who are persecuted for righteousness' sake.…Let your light so shine before men, that they may see your good works, and glorify your Father, who is in heaven" (Matt. 5:10, 16). He tested them at the high priest's court (Matt. 26:69–75).

There Peter refused to accept persecution for righteousness' sake. Instead of suffering for Jesus, he swore for Him, vehemently denying knowing Jesus: "Then he began to invoke a curse on himself and to swear, 'I do not know the man'" (Matt. 26:74, ESV). Instead of letting his light shine and glorifying his heavenly Father, Peter hid his light under a bushel and grieved his heavenly Trainer. Yet another teaching forgotten, yet another test failed.

Praying with persistence

Jesus taught His disciples to pray with persistence: "Keep on asking, and you will receive what you ask for. Keep on seeking, and you will find. Keep on knocking, and the door will be opened to you" (Matt. 7:7, NLT). He tested them in Gethsemane.

There, instead of persisting in prayer, Peter, James, and John persisted in sleep: "And he cometh unto the disciples, and findeth them *asleep*.…And he came and found them *asleep again*" (Matt. 26:40, 43). Again, they failed to link their circumstances to His instruction and to respond.

Not resisting evildoers

Jesus charged His disciples to "resist not evil" (Matt. 5:39). He later tested them when evil incarnate, the treacherous turncoat Judas Iscariot, came with an armed mob to arrest Him: "And…Judas, one of the twelve, came, and with him a great multitude with swords and clubs" (Matt. 26:47).

Instantly, Peter drew his sword to resist the evildoers—exactly what his Master had taught him *not* to do. Another divinely tailored opportunity to obey passed up!

"Have faith in God"

Jesus exhorted His disciples to "have faith in God" (Mark 11:22). He then chose to test them during the days immediately before and after the greatest contradiction possible to their kingdom-now-centered faith: His shocking crucifixion.

In this crucible also they proved to be "slow of heart to believe all" that He had spoken (Luke 24:25). Before His death, they disbelieved His repeated personal, direct warnings of His upcoming crucifixion. After He rose, they time and again dismissed the numerous eyewitness reports of His resurrection He graciously sent to revive their faith (Mark 16:9–14). Please, not again!

These chosen ones seemed to have a permanent disconnection between their learning and their living. Why were they so distressingly dull?

Several valid reasons come to mind. First, they had not received the Holy Spirit, who alone gives the spiritual sensitivity, or situational awareness, that connects biblical teaching with providential events. Being "yet carnal" in their thinking, and unaided by the *Paracletos*, they were understandably slow to see and say, "It is the Lord" (John 21:7). Second, Jesus didn't announce when, where, and how their tests were to come. Their examinations always arose suddenly and passed as quickly. Third, despite Jesus' implicit warning in the design of the Sermon on the Mount, the disciples did not realize He had predetermined to test them after each teaching. So ignorance of His ways explains in part their dismal failures.

But we know His ways. The disciples' experience tells us plainly that the Lord, who "[changes] not" (Mal. 3:6) and is "the same, yesterday, and today, and forever" (Heb. 13:8), still deals with us today as He did the twelve. He teaches us, then tests us. We hear, and then we must do.

For instance, we are instructed on love and mercy. Shortly afterward we have an opportunity to forgive an offender, do good to an enemy, or help a stranger. Or we undertake and complete a thorough study on faithfulness. The next week we suffer a flood of self-depreciating, negative, unbelieving thoughts. Tempted hard to consider our work as futile, we almost give up faithfully executing our duties.

Another possible scenario is that, after hearing the word of faith, severe trouble besieges us. We are constrained to believe God and wait for His promised help as never before. Or after meditating on a message expounding the words, "Ye cannot serve God and money" (Matt. 6:24), a lucrative job offer comes our way. But accepting it will mean leaving a position we know God has called us to—and from which He has not released us.

These "valley" experiences are not accidental but providential. They are the Lord's tests. They are the experiential "labs" in which we put His truth into practice. And they always follow, sometimes very quickly, our teaching sessions. We hear, and days, sometimes hours, later, an opportunity arises for us to practice precisely the biblical truths we have heard.

Like the disciples, we often seem afflicted with chronic spiritual blindness. The Father puts His tests right in front of us, but we don't recognize them. We're "slow of heart to believe all" Jesus has told us, slow to believe He has sovereignly created situations in our lives to see if we'll obey Him or not. We lack faith—that amazing spiritual insight that sees God in not only every scripture but also every occurrence and that trusts every problem to Him. We're dominated more by carnal reasonings than by spiritual thoughts. Jesus taught that even "the very hairs of your head are all numbered" by our heavenly Father (Matt. 10:30). How then can anything touch our lives that He is not in, working all things toward some eternally good purpose? God forbid that we end up taught but not transformed.

ENCHANTED BUT UNCHANGED

God told Ezekiel that the Jews of the captivity enjoyed hearing his preaching, as they would any other form of good, clean entertainment, but they were not doing what he was saying:

> And they come unto thee as the people come, and they sit before thee as my people, and *they hear thy words, but they will not do them*.... And, lo, thou art unto them as a very lovely song of one that hath a pleasant voice, and can play well on an instrument; for *they hear thy words, but they do them not.*
>
> —EZEKIEL 33:31–32

In other words, the exiled Jews listened, but they had no intention of obeying. They nodded their heads but hardened their hearts. They shouted, "Amen," but it all ended there. They never closely examined themselves or made real changes in their thinking, talking, or actions. They constantly applied the Word to others but rarely, if ever, to themselves.

Oswald Chambers referred to this class of Jews—and Christian believers—as "enchanted, but unchanged."[3] James calls such Christians self-deceived "hearers only" (James 1:22). The apostle Paul had them in mind when he wrote, "Ever learning, and never able to come to the knowledge of the truth" (2 Tim. 3:7). As quoted in our text, Jesus likened them to fools, building houses on shifting sands (Matt. 7:26–27). Let's be fully honest. Does our present manner of living put us in or uncomfortably near this undesirable category?

Our Basic Problem: Rebellion!

In the first century, Jesus "began again to teach…and he taught them *many things*" (Mark 4:1–2). He's still teaching us "many things" today through many different channels of communication: personal meditative Bible reading, systematic Bible study, sermons, seminars, spiritual retreats, Christian books, publications, CDs, DVDs, and most recently, Internet websites and programming. Yet many of us fail repeatedly when God tests us on the "many things" we have heard. It's not a matter of spiritual ignorance. We know what God says in His Word. Our problem, again drawing on Chambers, is spiritual "stupidity."[4] In a word, stupidity is *rebellion*; we know what we should do but refuse to do it. We stubbornly hold back from applying the spiritual intelligence we have. We love to hear biblical truth expounded, to be inspired and blessed, but we're unwilling to execute in the test.

The Christian Missionary and Alliance pastor and writer A. W. Tozer wrote:

> Christians habitually weep and pray over beautiful truth, only to draw back from that same truth when it comes to the difficult job of putting it into practice.…The mind can approve and the emotions enjoy while the will drags its feet and refuses to go along.…It appears that too many Christians want to enjoy the thrill of feeling right but are not willing to endure the inconvenience of being right.[5]

Being taught is so painless, so enjoyable, so easy. We "heareth the word, and immediately with joy receiveth it" (Matt. 13:20). But testing isn't fun. It's intense, demanding, costly, humbling when we obey, and humiliating when we fail to obey! The instant God begins to test us, many get huffed and "immediately…offended" (v. 21). The very idea of having to prove ourselves to anyone, even God, insults our pride and repels us! When the Father tested Jesus, Jesus embraced His trials and "humbled himself and became obedient unto death" (Phil. 2:8); when He tests us, we evade our challenges and remain proud. Like skilled escape artists, we dodge, ignore, or openly flee from foreseeable difficulties. Like Jonah, if the test lies to the east, we head west.

But we cannot long avoid the unavoidable. Omniscience, Omnipresence, and Omnipotence has a way of catching even the cleverest. Soon we acquiesce to the fact that everyone taught on the "mountain" of revelation must endure testing in the "valley" of humiliation. Spiritual rains, winds, and floods must eventually "beat" upon every Christian's house of character. Wise and foolish alike must endure stormy situations. All God's students must take their final examinations. The wise Christian accepts this now and gets busy preparing for, and passing, his or her tests.

WHY WE NEED TESTING

Why does the Lord persist in testing us? He does so for many worthy reasons. Here are three primary ones: to graft His word into our souls, to enlarge our capacity for truth, and to establish Christian character in us. Let's examine these objectives more closely.

To graft His Word

"Receive with meekness *the engrafted [grafted] word*, which is able to save your souls" (James 1:21). "Grafting" is a horticultural operation in which the bud or shoot of one plant is inserted into a slit or groove of another and continues growing until it becomes a part of that plant.[6] By successful testing, God "grafts" His Word into our souls, making it real to us, alive in us, and one with us. In a spiritual sense, the divine Word is, again, "made flesh" in all who both hear and do it (John 1:14). As we humbly obey it, the truth is inserted into the "branches" of our souls, and in the heat of the day of trial, it grows more deeply and firmly embedded. Thereafter it remains a permanent part of our personality and the cause and means of fruit-bearing. "Love, joy, peace, long-suffering"—these and other fruit of the Spirit cannot grow in us unless the Word is grafted through trial-obedience. Biblical information alone, however much and correct, produces no such organic transformation.

When we hear but refuse to do, this "grafting" process cannot occur. We become "hearers only" and begin deceiving ourselves, mistaking comprehension for compliance, and knowing what to do for doing what we know. Wisely, the half-brother of our Lord and a key figure in the early church, James "the Just" (or Elder), felt inspired to warn us of this grave danger:

> But be ye doers of the word and not *hearers only*, deceiving your own selves.
> —James 1:22

> But don't just listen to God's word. You must do what it says. Otherwise, you are only fooling yourselves.
> —James 1:22, NLT

"Hearers only" gradually lose touch with what we are really like. Hypocrisy sets in. The gap between our religion and our reality widens. If this continues, we end up a sanctimonious, deceived "Pharisee" Christian, savorless spiritual "salt" that's "good for nothing, but to be cast out, and to be trodden under foot of men" (Matt. 5:13). Why? We would not let God graft His Word into us.

The Word taught becomes the "grafted" Word only at the point we bow and obey it. Truth enacted is truth engrafted. Truth disobeyed is truth detached from the branches of our character. It is still true, of course, but not true *in us*.

At the judgment seat of Christ, the living Word will send away those in whom His Word is not grafted: "I never knew you; depart from me, ye that work *iniquity*" (Matt. 7:23). Their crime? "Iniquity," or literally, "illegality"; or violation of law;[7] or "the condition of [being] without law" due to violation of it.[8] They heard, read, or studied the liberating Christian "law" of grace, all the words of the New Testament, and especially the teachings of Christ, but they consistently refused to submit to it in their testing process.

To enlarge our capacity for truth

"Thou hast *enlarged* me when I was in distress" (Ps. 4:1). As David here attests, successful testing "enlarges" (Hebrew *rachab*, "to broaden, make room, make [open] wide"[9]) our capacity for spiritual truth, to know and teach it.

When we hear and do New Testament teaching, God rewards us by creating within us a new and enhanced ability to appreciate, understand, and apply divine truth. As we pass test after test, the Word gradually becomes more alive and full of meaning. Why? Jesus is "opening" our mind to grasp more of God's mind in His Word: "Then *opened* he their understanding, that they might understand the scriptures" (Luke 24:45).

Therefore, the more of the Word we do, the more of the Word we know. Jesus taught this: "If any man will *do* his will, he shall *know* of the doctrine" (John 7:17). God gives sharper, clearer insight to the "eyes of your [our] understanding" (Eph. 1:18). Scriptures come together, questions are cleared up, and we understand doctrine more readily and thoroughly. The spiritual well within us becomes deeper and wider, holding more of the precious "living water" of Spirit-illuminated truth. We can take in much more of what God has to say—and give it out to the thirsty. We have ears to hear things we never heard before—and pass them on to others whose ears God has opened (Isa. 50:4–5). Thus both we and those we mentor or teach become deeper in God.

Why all this deeper life and ministry? Simply, we practiced what Jesus preached: "Whosoever heareth these sayings of mine, and doeth them..." (Matt. 7:24). We paid the price of obedience, implemented His instruction, applied what we applauded, and passed our tests. This "enlarged" mind and ministry is a valuable reward God yearns to give us. Thus, by the Spirit's prompting, the apostle prayed, "That ye may be *filled with the knowledge of his will* in all wisdom and spiritual understanding" (Col. 1:9).

To establish Christian character

"Whosoever heareth these sayings of mine, and doeth them, I will liken him unto a wise man, who built his house [of character] upon a rock" (Matt. 7:24). Speaking figuratively here, Jesus refers to the building of a "house," not of domestic habitation but of personal character. The context teaches that successful testing establishes Christian character in us.

Our personal characters are the sum of our daily decisions and deeds in the actual conditions of life. Our trials provide us with opportunities to choose and do that which is *right in the Lord's sight*. By such *righteous* decisions and actions, we build righteous, or Christian, character. The bride of Christ will be "ready" for translation and eternal union, reward, and rulership with Christ when we are sufficiently clothed in righteous character: "His wife hath made herself *ready*...arrayed in fine linen, clean and white; for the fine linen is [symbolizes] the *righteousnesses* [righteous acts] of saints" (Rev. 19:7–8). The word "righteousness" (Greek *dikaioma*, "a righteous deed; act of righteousness"[10]) implies more than merely a legally imputed right relation to God; it speaks of such right standing before God being translated into right living before Him, or Christian character.

Through testing, we establish in tangible acts the fact that we do believe God, we do fear Him, and we do submit to and serve Jesus as Lord. God, men, angels, and demons look on and take note: "Now I know that thou fearest God, seeing thou hast not withheld thy son, thine only son from me" (Gen. 22:12). After such trials, none may protest or deny our faith. It is irrefutably proven by our consistent acts.

Salvation comes "by grace...through faith" and is "the gift of God" (Eph. 2:8). In it God gives the divine *nature* to all that believe. But Christian *character* is entirely different. It's not a gift but an attainment. It's the sum, not of God's decisions and actions, but of ours. It comes not by grace but by obedience. If we are ever to have it, we must build it ourselves. The indescribably awesome, unfailingly faithful, gracious aid of the Holy Spirit is ever with us throughout our character-building tests, but only to assist us in, not execute for us, our obedience. In the final analysis, we must decide, we must act, we must build, while grace ever urges but never forces obedience. So Jesus said the wise man "built" his house of character: "A wise man, who *built* his house upon a rock." It was not built for him.

All Christians are building character, but not all are building Christian—truly Christlike—character. All are building a *house*, but not all are building upon the *rock*. Those who hear and obey build an honorable Christian character on the rock. Those who hear Christ's sayings and don't obey them build a dishonorable character. By their actions in trial they establish *unrighteous* character, despite having received the nature of Christ when they were born again. Their consistently wrong thoughts and errant choices produce unspiritual, sinful, and offensive deeds evident to God and man. These are the "foolish virgins" Jesus spoke of in Matthew 25:1–13. They are like the "foolish man" who builds his house of character on the sands of disobedience (Matt. 7:26–27).

Strange as it seems, among the vast number saved by the blood of the Lamb, there will be both honorable and dishonorable characters. God's "great house," His kingdom, has in it vessels "to honor" and "to dishonor." "But in a *great house* there are not only vessels of gold and of silver; but also of wood and of earth; and some *to honor*, and some *to dishonor*" (2 Tim. 2:20). Daniel and Samson, two redeemed ones from the Old Testament period, symbolize this for us.

Daniel built his house of character upon the rock. He believed, obeyed, and overcame amid a variety of tests. Repeatedly, the record of his life shows him rising "to honor" at the end of his tests (Dan. 1:19; 2:46–49; 5:29; 6:25–28). Samson, however, built a dishonorable character. He preferred the sands of carnality to the rock of righteousness and repeatedly failed his tests (Judg. 14:8–9; 16:1, 4). Every time God tested him, he consistently disobeyed, until gradually the habits of unrighteous character became irreversibly imbedded in his spiritually asleep soul.

Finally, one day as he slept presumptuously in Delilah's arms, his house fell apart. And despite one final hurrah, "great was the fall of it."

Both Daniel and Samson enjoyed right standing with God, but only one was honorable. Both were God's children, but only one was wise. Both were used of God mightily, but only one pleased God. Both represented Yahweh, but only one glorified Him. Both will be in heaven, but only one will be held in honor there. Both built a house of character, but only one built Christian character. What established their respective characters? Not teaching alone but also *testing*! Their teaching informed them; their testing transformed them—one into a godly character, the other into an ungodly one.

Teaching and testing do the same for us today. Indeed, they are the alternating spiritual rain and sunshine we need to become strong "trees of righteousness, the planting of the LORD, that he might be glorified" (Isa. 61:3). So when the Father tests you, give Him thanks! He is trying to graft His Word into your soul, enlarge your capacity for truth and ministry, and establish Christian character in you. Be wise, dig deep, and build your "house" upon the rock of consistent, childlike Word-obedience: "Whatsoever he saith unto you, *do it*" (John 2:5).

And if in any situation you fail to do so, quickly confess your sin and look up, expecting the Lord to give you another chance.

ANOTHER CHANCE

And the word of the LORD came unto Jonah the second time, saying,
Arise, go unto Nineveh.

—JONAH 3:1–2

IF WE HUMBLY confess our sins and failures, the Lord faithfully
forgives us and immediately restores our fellowship with Him: "If
we confess our sins, he is faithful and just to forgive us our sins, and
to cleanse us from all unrighteousness" (1 John 1:9). But He doesn't stop
there. He immediately schedules another chance for us to obey, providentially arranging another situation spiritually similar to the one in
which we just failed.

Why? To punish us further by cruelly reminding us of our failures?
No, His kind purpose is just the opposite. He wants us to be able to
forget our failures completely. So He provides us with another chance
that we might avenge our spiritual defeats and live thereafter in the joy
of overcoming rather than the frustration of failure. He wants us to be
more than forgiven; He wants us victorious! Joyful! Soaring!

Not surprisingly, our Creator understands our deepest thoughts.
He knows that even when we believe we're forgiven, the memories of
our past failures tend to linger and vex us. Like David, we sometimes
feel as if "My sin is ever before me" (Ps. 51:3). In His mercy, therefore,
our Father arranges "replacement tests" or "supplemental exams" for His
discouraged students, so our troublesome memories may be cleared and
replaced forever with pleasant memories of tests overcome and victories won. As David also wrote, "For by thee have I run through a troop
[of enemies]; and by my God have I leaped over a wall [of opposition]"

(Ps. 18:29). Jesus' blood gives us the peace of forgiveness, but only our obedience in tests gives us the joy of overcoming. After redeeming our past defeats with fresh victories, we can close the chapter on our season of trials, the agitation of regret gone and "joy unspeakable and full of glory" abiding (1 Pet. 1:8).

ONE OF GOD'S WAYS

The ministry of second chances is one of God's ways taught throughout the Bible. Jonah and Peter exemplify it best.

Another chance for Jonah

When God first ordered Jonah to preach to Nineveh, the prophet flatly rebelled. Unwilling to offer God's grace to the ungracious, ungodly, bullying nation of Assyria, in which Nineveh was situated and of whom Israel and all Near Eastern nations were afraid, Jonah went straight in the opposite direction: "But Jonah rose up to flee unto Tarshish [Tartessus in southwestern Spain[1]] from the presence of the LORD" (Jonah 1:3). Jonah's rebellion brought swift divine chastisement: "But the Lord sent out a great wind into the sea, and there was a mighty tempest" (v. 4). After experiencing the terrifying storm and a three-day stay in a fish's stomach, Jonah cried out with genuine repentance. God faithfully forgave him, delivered him, and restored his fellowship with Him (Jonah 2:1–10). But the divine dealings didn't end there.

The Lord promptly arranged for Jonah to be tested again, exactly as he had been tested before: "And the word of the LORD came unto Jonah *the second time*, saying, Arise, go unto Nineveh" (Jonah 3:1–2). In this second call, Jonah clearly recognized that he was being given another chance and that he had a perfect opportunity to redeem his earlier failure—or refusal to try! He quickly seized the opportunity: "So Jonah arose, and went unto Nineveh, according to the word of the LORD" (v. 3). And just as quickly God gave him miraculous success. Wicked Nineveh, godless Nineveh, hated Nineveh, hardened Nineveh, hopeless Nineveh, repented! "So the people of Nineveh believed God, and proclaimed a fast, and put on sackcloth [indicating penitent grief], from the greatest of them even to the least of them" (v. 5). It was a miracle for the ages! Suddenly Jonah's bitter memories of his previous failure, with all their regret, frustration, and grief, were gone. In their place came the joy of overcoming and sweet memories of one of history's greatest spiritual revivals.[2]

Another chance for Peter

Under severe testing in the high priest's courtyard, Peter broke down and failed the Lord. When a young woman, after closely scrutinizing him, swore Peter was surely one of Jesus' companions, Peter swore and "denied him, saying, Woman, I know him not" (Luke 22:57). Two more dismal denials followed in rapid succession (vv. 58, 60). Then Jesus turned and looked upon Peter. That one look inflicted more pain than a thousand lashes. Peter had failed his Lord terribly, at the most crucial moment, and he knew it—and could do nothing about it! Or so he thought for the moment.

But God graciously gave him "godly sorrow" (2 Cor. 7:10), and in the throes of his greatest personal defeat to date, Peter wept his way through to repentance and confession: "Peter went out, and wept bitterly" (Luke 22:62). After his implied confession, he was immediately restored to fellowship with God. Consequently, on the morning of the third day, after Jesus rose from death, we see the humbled apostle again leading his brethren, this time in their quest to confirm the reports of Jesus' rising: "Then arose Peter, and ran unto the sepulcher..." (Luke 24:12). But despite this return to ostensible leadership, Peter, I believe, was far from happy. Why? His heart was still pained by the memory of his recent failure. Mercifully, the Lord didn't leave him long in this state, promptly arranging another chance.

It occurred during the interim between the Lord's resurrection and His ascension, when "Jesus showed himself again to his disciples at the Sea of Tiberias" (John 21:1). After fishing an entire night unsuccessfully, the disciples were weary, hungry, and low in spirit. So Jesus appeared and kindly prepared and served them a breakfast of "bread and fish" (vv. 12–13) and proceeded to encourage them.

After they had eaten, Jesus turned to Peter in front of the others and asked him the same question three times: "Lovest thou me?" (vv. 15–17). So three times Peter responded, "Yea, Lord; thou knowest that I love thee," publicly confessing his loyalty to Him.

Why the three identical questions in public? Jesus was giving Peter another chance. He had denied the Lord three times publicly, so now he was being given a spiritually similar situation, a replacement test or supplemental exam also in public. Peter's three public confessions totally erased the bitter memories of his three previous denials.

But not content with this, to demonstrate that Peter was fully restored in every way, Jesus gave Peter three other timely blessings: a solemn charge, a sustaining prophecy, and a vital correction.

The Chief Shepherd officially "ordained" Peter as an undershepherd with a threefold pastoral commission: "Feed [nourish with my word] my lambs [immature sheep]," "Shepherd [watch, warn, guide] my sheep [more mature ones]," and "Feed my sheep [also]."[3] Then He foretold long service for Peter, ending with the ultimate victory over the tempter, martyrdom. (See Revelation 12:11.) Peter would, He assured, live to "be old" and in the end "stretch forth thy hands" to submissively and trustingly suffer execution for Christ's sake—the very thing he feared when he denied the Lord! Then Jesus wisely tempered all this uplifting news with a sober warning against unchecked curiosity and unauthorized meddling in John's and other leaders' lives and leadings: "Jesus answered, 'If I want him to live until I come back, *that is not your business. You follow me*'" (John 21:22, NCV).

So when Jesus ascended several days later, Peter was more than a forgiven man. Thanks to his second chance, he was fully restored, recharged, and ready to lead!

Here is encouragement for every Christian. If we fail God under trial, we need not succumb to despair. Final defeat is not inevitable, nor is a lasting victory out of reach. Like Jonah, let's look again to our merciful Lord for another chance: "Then I said, I am cast out of thy sight; yet I will look again toward thine holy temple" (Jonah 2:4).

While expecting another chance, remember this: our next trial may be identical to the one we just failed, a déjà-vu experience like Jonah's "second time." Or it may be spiritually similar yet visually different. God may rearrange the "set" of your drama somewhat, testing the same character quality—faith, mercy, courage, generosity, patience, forgiveness, forbearance, and so forth—but on a different "stage" and among different "actors," as He did with Peter's replacement test. Also remember your supplemental exam may come immediately or eventually, days or years later. But come it will. God never misses a detail.

Whenever He sends you another chance, seize it. Where you feared before, trust. Where you held back earlier, give. Where you denied the Lord previously, confess. Where up till now you've been hardhearted, be kind and gentle. Where you formerly compromised Christ's righteousness, stand unyielding. Where you stopped short in the past, press on to the finish. Then you can exchange the shame and frustration of defeat for the irrepressible joy of an enduring victory. As Isaiah said, the Father will give you who have "mourn[ed] in Zion...the oil of joy for mourning [and] the garment of praise for the spirit of heaviness" (Isa. 61:3).

And that's not all He will give you.

Chapter Six

GOD IS WATCHING

And Othniel, the son of Kenaz, Caleb's younger brother, took it;
and he gave him Achsah, his daughter, in marriage.

—JUDGES 1:13

D
ON'T UNDERESTIMATE THE importance of the tests in which
you presently struggle. If passed successfully, they may not only
bring you the "oil of joy" but also open doors for you in God
that are "exceedingly abundantly above" anything you ever dreamed
or dared to ask (Eph. 3:20). God's increase may far exceed your small
imagination: "Though thy beginning was *small*, yet thy latter end should
greatly increase" (Job 8:7).

The Book of Judges reveals this in the experience of Israel's first
judge, Othniel.

GOD'S WATCHFULNESS OVER OTHNIEL

After Joshua's death, Israel began to more fully possess the territory it
had subjugated during his lifetime. The first recorded tribe to take its
land was Judah (Judg. 1:1–3). In one of the first battles, Caleb offered the
hand of his daughter Achsah in marriage to whoever successfully led
Judah against the city of Kiriath-sepher, which was also called Debir.
His nephew Othniel stepped forward and accepted his challenge. And
with God's help, Othniel led a raid that took the city. So Caleb "gave
him Achsah, his daughter, in marriage" (v. 13). Thus, by faith, Othniel
wrought a victory and gained a reward. And another small Old Testament episode ended. But not so fast.

Something else far more important had occurred. Othniel had

won the approval of God, who had been intently watching the seemingly insignificant situation as it developed. He observed Othniel's faith, courage, leadership, and military skills in action at Kiriath-sepher. After the skirmish ended, God knew He had Himself a good man in the son of Kenaz. While Othniel was rejoicing over his first earthly military victory, something much better was happening in heaven above. The angels were writing Othniel's name down on God's list of overcomers and reserving a bigger, better place for him in the days ahead.

Two to three years later,[1] Israel sinned and came under bondage to Cushan-rishathaim, king of Mesopotamia. After eight years of his bitter oppression, the children of Israel cried out to God for deliverance (Judg. 3:8–9). God then "raised up" Othniel to come forth and challenge the oppressor. A decade earlier he had taken a city; now he would have the chance to deliver a nation! And with God's help, he did just that: "The Spirit of the LORD came upon him, and he judged Israel, and went out to war; and the LORD delivered Cushan-rishathaim, king of Mesopotamia, into his hand; and his [Othniel's] hand prevailed against Cushan-rishathaim" (v. 10). In Othniel's brief history, we see one of God's ways of operating.

God often gives His big assignments to those who have proven themselves in "the day of small things" (Zech. 4:10). Jesus taught this principle in His parable of the talents: "His lord said unto him, Well done, thou good and faithful servant; thou hast been *faithful over a few* things, I will make thee *ruler over many* things" (Matt. 25:21). Othniel, who was given "many" new responsibilities, had indeed first been faithful over a "few" things.

As military engagements go, Othniel's first victory at Kiriath-sepher was a relatively small thing. Kiriath-sepher was no imposing fortress. It did not compare with the heavily fortified capitals of Assyria, Babylon, or Egypt. Its name (Hebrew *qiryat-seper*) is interpreted variously as "city of [the] book [or document],"[2] "city of writing,"[3] and "city of the scribe,"[4] all of which indicated it was a city of records. It probably had a library filled with scrolls and staffed by scribes (comparatively few could write in the ancient world) and so was an important record-keeping center, or tax or military registration office, such as a county seat in modern America. But it was not an imposing military bastion. It had as many peaceful men of pen and paper as it had fierce warriors of spear and sword.

Its fall was insignificant in the eyes of secular historians; it didn't rate mention in the works of Herodotus! Neighboring kings and tribal heads probably didn't even discuss the battle over their evening meal. To these, it was a small thing. But it was a victory nonetheless, and one that Othniel was glad to have. Sensational triumphs over mighty heathen nations would come later. For now, he was thankful to have taken a city. Any city.

Othniel was obviously a humble man. Other men of war might have turned down Caleb's offer, opting to wait for a larger conflict, something more impressive, more newsworthy. Those with the swollen pride of a Naaman or Goliath may even have scoffed that Kiriath-sepher was beneath them. They were too important to waste their time on small things. But not Othniel. He took the little things seriously.

He apparently realized that the size of the trial has nothing to do with the character qualities that God is testing and developing through that trial. Faithfulness is still faithfulness, whether the responsibility is large or small. Courage is still courage, whether the challenge is more or less. Patience is still patience, however long the struggle. Diligence is still diligence, whatever size the work load. Whether people think our test is laudable or laughable, these and other key qualities of overcomers are still being exercised and grown. Jesus taught this truth too. He said, "He that is faithful in that which is *least* is faithful also in *much*; and he that is unjust in the least is unjust also in much" (Luke 16:10). So from God's viewpoint, it's not important whether the test is "least" or "much," but whether we're faithful or unfaithful in it. Othniel humbly paid his "dues" at the battle of Kiriath-sepher, and God rejoiced to see it: "For who hath despised the day of small things? For they shall rejoice and shall see...they are the eyes of the LORD" (Zech. 4:10). Thereafter it was on the record, not in Kiriath-sepher's library but in heaven's, that Othniel was faithful in "the least."

His later conflict with the king of Mesopotamia, however, was no small thing. For Israel it was a crisis hour. The future of the chosen people was on the line. For Othniel it was a "great door, and effectual" opened before him (1 Cor. 16:9), the opportunity of a lifetime. If he succeeded, his entire nation would go free from the yoke of its oppressor; if he failed, the yoke would remain and likely tighten. His adversary, Cushan-rishathaim, was as bad as they come. Apparently he was *twice* as bad as they come, because his compound name means "Cushan of double wickedness";[5] another source says, "Cushan of the double crime."[6] Since "Cushan" means "a black countenance [of Cush or Ethiopia]; or full of darkness"[7] we may more fully interpret his character-reflecting name as "*a doubly wicked and criminal king of dark, brooding countenance.*" This is not someone you would want to tangle with—unless a doubly powerful God was with you! Furthermore, Mesopotamia's army was made up of proven, able warriors. Unlike the lesser battle at Kiriath-sepher, this clash was a frightful encounter with a formidable foe under wicked leadership. Yet with God's awesome, almighty Spirit strengthening, guiding, and protecting him and his fellows, Othniel prevailed: "The LORD delivered Cushan-rishathaim, king of Mesopotamia, into his hand" (Judg. 3:10).

This victory was by no account insignificant, either before God or men. It both commanded attention and demanded recording. It was the fall of one nation and the rising again of another, not the defeat of a single, isolated city. It was a joyous emancipation from heathen domination for all Jews, another "exodus" from sorrow and despair. It renewed their personal faith and national hope in the God of Israel.

The rewards of this latter battle were also great—for everyone. As the psalmist wrote: "In keeping of them [God's Word and will] there is

great reward" (Ps. 19:11). The Jews received forty years—a full generation—of peace and freedom: "The land had rest *forty years*" (Judg. 3:11).
Their deliverance honored God, revived their faith, and silenced their
enemies. Israel was blessed and happy again. And Othniel was installed
as the first "judge," or leader of God's people, after the Canaan conquest.
As such, his name is memorialized forever in the sacred Scriptures. I
wonder if he imagined this "exceedingly abundantly above" end, for
himself and his nation, during his humble beginnings at Kiriath-sepher?
I think not. But we can imagine.

God's Watchfulness Over Us

Don't think lightly of your present trials. The relatively small battles at
your Kiriath-sepher may seem unimportant to you and go unnoticed by
others, but they are not small.

They are big, terrifically big. Why? They will determine *your* future
in God's plan and your ability to be a blessing to His people. Why? He
is watching—every decision to please Him, every surrender to His will,
every seeking of His kingdom interests, every upholding of His righteousness, every act of kindness, every sacrifice to help those in need.
In these hidden, humble "cities of books and scribes," your "Father, who
seeth in secret" is present with you in your quiet days of small things.

Repeatedly His Word proclaims His watchfulness:

> The eyes of the LORD are in every place, beholding the evil and the
> good.
>
> —Proverbs 15:3

> The eyes of the LORD are upon the righteous.
>
> —Psalms 34:15

> Thou God seest me.
>
> —Genesis 16:13

The smallest matters become immensely important when God is watching. Nothing that holds the Immortal's attention is insignificant! It's also important that we understand how to win spiritual victories.

How Spiritual Victories Are Won

Bear in mind that spiritual victories are not always won in ways that appear victorious to the natural eye.

On Calvary, Jesus won by losing, by letting evil men nail Him to a cross without cause. We too may win our spiritual battles by letting others have their way, by not resisting mistreatment or demanding our rights. Spiritual strength at times appears to be weakness, and such "weakness," or acquiescence to divinely arranged crosses, when combined with perseverance in abiding and duty, builds in us the highest strength of character and power in ministry. An expert on this, the apostle Paul, wrote:

> I take pleasure in infirmities, in reproaches, in necessities, in persecutions, in distresses for Christ's sake; for when I am weak, then am I strong.
> —2 Corinthians 12:10

Paraphrased, this expert sufferer and spiritual champion is telling us:

> When Jesus asks me to endure all kinds of difficulties, stresses, or sufferings for His sake, I fully accept them; the more I am "weak," or *submissive and weak-willed toward God's will*, the more I grow "strong," or *established in Christ's character and empowered by His Spirit*.
> —Author's paraphrase

Like Paul, we overcome by surrendering and accepting things as our heavenly Father has arranged them. When enemies harangue or harass us, we "fight back" in the best, yet most unnoticed, way: by following God's instructions pertaining to our situation! We win our arguments, for instance, by simply stating our position, and then, if adamantly and unreasonably opposed, by refusing to indulge in further argument. Why?

God's Word says, "The servant of the Lord must not strive" (2 Tim. 2:24), and "Strive not about words to no profit" (v. 14).

Overcomers' ways are indeed paradoxical. We move up in God by stepping down among men. We make progress by refusing to bull ahead and by standing still in trust. Whatever the particulars of our trial may be, we can be sure of one thing: *spiritual victory comes simply by obeying God.* In every scenario, "Whatever he saith unto you, do it" (John 2:5). God doesn't care how things look just now—whether we appear strong or weak, victorious or defeated in the eyes of men—only that we trust and obey Him. That's how He measures victory, and so must we. God knows how and when to make our victory apparent to us and to others.

So remember, your part in the Lord's battles yet to come depends entirely on your present performance at your Kiriath-sepher. If you refuse to stir yourself to courageous obedience, the heavenly watchman will see this and, with a heavy sigh, note your failure in His book. But if you, as Othniel did, rise above the smaller challenges that surround you, God will know that He can count on you in the future. He will inscribe your name on His list of overcomers and reserve for you a bigger, better place in His master plan. And when the church's crucial hour of deliverance from its dark, doubly wicked and criminal enemy, Satan, and all his deceptive agents and distracting agendas comes, you will get His call: "Rise, he calleth thee" (Mark 10:49).

Be encouraged, overcomer. Today we take cities for God; tomorrow we conquer nations!

RISE ABOVE IT!

And he that overcometh...

—REVELATION 2:26

BEFORE WE'RE READY to conquer nations, however, we have to consistently rise above spiritual "thorns" and "mountains."

In our lives there are evil people who, like thorns in our flesh, vex us. There are also hindering circumstances that, like imposing mountains, block our way. Because of these spiritual "thorns" and "mountains," we experience painful, ongoing trials. Their continuing presence seems to prophesy endless misery, and we become convinced they will remain forever to vex and hinder us. But they will not. When they have served their purpose, their presence will cease. When we rise above them, the Lord will remove them.

God is the Creator of circumstances in our lives. He moves and shifts and rearranges the scenes in which we live. Constantly, His "seasons," or periods of times sent for specific purposes, blow over us: "He changeth the times and *seasons*; he removeth...and setteth up" (Dan. 2:21). Friends come and others leave. Our bosses leave and others take their places. We move to a different city, take a new job, attend a new school, join a new church, enter a new ministry, or launch a new mission. Though these circumstances constantly change, one thing never changes: God, not chance, controls every detail of our lives; not random forces, but the Redeemer initiates every change that comforts or challenges us. This unshakable confidence that *God controls all things, and always for the ultimate good of His people* (Rom. 8:28), is the only foundation strong enough to support the overcoming life. It's the spiritual bedrock upon which wise Christians build indestructible "houses" of character and ministry.[1]

To that end God sends *evil or vexing people* (thorns) and *hindering circumstances* (mountains) our way. By design He uses them to develop the character of His Son given us at spiritual rebirth. The Redeemer's objective is to reproduce Jesus' extraordinary characteristics in ordinary people like you and me. He aims to manifest the "beauty of the LORD our God" (Ps. 90:17) in us in this ugly world, to promote the health of "his holiness" (Heb. 12:10) through us amid the worldwide pandemic of sin, and to disperse the light of righteousness through us in our sin-darkened nations. Paul wrote the Philippians:

> For it is God who worketh in you both to will and to do of his good pleasure... that ye may be blameless and harmless, children of God, without rebuke, in the midst of a crooked and perverse nation, among whom ye shine as lights in the world.
>
> —PHILIPPIANS 2:13, 15

This is the reason God sends His thorns and mountains into our lives. They are His means to His ends in us, sent so we may be "conformed to the image of his Son" (Rom. 8:29).

This Christlikeness is synonymous with the "fruit of the Spirit." To be conformed to the image of God's Son is to have the Spirit's "fruit," or evidences of His presence and work, manifest and growing within us. Specifically, "The fruit of the Spirit is love, joy, peace, long-suffering, gentleness, goodness, faith, meekness, self-control" (Gal. 5:22–23). This *beautiful, healthy, and delicious spiritual development* not only pleases our heavenly Father but also honors Him. Jesus said, "In this is my Father glorified, that ye bear much fruit" (John 15:8).

Hungry for this "glory," God wants Christ's love and gentleness made real in us. So He chastens and instructs us until we become patient and kind even in long-suffering: "Love suffereth long, and is kind" (1 Cor. 13:4). God also thirsts for Christ's meekness and self-control to be found in us so that we remain submissive to Him and merciful toward our adversaries in the face of ongoing mistreatment. He's starving for Christ's goodness to fill us so that our motives, desires, and goals become purified and we forsake all malicious or spiteful intentions.

He's famished to instill in us Christ's untouchable joy and undisturbable peace so that we cannot be irked by even life's most insistent vexations. Above all, He hungers for us to possess overcoming faith—steady, Christlike confidence in Him when everything but His Word tells us that He and His promised help are nowhere to be found. This sweeping, transformational "harvest" of Christ-fruit doesn't happen overnight. Just as natural harvests result from maintaining right conditions, so this yield arises only as we sustain the right reaction to the difficult people and situations God sends our way.

The instant we surrender our wills to God and submit, acknowledging His hand in our adversities, we begin to grow in His purpose. He then begins to teach us how to overcome the difficulties, how to abide in Him when they remain for a season, how to put off our old attitudes and put on new ones, and how to maintain a patient faith in His present control and ultimate justice and reward.

We enter a new day and adopt the attitude of "more than conquerors" (Rom. 8:37) toward formerly dreaded people and situations when we realize that God sends everything, even things Satan hopes will tear us down, to build us up. Anxiety goes and joy rises within. Our spirit revives, and we begin enjoying life again—even in most unenjoyable circumstances! What's happened? New understanding has brought with it fresh inspiration. Soon we calmly face foes from whom we formerly retreated. Why? We see our adversaries from a new, spiritual viewpoint. No matter how diabolical their attitudes and purposes, we focus on the divine purpose present: God is using them to raise us up, to make us spiritually mature, to ripen the "fruit of the Spirit" in us. As Joseph said centuries ago, "Ye thought evil against me; but God meant it unto good" (Gen. 50:20).

Now the superiority of spiritual mindedness is lifting us above the circumstantial muck. We've taken the first important steps down the road that eventually ends in God's intervention and our full, outward deliverance. God lets us walk in this new viewpoint for a season.

THE ADVENT OF MASTER TRIALS

After we have learned to walk in God's ways in minor tests, and our spiritual state is strong enough to handle it, God sends a master trial our way. These distinctly more difficult tests shock us with dismay. Our spiritual equilibrium is temporarily lost as we reel with the surprise of it all. We are knocked down but not out. As Paul wrote, "Persecuted, but not forsaken; cast down, but not destroyed" (2 Cor. 4:9).

Smitten and wounded in spirit, we feel overwhelmed. David expressed it this way: "The enemy hath persecuted my soul; he hath smitten my life down to the ground.... Therefore is my spirit overwhelmed within me" (Ps. 143:3–4). "Overwhelmed" here means *envelop in feebleness, faintness, and weakness.*[2]

Our sense of justice is outraged. We can hardly believe what has happened. In despair we cry out to God and hold on... at times for dear life! We do well to survive such times without turning away from God— or dying: "Thou hast kept me alive" (Ps. 30:3).

Like Jacob after God injured him, we cling to God until we regain our spiritual composure. Temporarily unable to advance, we take refuge in God, hold our ground, and endure. Again the oft-tried David says it best: "Yea, in the shadow of thy wings will I make my refuge, until these calamities be passed by" (Ps. 57:1). When able to do little else, we draw near and wait upon the Lord in thanksgiving, prayer, and thoughtful Bible reading, running chain references and exploring other biblical passages that come to mind as we prayerfully feed our faith.

As we hold fast in our woeful day, a wonderful thing happens. The Spirit of life from God reenters our feeble frame, and our confidence and strength revive. Why? We've learned the great secret of spiritual restoration—quiet, prayerful, worshipful waiting upon God in His wonder-working Word. Again David expertly advises, "Wait on the LORD; be of good courage, and he shall strengthen thine heart" (Ps. 27:14). So, being supernaturally strengthened by God, we stand to our feet, physically and spiritually, and face again the thing that knocked us down—and almost out.

What has happened? We have endured to the "end" of our present strength, and the Lord has "saved" us from going under: "But he that shall *endure unto the end*, the same shall be *saved* [released, restored]" (Matt. 24:13). We have advanced beyond our former spiritual limits of endurance and risen to a new, broader place of living: "He brought me forth also into *a large place*; he delivered me" (Ps. 18:19). It was touch and go for a while, but by God's grace we've come through. Now we're more prepared to handle mean people and all the miserable messes and madness they make.

ABOUT OVERCOMING MEAN-SPIRITED PEOPLE

You may wonder, "How do I overcome mean-spirited people with whom I live, work, or attend worship?"

For once a worldly proverb has it right: *Kill them with kindness!* Although this may be and often is practiced with a vindictive motive— sweet-sounding words used to convey bitter feelings—it nevertheless expresses perfectly how we must handle the evil people God sends into our lives to try us. By patience and kindness we de-thorn our thorny adversaries: "A soft answer turneth away wrath" (Prov. 15:1), or "A gentle answer will calm a person's anger" (NCV). By our overcoming attitude, we bind the evil spirit that moves them. Obedience to our Master's teaching makes us spiritually untouchable. Because they sense they cannot get to us, our enemies are frustrated in their attempt to cause us to stumble. This overcomes their mean spirit toward us. It also quenches their sinful joy.

When they cannot make us "fall," or react in an ungodly or unspiritual way and thus stumble in our walk with God, our enemies have no peace. Sometimes this gnawing frustration causes insomnia: "For they sleep not, except they have done mischief; and their sleep is taken away, unless they cause some to fall" (Prov. 4:16). Yet even this is the mercy of God. It's the Holy Spirit's way of working on their consciences to bring them to the acknowledgment of the truth so they may repent: "He gets their attention and commands that they turn from evil" (Job 36:10, NLT). If they respond by telling Him the truth about their sin, He will give them grace to fully and openly repent, changing their minds, ways, and talk to henceforth walk in fellowship with Him and His people: "If God, perhaps, will give them repentance to the acknowledging of the truth" (2 Tim. 2:25).

So by "overcoming" our human antagonists, we're not harming them but rather helping them. Through our non-retaliatory actions, God is leading them to repentance: "The goodness of God [through His people] leadeth thee to repentance" (Rom. 2:4). Thus overcomers liberate those they overcome from the malevolent attitudes that overcome them: "That they may recover themselves out of the snare of the devil, who are taken captive by him at his will" (2 Tim. 2:26). In this way we fulfill the weighty scriptural command, "Be not overcome by evil, but overcome evil with good" (Rom. 12:21).

OUR ADVERSARIES' OPTIONS

As we learn to consistently overcome our adversaries' mean-spirited mischief, we enter a new season.

Since our ways of reacting to our spiritual enemies are pleasing to our heavenly Father, He begins intervening on our behalf to subdue them: "When a man's ways please the LORD, he makes even his enemies to be at peace with him" (Prov. 16:7, ESV). The pressure of His almighty hand bears down heavily on those who have heavily oppressed us with injustices, offenses, or cruelties. Since by our consistent responses to them we have proven our obedience to God, the issue now is entirely between them and God. The question no longer is will we submit to God in adversity, but rather will our spiritual opponents repent or be removed? One or the other must inevitably follow, because it is a serious thing to oppose even one of the least of Christ's "little ones."

Jesus' warning here is shockingly clear and sobering:

> Whosoever shall offend one of these little ones who believe in me, it were better for him that a [large] millstone [pulled by a donkey[3]] were hanged about his neck, and that he were drowned in the depth of the sea. Woe unto the world because of offenses! For it must needs be that offenses come; but woe to that man by whom the offense cometh!
>
> —MATTHEW 18:6–7

Here the normally tender Jesus promises a terrible judgment for anyone who offends one of His "little ones"—they will be tossed into the ocean depths with a massive, animal-pulled millstone strapped to their neck! Why is Christ so adamant?

Mainly this severe judgment reflects His passionate love for all children, but especially His adopted children—born-again Christians: "one of these little ones *who believe in me*" (v. 6). In this context "little ones" (Greek, *micros*[4]) refers to (1) children young in years, (2) Christians young in faith, and (3) others humble in attitude ("little," or not overinflated, in the "sight" of their self-esteem; see 1 Samuel 16:7). Jesus' love is so strong for these "little ones" that He righteously detests, and will one day punish, all who impenitently harass, hinder, or harm them.

His stern warning also reveals the seriousness of doing "despite unto the Spirit of grace" (Heb. 10:29), or steadily refusing to respond to the Holy Spirit's repeated gracious attempts to turn our hearts toward Jesus. Every time we rise above our antagonists' mean-spirited words, actions, or inactions, the Spirit warns them of their wrong being and behavior and woos them to lay down their arms and capitulate to their compassionate Creator's loving overtures. Our Father is extremely forbearing with these enemies, yet His seemingly endless patience has an end. When that terrible terminus is reached, if our antagonists continue persistently refusing to allow God's *mercy* to lead them to repentance,

His *justice* will lead them to judgment. There are no other options for the obstinate opponents of Omnipotence.

David's experiences with King Saul illustrate this for us.

DAVID AND KING SAUL

King Saul stood as a towering "mountain," an apparently immovable obstruction, before the anointed but severely tested son of Jesse. Saul had to either repent or be removed before David could build a highway of righteousness through the land.

Through David's repeated kind reactions, God graciously warned and wooed Saul, giving him ample opportunity to repent. Twice David demonstrated the amazing grace of God to Saul by sparing his life when it was his to take. (See 1 Samuel 24:1–22; 26:1–25.) By these and other consistent acts of mercy toward his merciless antagonist, coupled with his ongoing devotion to God's Word, worship, and work, David proved his submission before God and man. Thus he rose above his imposing "mountain" by demonstrating obedience, integrity, and compassion.

But in spite of David's kindness, Saul would not change. He continued to defame and persecute David at every opportunity. And while he admitted his sins on several occasions, he never repented. His stubborn stand left God no alternative but to remove him. Because Saul adamantly rejected mercy, justice took over. God intervened and moved Israel's apostate king out of the way of its approved king—permanently. Incidentally, David's "mountain" was removed on a mountaintop. On Mount Gilboa, "the battle went heavily against Saul, and the archers hit him....So Saul died" (1 Sam. 31:3, 6).

His oppressive obstacle removed, David began building a wide highway for God, His people, and righteousness—right where his "mountain" previously stood.

In the end, the Lord avenged David because he obediently refused to avenge himself, choosing instead to trust God to judge the bitter controversy in His time and way. Paul urged us to do the same: "Beloved, *never avenge yourselves,* but *leave the way open for [God's] wrath;* for it is written, Vengeance is Mine, I will repay (requite), says the Lord" (Rom. 12:19, AMP).

Never did David intend or attempt to harm Saul! Never! All he desired was to obey and live and fulfill God's will. Yet his non-retaliatory actions brought on God's intervention. God struck Saul in judgment, as He had Nabal earlier (1 Sam. 25), because David's actions firmly established that he would never avenge himself, though even his closest associates occasionally counseled him to do so. When Abishai asked permission to slay Saul as he slept, David responded:

> Destroy him not....As the LORD liveth, the LORD shall smite him; or his day shall come to die; or he shall descend into battle, and perish. The LORD forbid that I should stretch forth mine hand against the LORD's anointed.
>
> —1 Samuel 26:9–11

This memorable response to the spirit of revenge proved to be David's final "thesis" in the school of the Spirit. When the Father read it, He gave David an "A" and set the date for his graduation *summa cum laude!*

As we see in David's life, God avenges only those who forsake the spirit of vengeance. He will not fight for those who still have the "fight" left in them. The reality and thoroughness of David's freedom from vengeance is seen in the fact that he was genuinely grief-stricken at the death of Saul (2 Sam. 1:17–27). Nothing in David could rejoice.

You may wonder why God didn't remove King Saul years earlier. God gave David a swift victory over the imposing "mountain" of a man, Goliath. Could He not have constrained Saul to step aside quickly and make room for his anointed successor? Why did the good Lord allow those awful years of harassment? Why didn't He step in much sooner than He did to end the conflict and bring David to Israel's throne?

God's reason was simple: *He was using King Saul as David's training ground.* Practice makes perfect, so God's plan was to let David practice the forgiveness of God upon Saul until David was "perfect," or thoroughly developed in the mercies and methods of God. The many injustices and cruelties Saul dealt David were spiritual hurdles to leap over. "By my God have I leaped over a wall," observed David (Ps. 18:29). Every time Saul offended him, David would rise above the wrong by forgiving Saul in his heart and going on with God, thanking Him for the opportunity to learn how to overcome and embodying the New Testament phrase, "forgetting those things which are behind, and reaching forth unto those things which are before" (Phil. 3:13). Had he not done this, unforgiveness would have fatally embittered him. Instead of training his faith, his wilderness experiences would have terminated it—and him.

But David chose to be trained. There were many such hurdles in the race set before him: Saul reneged on his promise to give his daughter, Merab, to David in marriage; he twice tried to kill David with his spear; he sent his servants to assassinate David when he was reportedly sick; he forced David out of his job, his home, and his marriage; he gave David's wife Michal to another man, Paltiel, in marriage; he slandered David's good name throughout Israel; and he and his most elite military units hunted David for years in an attempt to physically extinguish his life. But David rose above each offense by simply obeying God's commands to show mercy (Ps. 18:25; Prov. 3:3; 11:17), not harbor any grudges (Lev. 19:18), and commit judgment to God (Deut. 32:35). Thus by thinking scripturally, he thought spiritually instead of carnally.

After years of this spiritual training, David became consistently spiritual in thought, word, and deed. When one day he arrived at the finishing line of his divinely appointed course of training, the Creator of circumstances removed the "hurdles"—King Saul and all his evildoing passed away. Then He promptly promoted David from the training ground to the throne room—first, to rule Judah, and later, all Israel. It's the same with us today.

The *thorny* and *mountainous* oppressors in our lives, the troublesome circumstances that we must endure, these all have a distinct purpose. They are not meaningless objects flung carelessly in our way but divinely designed "hurdles" placed with utmost care. To fulfill our callings and ministries, we must learn to leap over them efficiently and effortlessly by obedience to God's Word. This will not happen suddenly or easily. It will take practice, practice, and more practice for us to perfect the mercies and methods of God. This demands of us diligence, determination, and the willingness to suffer for Christ's sake. David paid this price. Will we?

It is the character of Christ, the fruit of the Spirit, that our heavenly Father seeks to develop and mature in us. Human "thorns" and "mountains" are just instruments He uses to achieve His ends. When His heavenly purposes are achieved, He will lay down His earthly instruments. When we have manifested the spirit of a conqueror toward our "Sauls," God will relieve us of them. He will either bring them to repentance or in some way remove them from our lives. They will either wither in willing surrender to God or be cut down by divine judgment (Ps. 37:1–2). In either case, our divinely appointed course of training, like David's, will come to an end. David's son, King Solomon, wisely assures us, "Surely there is an end, and thine expectation shall not be cut off" (Prov. 23:18).

In the middle of our apparently endless trials, we may take comfort in this: *as soon as we consistently rise above our trials, God will remove them.* Isn't this sufficient incentive to overcome? May God stir us as never before to gird up the loins of our minds and rise above it!

> Now rise up, said I, and get you over.
> —DEUTERONOMY 2:13

Oh, and you'll have to rise above some "snakes" too.

TAKE THE SERPENT BY THE TAIL

And the Lord said unto him, What is that in thine hand? And he said, A rod. And he said, Cast it on the ground. And he cast it on the ground, and it became a serpent; and Moses fled from before it. And the Lord said unto Moses, Put forth thine hand, and take it by the tail. And he put forth his hand and caught it, and it became a rod in his hand.

—EXODUS 4:2-4

I n EXODUS 4:1-9, God gave Moses final instructions before sending him on his great mission to deliver Israel from Egyptian bondage. In verses 1-5, He gave him power over all satanic power; in verses 6-8, power over all sickness; and in verse 9, power over the natural creation. Thus supernaturally empowered by God, Moses went forth to embrace the super-difficult task of delivering his downtrodden, depressed, despairing brethren.

But verses 1-5 reveal that before Moses could withstand, confound, and defeat mighty Pharaoh,[1] he first had to get the victory over a much less formidable opponent—one little serpent!

MOSES' VICTORY OVER THE SERPENT

Exodus 4:1-9 describes a moment in time in which one little serpent held the upper hand over one big man of God! Why? Moses was scared of it and "fled from before it" (v. 3).

What uncharacteristic behavior! Moses, the chosen deliverer, flee? A man of exceptional knowledge and energetic action, "learned in all the wisdom of the Egyptians, and...mighty in words and in deeds" (Acts

7:22), Moses retreated from nothing and no one. Why did he flee from this low, small, scaly reptile? Evidently he thought the serpent was something he could not deal with, something beyond his present capabilities. When mighty Moses fled from this minuscule challenge, heaven must have been embarrassed: the devil had the deliverer on the run! For now.

Then came God's call to courage: "Put forth thine hand, and take it by the tail" (Exod. 4:4). God had seen Moses flee in fear, so His call was tailored to make him reach out and conquer the thing he feared. He had to square his shoulders and face that squirming, venomous enemy, catch it by its tail, and bring it under his control—trusting the One who called to provide all the strength, skill, and protection he needed. Paraphrasing God's call:

> Go ahead, Moses. Don't be afraid of this serpent. I AM with you and will help you. Use the skills I've taught you during your forty years of shepherding; you dispatched snakes many times when they threatened Jethro's sheep. Overcome this challenge too; master it and defeat it. Don't let a miserable little serpent keep you from fulfilling your noble destiny as the liberator of My people!

Like Mordecai's later stirring of Esther, this divine challenge paid huge dividends. It stung Moses' manly conscience and awakened his dormant courage. Immediately, and in faith, he acted: "And he put forth his hand, and caught it" (Exod. 4:4).

Just where Moses had formerly slipped and come under a challenging situation, he now came over it. His panicky flight ceased and a controlled advance began—a mighty spiritual march that didn't end until a string of miraculous victories had been wrought, a nation delivered, and the name of Jehovah glorified for all time and eternity! And that's not all. Moses' victory was more than a minor win over a stray reptile—much more.

In the Scriptures, the serpent symbolizes satanic power and those through whom it operates. (See Matthew 23:33; Revelation 12:9; 20:2.) This serpent Moses faced, however, was more than a symbol. By divine planning and power, this stick-become-snake was, for a brief moment, an embodiment of satanic power—the devil himself in snakeskin. Moses' opponent was the same subtle but powerful creature who overthrew the first Adam in the garden (Gen. 3:1–6) and confronted the second in the Judean wilderness (Luke 4:1–13). Therefore, when Moses put forth his hand and "caught it" (Exod. 4:4), his actions foreshadowed Christ's victory over Satan in the wilderness. Indeed, as his Lord would later do, Moses met the evil one in a great test on holy ground and came away victorious. Then his previously embarrassing situation was completely reversed: the deliverer had the devil on the run! And heaven breathed a sigh of relief.

What followed Moses' victory? Immediately the conquered serpent "departed from him for a season" (Luke 4:13), and the object Moses held in his hand became again a shepherd's rod. But it was no ordinary rod. It was now a noble scepter filled with the supernatural power of the living God. How do we know this? With that rod Moses wrought miracles, judgments, and signs. With that rod he humbled haughty Pharaoh and confounded his mischievous magicians. With that rod he invoked the plagues upon the Egyptians and opened and closed the Red Sea. With that rod he opened a gushing river from a rock and controlled Israel's crucial initial battle with fierce Amalekite tribesmen. One author wrote that Moses' rod symbolized "the authority of God committed to human hands."[2]

So we see, then, that God put His power into Moses' hands *after* he accepted God's challenge and took the serpent by the tail. There's a vital lesson here for us.

OUR "SERPENTS" AND VICTORIES

Today God has many men and women called after the order of Moses. They may not lead millions, as Moses did, but they are deliverers in the making, developing disciples and leaders who have the potential for being "strong in the Lord, and in the power of His might" (Eph. 6:10).

Why do they hold such promise? By God's works of grace, the nature of the Deliverer, Jesus Christ, is in them and His Spirit upon them. In this late hour, the church's weary, confused ranks need deliverers as desperately as Israel's exhausted slaves needed Moses. But however redeemed, well taught, and zealous we may be, before we can receive divine *power* to deliver needy Christians and non-Christians, we must first "take the serpent by the tail"—not literally, as Moses did, but spiritually.

To us, the "serpent" represents satanic attitudes and acts, not in snake but in human skin. Our contest is not with a wily viper but with crafty, evil-minded people. Satan, God's and our perpetual enemy,[3] works against committed disciples and effective ministers through any (and sometimes every!) soul that refuses to yield wholly to Christ. These unbelievers and disobedient Christians are "taken captive by him at his will" (2 Tim. 2:26) and used as his instruments to oppose those who earnestly seek to follow the Lord wholly. This is the invisible explanation behind all visible persecutions that arise for righteousness', Christ's, or the Word's sake. It illuminates, for instance, the patriarchs' cruel mistreatment of their brother, Joseph; Saul's murderous campaign against his son-in-law David; Judas' murmuring against Mary of Bethany's "waste" of spikenard; the Pharisees' relentless accusations against Jesus; and Peninnah's ceaseless needling of Hannah. The inspired description of the latter's harassment speaks for so many others: "Her adversary also *provoked her relentlessly, to make her fret*" (1 Sam. 1:6). Satan makes these, his human agents, as vexing as thorns in our flesh and as crafty and deadly as snakes. They constantly create trying situations for us to deal with, situations from which we, as Moses did, often flee. Why? We dread confrontation. We fear failing God—again! We believe we are unable to handle the difficulty involved. Or we are so weary and fed up we just don't want to bother facing another challenge!

But God, who never tires, is trying to make us like Him. He is trying to build such exceptional strength in us, such indomitable confidence in His faithfulness, that we will stand firm and handle the "serpent" whenever, wherever, and through whomever we encounter him. This is legitimate New Testament "snake handling," not the foolish testing of God practiced presumptuously by those who voluntarily handle venomous snakes. It is the spiritual interpretation of Jesus' prophecy: "These signs shall follow those who believe: in my name... *they shall take up serpents*" (Mark 16:17–18). (The rare literal interpretation is illustrated on Malta, where Paul *accidentally* encounters a snake and its deadly bite and survives by God's miraculous power; see Acts 28:1–6.) When Satan seeks to hold us at bay through the malicious plans, words, and acts of his servants, we must outwit his strategy. For that we must be as alert, quick-witted, and subtle as our enemy. Jesus commanded us, "Be ye, therefore, *wise as serpents...*" (Matt. 10:16). Yet we must never use this wisdom to intend, invoke, or inflict harm on our adversaries: "...and harmless as doves." That's a tall order.

To fill it, we must remind ourselves constantly that "we wrestle not against [mere] flesh and blood, but [also, at core]...against spiritual wickedness" (Eph. 6:12). Although people do "wrestle" against us as we walk and work with God, spreading His love and truth, they are not the real source of the opposition. They're just instruments; the real enemy is *Satanas*. To consistently overcome, we must habitually *see through* our human opponents and discern our real adversary, "spiritual wickedness" (or "evil spirits," NLT) doing Satan's bidding through people subject to his influence or control.

Paul's "Serpent"— a "Thorn in the Flesh"— and Victory

Ironically, the man who wrote, "We wrestle not against flesh and blood," found himself constantly grappling against human antagonists.

Everywhere Paul ministered, Jews or Gentiles gathered together against him. Time and again he was falsely accused, hauled into court, beaten, whipped, stoned, or run out of town, always without just cause.

Soon Paul went to the Lord with a petition of complaint, seeking relief from the overwhelming human opposition that dogged him (2 Cor. 12:7–10). The Lord then revealed to him that his real enemy was not any one person who had harassed him but a "messenger of Satan" sent "to torment me" (v. 7, NIV). "Messenger" is translated from the Greek *angelos*, which means simply "messenger or angel."[4] *Angelos* is rendered "angel" 167 times out of 175 occurrences in the New Testament (KJV). So Paul here refers to a fallen angel, a satanic spirit or demon that Satan appointed to torment him with persecution and tribulation. Symbolically, he called it a "thorn in the flesh," comparing its affliction to the constant and inescapable pain caused by a *large thorn* lodged in one's hand or arm; or perhaps, some sources say, a larger *pointed stake* upon which one was impaled or crucified.[5] (Neither the original language used here, nor this context, nor any other in the New Testament indicates that Paul's "thorn" was an eye sickness.[6])

Why was Paul given a "thorn in the flesh"? Two reasons for this existed simultaneously, one divine and the other diabolical:

1. To keep Paul humble, because of the many spiritual revelations given him to pass on to the church. "Lest I should be exalted above measure" (2 Cor. 12:7) is stated *twice*, reflecting the weightier divine intent.

2. To stop Paul from continuing to minister the light of God's Word, or the "revelations" given him, to the church. This is not stated but implied plainly enough in the Book of Acts and in 2 Corinthians 11:23–33, in which Paul lists the many ministry-hindering troubles the "thorn" caused him.

So the same serpent that confronted Adam, Moses, and Christ also tried to overthrow Paul. His goal was to cause Paul to become offended with God at his constant adversity and stop walking and working with God; yet God wisely let Satan continue his pernicious assaults on His servant, knowing they would counterbalance the spiritual exhilaration Paul often felt when visited by the Lord, angels, visions, or inspired openings of the divine Word, plan, or prophecies.

Once Paul understood this, he yielded and fully and permanently accepted his "thorn in the flesh" as a necessary cost of exceptionally effective ministry. Realizing the presence and plan of his real hateful enemy, Satan's *angelos,* and the higher purposes of God made it easier for Paul to forgive his many human offenders. Satan was just using them— and the Father was working it all together for good! Thus, by submission and obedience to Christ, Paul "took the serpent by the tail," overcoming his strategy. It was out of this enlightening personal experience that Paul penned his instructions to us, "We wrestle not against [mere] flesh and blood, but [also, at core]...against spiritual wickedness."

With Paul's experience and epistle in mind, it becomes much easier for us to forgive our human offenders too and to refuse to be offended with God, but instead wait patiently for His help. It also stirs us to realize that we either overcome the serpent or he cuts short our destiny.

WILL YOU TAKE YOUR "SERPENT" BY THE TAIL?

After initially having fled from the serpent, Moses faced and overcame him. We must also.

Wherever we have backed down from our diabolical adversary, wherever we have appeased people merely to maintain a false peace, we must now dismiss our dread and stand firm. Wherever we have repeatedly yielded and indulged in strife and anger, we must now overrule our prideful self-will and be content to answer simply yes or no, without trying to prove we're right (Matt. 5:37). Wherever we have experienced repeated spiritual failures of any kind, we must now reverse the trend of fear, flight, and failure and establish a new pattern of volition, valor, and victory. It's time for us to get the devil on the run!

To do so we must abandon the defeatism of unbelief. We'll never take the serpent by the tail if we remain hesitant, half-hearted, and double-minded. We must throw ourselves into this holy task with an iron will. Where will this courageous resolve, this undefeatable faith, come from? From only one source: renewed confidence in the promises of God's Word. The apostle of faith instructs us, "Faith cometh by hearing, and hearing by the word of God" (Rom. 10:17). Note it was when Moses heard God's voice, His Word, that he began reversing his course: "And *the LORD said* unto Moses, *Put forth thine hand*, and take it by the tail. And [then, responding,] he put forth his hand, and caught it" (Exod. 4:4). The Lord's voice, then, strengthened him to face down the serpent. It lifted him above the discouragement his previous failure caused.

The same *voice of the Lord* speaks to us today through the Scriptures, seeking to strengthen us to take our serpents by the tail. God wants to deliver us from fear, from the insidious uncertainty that inevitably arises in the wake of repeated spiritual failures. As we listen receptively to His voice through the pages of Scripture, our shakiness becomes sturdiness; our doubt, dynamic confidence.

Listen to the voice of the Lord in these Scriptures:

Behold, I give unto you power to tread on serpents and scorpions, and over all the power of the enemy; and nothing shall by any means hurt you.
—LUKE 10:19

Greater is he that is in you, than he that is in the world.
—1 JOHN 4:4

Stir up the gift of God, which is in thee....For God hath not given us the spirit of fear, but of power, and of love, and of a sound mind.
—2 TIMOTHY 1:6–7

Fear thou not; for I am with thee. Be not dismayed; for I am thy God. I will strengthen thee; yea, I will help thee; yea, I will uphold thee with the right hand of my righteousness. [And] behold, all they that were incensed against thee shall be ashamed and confounded.
—ISAIAH 41:10–11

Have not I commanded thee? Be strong and of good courage; be not afraid, neither be thou dismayed; for the LORD thy God is with thee wherever thou goest.

—JOSHUA 1:9

We all know these Scriptures; now we must put them to use. Immediately, and in faith, we must act upon them. We must exercise the power we already have—the power of the Word—if we would qualify to receive the power of the Spirit. In His wilderness trials, Jesus used the power of the Word to turn back the serpent, time and again overcoming him by submitting to and speaking God's authoritative Word: "It is written...it is written...it is said" (Luke 4:4, 8, 12). Then He emerged, enlarged and equipped "in the power of the Spirit" (v. 14). If Jesus had not taken the serpent by the tail, we would never have heard the good news of "how God anointed Jesus of Nazareth with the Holy Spirit, and with power; who went about doing good, and healing all that were oppressed of the devil" (Acts 10:38).

To follow Jesus' and Moses' examples, we must change our naturally negative attitude into a scripturally positive one. This happens only as we practice the *confession of our faith* by saying aloud what we believe in our hearts. The Bible exhorts us, "Let the redeemed of the LORD *say so*" (Ps. 107:2). It further informs us, "If thou shalt confess with thy mouth...thou shalt be saved [in trials and troubles]" (Rom 10:9), adding, "with the mouth confession is made unto salvation" (v. 10), or "with the mouth he confesses, resulting in salvation" (NAS). So the confession of our faith is the key that results in, or releases, God's salvation, or saving help in our adversities.

In distress, therefore, we should repeatedly confess every positive scriptural assertion we know and believe. For instance, "I can do all things through Christ, who strengtheneth me" (Phil. 4:13). This inspired "say so" needs to be sincere, firm, and present tense. Not later when difficulties have departed, but right now while they still persist, we choose to believe, confess, and trust God to release the help we need!

The godly positivism this produces is powerful! We not only think and feel, but now *know* that, through Christ who empowers us *we can* take our serpents by the tail! We can traverse fields of testing filled with spiritual serpents and scorpions and all the power of the enemy and come out without injury. We can "resist the devil" (James 4:7) without fretting at the people through whom he is working. We can divide the flesh from the spirit and forgive our human offenders every time, knowing inwardly that we're really contending with evil spirits. We can withstand reproach and persecution and walk steadily forward with God when "all hope that we should be saved" is "taken away" (Acts 27:20). We can handle impossible people who try us to tears—and beyond! We can master timidity and "having done all…stand" (Eph. 6:13) where in the past looks, works, and thoughts moved us. We can believe all things, bear all things, overcome all things. All we need is the grace of "grit," and our heavenly Father has all we need: "*My* grace is *sufficient* for thee" (2 Cor. 12:9).

To sum up, if Moses had not stopped fleeing from the serpent, he would never have received power, fulfilled his destiny, or delivered his oppressed people. If you keep thinking and saying, "I can't overcome my serpent," you will remain powerless. You will not finish the race set before you, and you will leave many needy Christians and non-Christians unhelped and languishing in despair. Is that what you want?

Today—this moment—take your serpent by the tail! To do so, you'll need determination.

DETERMINATION

And they who went ahead rebuked him, that he should hold his
peace; but he cried so much the more, Thou Son of David, have
mercy on me.

—LUKE 18:39

BESIDES SERPENTS, YOU'LL also have to overcome your share of
saints. The Gospels unwrap this surprise.

Astonishingly, Jesus' handpicked disciples—those closest to
Him—sometimes misunderstood, criticized, and actually opposed other
believers who were moving in true faith and by the leading of the Holy
Spirit. This strange resistance, however, was also part of God's plan. He
used it to force seekers to exercise their determination.

Determination is a fixing of the mind to persist in one's cause or
quest despite prevailing opposition. It's psychological and volitional steel
composed of the elements of passion, steadfastness, and tenacity forged
in fires of unrelenting difficulties. Christian determination is an indefati-
gable resolve to do God's will, a steady and sturdy refusal to quit, based
upon the conviction of the Holy Spirit within. Christian determination
is a mark of spiritual maturity. The spiritually mature Christian keeps
pursuing God's call, step by step, day by day, despite hateful resistance,
discouraging lack of support, and unexplained delays.

DETERMINED ONES

The Bible sets forth several clear examples of this mature determined
attitude and of the unusual opposition that at times arises from Christian sources.

Blind Bartimaeus

As blind Bartimaeus sought help from Jesus, the Lord's disciples opposed him: "And they who went ahead rebuked him, that he should hold his peace" (Luke 18:39). But their opposition only fueled his determination. He "cried so much the more" until he caught the Master's attention: "And Jesus stood, and commanded him to be brought unto him" (v. 40).

If Bartimaeus had not been a determined man, he would never have received his sight, Savior, or salvation!

The Syrophenician Woman

When the Syrophenician woman came to Jesus (Matt. 15:21–28), what was the apostles' immediate reaction? Did they praise God? Were they blessed and thankful that a woman of great faith had come to pay a visit—one that would help her tormented daughter, honor God, and become a shining example of persistent faith to henceforth bless all Christendom? No! Instead of being blessed, they were bothered! Exasperated by her repeated requests, they came to Jesus and begged Him to send her away! "And his disciples came and besought him, saying, Send her away; for she crieth after us" (v. 23). Yet, despite this rude treatment, the woman persisted and finally prevailed, for her daughter, herself, and us all.

Mary of Bethany

When Mary of Bethany broke open her alabaster box of expensive ointment and honored the Lord by anointing His head (Mark 14:3–9) and feet (John 12:3), did the apostles rejoice? Did they commend Mary for her great devotion to Jesus? No! Rather than rejoice, they reproached! Instead of supporting her, they joined in with Judas to criticize her sweet, wisely timed sacrifice as a foolish, uneconomical waste: "And there were some that had indignation within themselves, and said, Why was this waste of the ointment made? For it might have been sold for more than three hundred denarii, and have been given to the poor. And they murmured against her" (Mark 14:4–5).

But their roadblock of reproach didn't stop Mary. She continued steadfastly ministering to the Lord…until He silenced His disciples and praised and memorialized her determined devotion! "Verily I say unto you, Wherever this gospel shall be preached throughout the whole world, this also that she hath done shall be spoken of, for a memorial of her" (v. 9).

The apostle Paul

When the apostle Paul set his face like a flint to go to Jerusalem (Acts 21:8–14), did his brethren encourage him to pursue this path that God put in his heart, however difficult? Did they bolster his faith by telling him that God would see him through, no matter what the opposition or danger? Did they assure him that Christian sufferings lead to closer fellowship with God, deeper knowledge of His will, greater power in ministry, and eternal glory? No! Rather than support his faith, they tried to shake it! His dear believing friends at Philip's house church and his closest ministry team members—Doctor Luke, physician and inspired writer extraordinaire among them—begged him feverishly *not* to go to Jerusalem. Luke acknowledges, "And when we heard these things, both we, and they of that place, besought him *not* to go up to Jerusalem" (v. 12). No doubt they shook their heads in disbelief at Paul's intention to embrace God's hard will. But they didn't shake his faith or firmness. Determined, he held fast his course, putting them off with this polite but pointed "get thee behind me!" "What mean ye to weep and to break mine heart? For I am ready, not to be bound only but also to die at Jerusalem for the name of the Lord Jesus" (v. 13). Only after testing his resolve to the limit did they cease trying to turn him back: "And when he would not be persuaded, we ceased, saying, The will of the Lord be done" (v. 14).

And "done" it was! Paul's holy determination to finish his course carried him through beatings, imprisonments, death plots, mock trials, hurricanes, shipwrecks, snake bites, public denunciations and deifications, delays, and, finally, on to ministry in Rome!

In the examples above, the determined seekers did not allow their sincere but misguided brethren to weaken their clear sense of purpose. When pressed against, they pressed on. Bartimaeus kept calling out for Jesus until He responded. The Syrophenician woman kept approaching Jesus until she received assurance that her daughter would be delivered. Mary of Bethany continued to anoint Jesus while the apostles murmured. And Paul kept journeying toward Jerusalem, and on to Rome, despite the strenuous objections of his sincere but momentarily blinded brothers.

In Miletus, Paul expressed perfectly the spirit of godly determination: "And now, behold, I go bound in the spirit unto Jerusalem, not knowing the things that shall befall me there, except that the Holy Spirit witnesseth in every city, saying that bonds and afflictions await me. *But none of these things move me*" (Acts 20:22–24). Unwittingly, he spoke for all determined disciples everywhere. Down through the entire Church Age, from Paul, to Athanasius, to Wycliffe, to Luther, to Bunyan, to Wesley, to Finney, to Wang Mingdao and other Chinese house church leaders during Mao Zedong's oppressive regime, to a person their attitude is one: "None of these things move me!"

It is likely they built their firm faith on foundations such as these:

I have set the LORD always before me; because he is at my right hand, *I shall not be moved.*

—PSALMS 16:8

I said, *I shall never be moved.*

—PSALMS 30:6

God is in the midst of her [Zion, and its remnant people]; *she shall not be moved.*

—PSALMS 46:5

He [God] is my defense; *I shall not be moved.*

—PSALMS 62:6

That *no man should be moved* by these afflictions; for ye yourselves know that we are appointed to these things.

—1 THESSALONIANS 3:3

These embraced, endured, and overcame their opposition. Opposition is only a stage God builds in the life of the Christian, upon which he "works out," or exercises to full manifestation, his determination before God and men. Paul challenged us, "*Work out* your own salvation" (Phil. 2:12). How can we exercise determination when all conditions are favorable and all bystanders supportive? Something must come against us. We must have some adversity. There can be no victory without an opponent, no prize without a contest. We cannot become overcomers without having something or someone to overcome. That's why God permits opposition to confront us. So, to God's determined ones, *opposition is opportunity.*

Our determination shines brightest when circumstances are the darkest, when it's blackest midnight and all hope for a dawn of deliverance is gone, when discouraging evidence abounds on every side. It is then that friends turn away and some Christians lose faith and question us. Deep inside, part of us would love to quit and just be done with all the trouble! But something deeper in us whispers, "Don't give up; hold steady; God is faithful!" Why? The sprout of Christian determination is springing up from the unfailing seed of God's Word planted there. Though contradictions, discouragements, and the specter of failure loom, we still have God's promise concerning our troubled walk or sputtering work or embattled ministry. So there's just one thing to do: press through the opposition to lay hold of what the omnipotent One has for us. Jesus spoke of this when He said, "The kingdom of God is being preached, and everyone is forcing his way into it" (Luke 16:16, NIV) and into every kingdom work, ministry, promise, movement, and vision. This is the spirit of Christian determination—and our Father loves it!

His special approval awaits every determined disciple of Jesus. As

Job held up under Satan's vicious assaults, God voiced His approval before Satan: "Hast thou considered my servant, Job, that there is none like him in the earth?...Still he holdeth fast his integrity, although thou movedst me against him, to destroy him without cause" (Job 2:3). To the Syrophenician woman, Jesus said, "O woman, great is thy faith" (Matt. 15:28). And, as stated earlier, He ordered that Mary of Bethany's lavish sacrifice be recited and revered wherever the gospel is preached world-wide—an honor granted to no other believer in the Gospels!

Could any honor bestowed by men begin to compare with this special divine commendation? What could be greater than the public praise of the Son of God? Truly, determined disciples bring honor to the cause of Christ, and for that cause He honors them. Samuel encapsulated this timeless law of God: "Them who honor me I will honor" (1 Sam. 2:30). In God's time determined disciples' ears will hear the blessed words, "Well done, thou good and faithful servant" (Matt. 25:21, 23), and "Friend, go up higher" (Luke 14:10). That is, if they overcome not only serpents and sinners but also saints!

WHY EVEN CHRISTIANS SOMETIMES OPPOSE US

Sooner or later, circumstances compel every serious-minded student-follower of the Savior to ask, "Lord, why do even my Christian friends sometimes resist me as I pursue Your Word, ways, and works?" I offer the following explanations as to why some of our antagonists may be Christians:

The Christians in question may be disobedient to the Lord.

Disobedient souls constantly oppose obedient ones. Their lives are headed in completely opposite directions: "He that is not with me is against me" (Matt. 12:30). Therefore, collisions occur frequently.

They may have stumbled spiritually.

Some Christians may have been offended by some unfortunate occurrence in their walk with God and never lifted and sustained by spiritual mindedness. Loss of confidence in God invariably follows; then, in spiritual decline or even apostasy, they inevitably give bad counsel. Disillusioned with the heavenly vision, they advise tempted Christians to lean on the arm of flesh rather than stay faithful and keep trusting in God's help. These turn back many from their spiritual quest.

They may be envious.

Our opposing friends may be angry and discontent that someone else has something they want themselves. Lukewarm Christians despise serious disciples yet envy their devotion. After envy enters, even the closest friends begin drifting apart. Soon the sweetest fellowship becomes the bitterest contention: "And [King] Saul became David's enemy continually" (1 Sam. 18:29). Christians with an "evil eye" of envy always try to throw cold water on our fervent devotional fires.

They may be false Christians.

The Bible warns us plainly about false prophets, false apostles, false teachers, workers of iniquity, angels of light, and wolves in sheep's clothing. Paul encountered false Christians in Antioch: "False brethren...who came in secretly to spy out our liberty which we have in Christ Jesus, that they might bring us into bondage" (Gal. 2:4). As there was a "mixed multitude" in Israel, so there are unconverted ones mingled with converted ones in the church. Some possess real Christianity; others only profess it: "For some have not the [true, personal, saving] knowledge of God" (1 Cor. 15:34).

They may be true Christians influenced by false doctrines.

Some sons and daughters of God are presently bound by the erroneous teachings of men. Their wrong beliefs—cheap grace, liberal theology, moral relativity, political partisanship, materialism—may cause them to oppose the stand we have taken.

Or they may have odd, private scruples, strange notions, or unscriptural "Pharisaic" religious standards to which we do not measure up. So they write us off as worldly and worthless: "And when they saw some of his disciples eat bread with defiled, that is to say, with unwashed, hands, they found fault...holding the tradition of the elders" (Mark 7:2–3).

They may be relatively new converts.

Some new converts lack teaching and aren't able to understand the spiritual matters with which we, and other more experienced believers, grapple. Thus they find fault with us in ignorance, lacking insight into the deeper things of walking with God. Though written of his preconversion resistance of Christians, Paul's testimony here speaks for many true but untaught converts: "I obtained mercy, because I did it ignorantly in unbelief" (1 Tim. 1:13).

The Lord may have blinded them.

They may be good, faithful Christians whom the Lord has smitten with temporary spiritual blindness to test us. He may have shut their eyes to the things He has enabled us to see to find out if we will press on with determination when, our best Christian friends having disagreed with us, it seems God has "withdrawn" His favor or help: "God *withdrew* from Hezekiah in order to test him and to see what was really in his heart" (2 Chron. 32:31, NLT).

Have you put your hand to the plow and encountered surprisingly stiff opposition from, of all sources, brothers and sisters in Christ? Have some of God's called ones—the very children of the kingdom—called for your censure or ostracism or discipline? Are they criticizing your sacrifices, telling you to hold your peace, or forbidding you to continue asking Jesus to deliver your troubled child? Are they trying to dissuade you from the cross-strewn path of ministry or duty to which the Holy Spirit has plainly called you? Don't faint.

Joseph, Moses, and David were all opposed by their brethren at first, only to be beloved and supported by them afterward. They had to press through their opposition and lay hold of the purpose for which God called them. This *rejection first–reception later,* or "cornerstone" principle, is seen in Jesus' life; though rejected by His people at His first advent, He will be received and revered by them at His second: "The stone that the builders rejected has now become the cornerstone. This is the Lord's doing and it is wonderful to see" (Ps. 118:22–23, NLT). The true prophets experienced the same during periods of spiritual darkness. Since this puts us in good company, Jesus taught us to meet our frustrating rejection with full, fresh praise to God: "*Rejoice* ye in that day, and *leap for joy*...for in the like manner did their fathers unto the prophets" (Luke 6:22). What else should you do?

After rejoicing, refocus. Don't doubt the Spirit's confirmed leading: "As many as are led by the Spirit of God, they are [living as] the sons of God [and *the* Son of God]" (Rom. 8:14). Settle it: Guidance by the Spirit is not guidance by the saints. Then resume your walk. Go forward with what God has told you to do: "Whatsoever he saith unto you, *do it*" (John 2:5). And retrain your thinking, time and again, until it's spiritual—the surprising opposition confronting you is not accidental but providential. Our Father has permitted it—sent it, really—to call forth your Christian determination. It's your stage. So act out the part, or "work out" the biblical script, of the unmoved disciple: "None of these things move me" (Acts 20:24).

Let none of "these things" move *you!*

> *I press on* to take hold of that for which Christ Jesus took hold of me....*I press on* toward the goal....All of us who are mature should *take such a view of things.*
> —PHILIPPIANS 3:12, 14–15, NIV

As you "press on" with "such a view of things," you'll discover God's distinctive way of removing your faults.

Chapter Ten

GOD'S SANDING PROCESS

But let patience have her perfect work, that ye may be perfect and
entire, lacking nothing.

—JAMES 1:4

H AVE YOU EVER noticed how God uses the faults of others to rid
us of our own faults? Surprisingly, the furniture industry helps
us understand this.

As a longtime resident of High Point, North Carolina, the self-
proclaimed "furniture capital of the world" and home to the International Home Furnishings Market,[1] I've observed a few things about
manufacturing furniture by osmosis. Fine wood furniture must endure
a great amount of sanding. Before the recent decline in American manufacturing, which decimated the once-thriving Western North Carolina furniture and accessories industries, sanding departments in great
companies such as Broyhill, Thomasville, Henredon, and others buzzed,
hummed, and roared out their home furnishings gospel: All the rough
places—the nicks, burrs, and splinters—*must* be sanded until they are
perfectly smooth, unnoticed by the eye and unfelt by the hand. Only
when quality control personnel confirm this has occurred is the wood
furniture ready for the finishing process, and, later, the merchant's store
and buyer's home. This industrial lesson has an inspiring application.

God too is in the home furnishings business. He's busy now making
"fine furniture," or manufacturing Christians of high character and value,
with which to fill His "house," or eternal kingdom. The Savior has died,
the Spirit has come, and the fivefold ministry has been sent for one prime
purpose: to make every born-again individual "a vessel unto honor."

Paul reveals, however, that not all Christians build high character in this world. Ultimately, some will have characters "to honor, and some to dishonor":

> In a great house there are not only vessels of gold and silver, but also of wood and of earth; and *some to honor, and some to dishonor.* If a man, therefore, *purge* himself from these, he shall be a *vessel unto honor,*[2] sanctified, and fit for the master's use, and prepared unto every good work.
>
> —2 Timothy 2:20–21

To manufacture godly character in us, God must "purge" us of our chronic character flaws, walking us through His sanding and finishing processes until we reach "perfection," or spiritual maturity. We'll never be "vessels unto honor" if we allow "rough places" of untouched carnality and stubborn selfishness to remain in our characters. They must go! God's "quality control Manager," the patient, passionate, persistent perfectionist we call the Holy Spirit, insists on it! As we allow spiritual sanding to progress, Christ in us is edified, trained, and polished, until eventually God's "glory"—the beautiful character traits of Jesus or "beauty of the LORD our God"—is seen "upon us" (Ps. 90:16–17). Then we are assured honorable placement and use in God's "house"—now in the Church Age, later in Christ's thousand-year kingdom, and, finally, in the Father's eternal kingdom, New Jerusalem.

To accomplish this high end, God sends some low tools, His "sanders," into our lives.

GOD'S SANDERS

God's "sanders" are people with obvious personality faults. They are impatient people, mean people, lazy people, ignorant people, arrogant people, inconsiderate people, bull-headed people, irresponsible people, rebellious people, strange people—personalities that go against the grain of our personality and rub us wrong. Very wrong! And very often! God deliberately places these abrasive souls near us because He wants them to come in contact with us daily. They must rub against us as sandpaper rubs against unfinished wood furniture. As we react rightly to this steady spiritual abrasion, one by one, day by day, our faults, weaknesses, and bad attitudes go from us, even as the nicks, burrs, bumps, and splinters go from well-sanded wood surfaces. Our attitude toward these offensive people is crucial.

When we first encounter them, most of us rebel. These sandpaper types chafe us, grating, annoying, and vexing us until we nearly go crazy! Complaints begin arising in our irritated hearts and escape through our lips: "Why do I have to deal with this person? Am I being punished?" Reflexively, our super-fast cerebral computers run their own interior searches for R E L I E F!

The first search result to pop into our minds is P R A Y! So, in our distress, we turn to prayer, as well we should. But this prayer is very narrow and focused on selfish ends, not humble-hearted and open-minded as it should be. God's will isn't consulted because we've already set our will: We want to pray these people, who seem to have large grains of sand glued all over their skin and clothes, *out of our lives*! We feel about them as the Jerusalem Jews did Paul: "Away with such a fellow from the earth; for it is not fit that he should live" (Acts 22:22), or something equally kind and generous-hearted! Persistently and urgently our petitions rise: "Lord, please send this man, this woman to another city, employment, or church. Liberate your 'turtledove' from this oppressive, predatory beast. *Please* don't let this person oppress me anymore!" Confident God is on our side, we stand on our prayer tower, watching and listening. But, strangely, our impassioned pleas bring no response. Heaven is silent—and we sink into despair. Then, suddenly reinspired by more self-centered thinking, we search again for R E L I E F!

The next search result that pops up on the monitor of our conscious mind is C H A N G E   T H E M! So we reset our attention and petitions on changing our sander's faults. God knows they're obvious, and much worse than ours, we reason, so if we can just get Him to change them, our chafing will cease. We launch a new round of fervent prayers, no longer for their removal but their redemption: "Lord, please deliver this man from his meanness, this woman from her hardness, this person from their impatience. Please save them, sanctify them, make them holy, conform them to Jesus' image!" Again, strangely, no answer comes from above—nor any change in our sander or situation below!

Slowly but surely, the Spirit releases God's higher perspective into our earthbound minds like dew descending on parched ground. Soon we begin thinking the unthinkable: God isn't going to remove them or redeem them for the time being. Why? He personally shaped, approved, and sent them into our lives for a higher purpose: C H A N G I N G   U S! Oh, how blind we were!!

With this dew of the Spirit comes new light, and, for the first time, we clearly understand God's obscure sanding process. We were seeking our comfort, but our Father was building our character. We assumed we were a finished product, but our Father knew we were unfinished furniture. We fixed our attention on our sander's faults, but our Father's eyes were riveted on ours. Their actions vexed us to anger, but our reactions grieved our Father to tears. We yearned for these troublemakers, young and old, to go, but our Father yearned for our "old man" and its spiritual immaturity to go! We passionately wanted them reformed...to relieve us, but our heavenly Father passionately wanted us transformed...to rejoice His heart! Will His higher purpose be realized?

Two factors above all others will determine this: (1) our perspective toward our sanders, and (2) our consistent reactions to them.

We must see our sanders as coming straight from God's hand. To the spiritually minded, there are no second causes. As stated earlier, the Book of Job shows us that nothing can touch our lives without our Father's personal approval and precise control (Job 1:12; 2:6). Jesus knew and lived this truth, even saying of Judas' stinging betrayal, "The cup which *my Father hath given me*, shall I not drink it?" (John 18:11). So we must think, as the prophet said, "This thing is from me" (1 Kings 12:24).

Why? He plans to use the chronic personality faults of our sanders to give us the opportunity to acknowledge and rid ourselves of our chronic faulty reactions. But this won't happen automatically.

Our consistently obedient reactions are required. If we rebel and regularly refuse to humble ourselves and practice God's Word in regard to our sanders, we will remain unfinished vessels, imperfect and unfit for the Master's use or house. Frankly, and tragically, many Christians remain in this state their whole lives; others begin this quest for maturity only to turn back when their trials become exceptionally hard or long. But if we consistently yield to and obey God's Word in our responses to our sanders, the mighty, living, re-creative Word will rub away our imperfections. Gradually our faulty reactions will occur less frequently until, eventually, they cease to be a part of our lives. After a season of polishing our obedience in God's "finishing room," we emerge from God's character manufacturing process spiritually mature, consistent, finished, and ready for God to place and use in the present manifestation of His "house," the church.

SAMPLE SANDING SESSIONS

To help us understand God's sanding process more clearly, let's consider some sample "sanding sessions." These scenarios, or very similar ones, are likely to occur in our lives.

Sample one

The Lord exposes you to those who openly do "evil"—biblically wrong, unjust, cruel, immoral, illegal, unethical, injurious acts or omissions. Why? He arranges this to give you an opportunity to "fret not thyself because of evildoers" (Ps. 37:1). Your "evildoer's" evil doings are not presently at issue; their reckoning will come as sure as the dawn. But presently your Father is trying to sand away your fretfulness over their ungodliness, your angry response to their angry deeds. He wants you to "cease from anger, and forsake wrath" (v. 8), and then begin to react according to His Word. That will mean praying for those who have been wronged and helping them, if possible, and praying for repentance for the "evildoer" and exhorting them to repent, if you have a door to speak.

Thus you learn neither to "fret" (smolder with suppressed anger), nor rage with loud protests, nor lash out impetuously to, in your way and time, "recompense...evil for evil" (Rom. 12:17), as Moses did when he saw grievous injustice in Egypt (Exod. 2:11–15). Instead you choose to take your line of response from God's Word, "resist[ing] not evil" (Matt. 5:39) and committing judgment to God or the proper authorities: "Commit thy way [circumstances] to the Lord; trust also in him, and he shall bring it [justice] to pass" (Ps. 37:5). You then guard against condemning the wrongdoer in your mind to avoid "sitting in the seat of the scornful" (Ps. 1:1). And you stand ready to help the wrongdoer the moment he (or she) changes or do him good presently, if you have a chance, remembering that "the goodness of God leadeth thee to repentance" (Rom. 2:4). In the end, God has changed you: No longer "overcome by evil," you're now learning to "overcome evil with good" (Rom. 12:21).

Sample two

You find yourself working for a demanding, inconsiderate employer or superior. Immediately self-pity—an unhealthy, obsessive sorrow for yourself arising from a selfish viewpoint of your troubles—cries, "Why me, Lord?" The reason is God wants to use your "boss" to sand away your slothfulness, disorganization, and inefficiency. He wants to grind down your destructive tendency to excuse and pamper yourself. He's being tough with you so you will become tough on yourself.

If you continue to indulge yourself, you will be of no value to the Chief Executive Officer of the church, who, though gracious, also seeks excellence of us. His corporate directive reads: "Whatever ye do, do it heartily [with enthusiasm and excellence], as to the Lord [as if He asked you to do it], and not unto men" (Col. 3:23). Are you discharging your vocational duties as if *Jesus* had personally appeared to assign them to you? The instant you become tough on yourself, your job becomes easy, and you discover that it's true, "I can do all things through Christ, who strengtheneth me" (Phil. 4:13). Why? *When the way grows harder, His grace grows stronger.* Or, "My grace is sufficient for thee" (2 Cor. 12:9).

Sample three

You live or work with someone given to strife. Everything you say, they contradict or mock it to incite debate. The psalmist had his own contentious sanders: "My soul hath long dwelt with him that hateth peace. I am for peace; but when I speak, they are for war" (Ps. 120:6–7). Daily, sometimes hourly, the temptation to argue futilely is present. Your proud carnal nature, which is quick to prove you're right and slow to back down, lusts to have the last word. Why has God put you near this son (or daughter) of strife?

He is giving you an opportunity to not strive back at them. There is no occasion to learn this when all our companions are sweet natured, gentle, and humbly unconcerned with proving they are right all the time. It's when we have pugnacious people pressing us that we have a stage on which to "strive not about words to no profit, but to the subverting of the hearers" (2 Tim. 2:14). The more we endure this sanding, the more gracious, self-controlled, and humble we become, because "only by pride cometh contention; but with the well-advised is wisdom" (Prov. 13:10); or "A vain man through pride causeth debate, and with the counselled is wisdom" (YLT).

Sample four

Your spouse is consistently inconsiderate. He (or she) deliberately ignores your wishes and, at times, your needs. And, despite your pleading prayers, God does nothing about it! Why?

He's not dealing with your spouse but you. You are His top priority. His Word declares, "Judgment must begin at the house of God" (1 Pet. 4:17). The principle in this verse teaches us that whenever and wherever He visits, God always deals first with those closest to Him. This may explain why He's presently insisting that while your spouse is inconsiderate of you, you carefully and consistently consider what Christ's teaching tells you to do and do it. Every time. If so, the Spirit will sanctify you entirely as He sands away your selfishness, willfulness, and stubborn insistence that you be treated right all the time. Nabal and Michal were not fun to live with, but interacting with them in a godly way made saints of Abigail and David!

Sample five

At church your Christian brethren always look to you to take the responsibilities, make the decisions, do the work, and see that things get done properly, while they help you as little as possible. Soon you get irritated by their evident apathy and irresponsibility.

Okay, Little Red Hen, don't lose it because the other "sheep" in God's "barnyard" run away while you bake your cake yet rush to eat it! Father knows all about their little tricks. Why? He arranged it. How come? They mean it against you "for evil," but God means it "unto good" (Gen. 50:20), specifically to use their irresponsibility to rub away your irresponsibility; the less responsible they are, the more responsible you must become. And He wants the burden to drive you to Him so *He* may give you more grace, wisdom, and assistance. You'll find the Father always ready to help and sufficient to raise new helpers, reveal new methods, and revive with new strength when those who should help carry the load look away. In great distress Paul learned this:

> At my first defense no man stood with me, but all men forsook me.... Notwithstanding, the Lord stood with me and strengthened me, that by me the preaching might be fully known.
> —2 TIMOTHY 4:16–17

When abandoned by the saints, this "Little Red Apostle" leaned harder on his Lord and emerged with more confidence in His unfailing faithfulness to help him discharge any duty in His will! Also, any lingering irresponsibility and self-pity he may have had were sanded away! Paul is an example to follow.

Let the buck stop with you. Let God refine your dependence on Him and your view of others. Stop fomenting and start forgiving those who should but won't help. Paul did: "I pray God that it may *not* be laid to their charge" (2 Tim 4:16). Continue accepting every duty God assigns you, discharging it joyfully with His unfailing strength and wisdom. And the sanctifying sanding goes on.

Sample six

Your children disobey you constantly. You have made, announced, and enforced family rules, yet your "olive plants" still fail to submit to your authority. Daily their rebelliousness rises to challenge you. Again you wonder, "Why, Lord?"

The heavenly Father is indeed deeply concerned about rebellious children, but He's even more concerned about rebellious parents. One of the hardest things to do well is not rebel at rebels, to not misbehave when insubordinates misbehave, to remain under authority to God when others refuse to respect your authority from God. God will bring your children under your authority—that's His plainly written will (Eph. 6:1–3)—but first He wants to use their rebellious actions to sand away your rebellious *reactions*. When Ezekiel faced rebellion from God's children, the Jews, God instructed him, "Be not *thou* rebellious like that rebellious house" (Ezek. 2:8). Rebellious parents cannot raise submissive children; if your kids see you "go off" on them all the time, how will they respect your authority and grow into cool, calm, collected Christians?

So you are God's primary objective; they are His secondary piece of work. The sooner you begin to "let patience have her perfect work" (James 1:4) in your dealings with your children, the sooner God will make them respect your authority and respond to your counsel. Good behavior compels imitation, but bad behavior repels it—or worse, reproduces it! So the more you obey God, the more your kids will obey you. The more consistently you submit to God's Word, the more readily they will submit to yours. Like the centurion, as you stay under authority, you'll grow in authority: "For I am a man under authority, having soldiers under me" (Matt. 8:9). Have no doubt, parent! These principles hold even if your spouse rejects parental responsibility or deliberately tries to undermine your influence on your children!

In these and many other ways, God seeks to sand away our character faults, raise us to a new level of maturity, and conform us to Jesus' image. And He's easily able to accomplish this, to rub away every nick, splinter, and bump, "that ye may be blameless and harmless" (Phil. 2:15) and "stand perfect and complete in all the will of God" (Col. 4:12). We are the only ones who can stop this character-manufacturing process. How? By refusing to react to our sanders with consistent obedience to God's Word.

Then we face the alternative. If we won't let God use our sanders to transform us, Satan will use them to control, transform, and spoil us. We'll find ourselves manipulated by the condition of our sanders: when they're up, we're happy; when they're stirred up, we're angry; when they're down, we're depressed. Why? We're reacting humanly, not spiritually; emotionally, not scripturally. We're obeying our flesh, not our Father. Paul warns us, "Don't you know that when you offer yourselves to someone to obey him as slaves, *you are slaves to the one whom you obey*—whether you are slaves to sin, which leads to death, or to obedience, which leads to righteousness?" (Rom. 6:16, NIV). This too is transformative. The more we continue our faulty reactions, the more they transform us into the image of our sin-master, Satan. This, then, spoils our usefulness to God, leaving us not a fine but a flawed piece of furniture.

So let God finish His sanding process in you. The writer to the Hebrews exhorts, "Let us go on unto perfection" (Heb. 6:1). Stop complaining about others' faults and face your own. Hold yourself to the higher standard of "his righteousness" (Matt. 6:33) and react accordingly, no matter how unrighteously others act toward you. Then you'll be fine, not flawed, furniture, "a vessel unto honor, sanctified, and fit for the master's use, and prepared unto every good work" (2 Tim. 2:21).

And you'll be prepared to endure reproach—rivers of it!

Chapter Eleven

MERCILESS CRITICISM

And they watched him…that they might accuse him.

—MARK 3:2

J ESUS LIVED UNDER the constant scrutiny of merciless enemies. Everywhere He went the scribes and Pharisees anxiously awaited Him, looking for apparent imperfections in the perfect One. Humanly speaking, this put our Lord under terrific pressure. Yet He accepted this pressure, came to expect it, thrived under it, and graciously overcame His critics time and again. He was the consummate overcomer.

He even tried to help His antagonists. While they busied themselves seeking an indictment against Him, Jesus sought to instruct them, voluntarily sharing with them glorious divine truths. By teaching His critics, He "loved" His enemies, as He taught us to do, and embodied the proverb: "The bloodthirsty hate the upright, but the just seek his soul" (Prov. 29:10). Jesus repeatedly perceived the wicked intent of His detractors, confounded them with His unassailably wise speech, and then gave them a rich portion of truth that, if heeded, would have saved them from their errors. No passage exemplifies this better than Matthew 22:15–46, in which in rapid succession Jesus dispatched the devious plots of the Herodians, Sadducees, and Pharisees and sent them home thoroughly silenced—and pondering yet more of His profound teaching!

Our heavenly Father wants to replicate this amazing grace in us. The apostle John wrote, "As he is, so are we in this world" (1 John 4:17). As "they watched him…that they might take hold of his words" (Luke 20:20), so they will watch us that they might find fault with our words— or if not our words, then our looks, our dress, our education, our friends, our hobbies, or anything else they can mock, belittle, or berate! Our every step brings new scorn. Anticipating our sufferings for Christ's sake, the Hebrew psalmist Ethan prayed, "Remember, Lord, how your servant has been mocked, how I bear in my heart the taunts of…your enemies…*they have mocked every step of your anointed one*" (Ps. 89:50–51, NIV). Yes, if we belong to Jesus, we will receive the same suspicious stares and stir the same malicious misjudgments and gossipy whisperings that He endured. Why? "The servant is not greater than his lord. If they have persecuted me, they will also persecute you," declared Jesus (John 15:20).

The children of this world, religious and nonreligious, are not only indignantly prejudiced against but also incurably preoccupied with the children of the kingdom. With insatiable curiosity, they constantly examine us as King Saul did David: "And Saul *watched enviously David* ["watched David closely," NCV] from that day and onward" (1 Sam. 18:9). One slip of the tongue, one false step, one obvious sin, one contradiction of our professed faith in God's promises or power, and our slip-up is quickly noticed and enthusiastically recorded and broadcast against us. Not once in a while, mind you, but this happens every time! Our enemies, for whom God commands us to have mercy, have no mercy—at least for us! They release surging floodtides of cruel comments against us from their mouths,[1] hoping to sweep us off our feet, away from God, and out of His will: "The mouth of the wicked and the mouth of the deceitful are opened against me. They have spoken against me with a lying tongue…with words of hatred" (Ps. 109:2–3). The current of their hatred is strong. David cried, "Consider mine enemies; for…they hate me with cruel hatred" (Ps. 25:19). Such is the nature of the merciless criticism every serious disciple of Jesus must face.

But we must learn not to complain, because *God Himself is behind this severe spiritual scrutiny.* While our antagonists pray their floodtide of reproach will drown us, God wants us to learn to "surf" their diabolical tide of taunts. To do so, we must remember that because our Father has sovereignly permitted this flood of bitter words to touch us, it falls within the scope of His grand promise in Romans 8:28. We don't know when it will end or how wide it will flow, but "*we know* that God causes *all things* [including this roaring river of reproach] to work together *for good* to those who love God, to those who are called according to His purpose" (NAS). Only two responses to this raging river are possible: fight it, or flow with it; resist it, or ride it.

If we believe Romans 8:28, we'll flow with it. We'll realize that if we fight our critics, word for word, lie for lie, misrepresentation for misrepresentation, strife will consume us. Wisely the apostle Paul warned, "If ye bite and devour one another, take heed that ye be not consumed one of another" (Gal. 5:15). Resentment and bitterness will fill our veins, our relationship to God will sour, our usefulness to His people will cease, and we'll drown in unbelief—exactly what Satan wants the "flood" to do! But if we accept the pressure of reproach as coming from our loving, all-powerful, all-wise Father, whose ways are higher than ours, and trust He'll turn it for our good in His time and way, then we'll grow from our tongue lashings just as surely as the Hebrews grew under Pharaoh's scourges: "But the more they afflicted them, the more they multiplied and grew" (Exod. 1:12). And we'll ride the tide of terrible words to a safe landing on the shores of spiritual maturity.

David learned to ride the waves of his reproach. As we will learn in the next chapter, when Shimei bitterly reviled David, David acknowledged that God permitted the verbal abuse for His own higher purposes, going so far as to say He "bid," or prompted it.[2] (See 2 Samuel 16:11.) This faith, and the attitude of acceptance it produced, enabled David to flow with his reproach instead of fight it. His amazing graciousness also anticipates Jesus' teaching, "Resist not evil" (Matt. 5:39).

Are we ready to flow with Christ's teaching and David's example? Are we willing to stop resisting and start embracing the endless stream of "evil" criticisms flowing our way so we can ride them? Are we submissive enough to God to neither rebel against nor fear "the reproach of men" (Isa. 51:7)? If so, the "fruit of the Spirit" will grow rapidly in our souls (Gal. 5:22–23). Our nonretaliatory attitude, based not in cowardice but in true spiritual-mindedness, will deeply please and glorify God and enable Him to bless us with fresh supplies of the Holy Spirit. Peter promises, "If ye be reproached for the name of Christ, happy [blessed] are ye; for *the Spirit of glory and of God resteth [afresh] upon you*; on their part he is evil spoken of, but on your part *he is glorified*" (1 Pet. 4:14). Such an attitude, if persisted in, will eventually silence even our worst critics. Like the swelling Jordan before Joshua, their flood of bitter words will be cut off. Again Peter writes, "For so is the will of God, that with well-doing ye may *put to silence the ignorance [groundless criticisms]* of foolish men" (1 Pet. 2:15).

MERCILESS CRITICISM: A GOOD EVIL

Merciless criticism is a useful "thorn in the flesh." Paul listed "reproaches" (criticisms) as one of the thorny afflictions *the* "thorn," Satan's messenger, used to constantly vex him (2 Cor. 12:7, 10).

Initially Paul tried his best to pray away these criticisms: "For this thing I besought the Lord thrice, that it might depart from me" (v. 8). But the Lord, surprisingly, denied the mighty apostle's earnest request: "He said unto me, My grace is sufficient for thee" (v. 9). He then added that His plan was to use the "weakness" (weariness) his thorny reproach caused, not only to humble Paul (v. 7) but also to "perfect" (mature) him in divine strength: "for my strength is made perfect in [your thorn-induced] weakness" (v. 9). By learning to handle his painful criticism, Paul would grow more dependent on divine strength, more efficient in receiving fresh supplies of it, and more consistent in his walk and ministry. When Paul accepted this answer, he immediately received a new attitude toward his old critics. Instead of eschewing them and their complaints, he started embracing them: "Therefore, *I take pleasure ... in reproaches ...* for Christ's sake" (v. 10). From then on, instead of resisting his disturbing opposition, he restfully accepted it. This humble submission to God's difficult will enabled the Spirit to so empower Paul that he overcame all his critics: "For when I am weak [submitted to God's will], then am I strong [sure, stable, and wise before my adversaries and adversities]" (v. 10).

We must do the same. As long as we stay close to the Lord and pursue our calling, our critics will keep talking. They must; it is the nature of satanic warfare. Periodic reproach is the unavoidable price of growing spiritual life and Spirit-led ministry. We must, therefore, keep ourselves strong to bear this criticism, remembering it is a useful thorn, a good evil, in God's hands.

CRITICISM: A CROSS OR A CORRECTION?

We must also be quick to discern any part of our reproach that may be justifiable.

Peter writes, "For what glory is it if, when ye are buffeted for your faults, ye shall take it patiently?" (1 Pet. 2:20). Unjustified reproach is a cross by which we are counted worthy of the kingdom and our Lord is honored. But justified reproach is divine correction, parental discipline from Father, by which we are painfully but necessarily reminded of things we should have already dealt with, things that bring Him not glory but grief! Paul alertly and wisely recognized that the criticism circulating concerning the Cretan Christians was all too true: "One of themselves...said, The Cretans are always liars, evil beasts, lazy gluttons. *This testimony is true*" (Titus 1:12–13). Instead of recommending that Titus praise them, he charged him to rebuke them—and sternly! "Wherefore, *rebuke them sharply*, that they may be sound [strong and blameless] in the faith" (v. 13). Why? He knew God sometimes uses even destructive criticism for constructive purposes—to call us back to His high standards so we will reflect Jesus accurately and bring Him glory in this spiritually hostile environment. Do we share Paul's humble perspective?

When criticism comes calling, it's time to wake up: we too are in enemy territory in this satanically ruled social order and must strive to bring Jesus honor, not dishonor, in it. Again, David's life speaks to us.

Though so different, the Philistines and King Saul were alike in one point—both hated David and sought his downfall. Why? Their dominant spirit was of this world, and David's was of God. Just as David's Jewish and Gentile detractors united to denounce and destroy him, all who are worldly (Christian and non-Christian) long to find fault with, and cause to stumble, believers who are becoming spiritual. Paul teaches, "But as then he that was born after the flesh persecuted him that was born after the Spirit, even so it is now" (Gal. 4:29). So we must be doubly sure that we do not give our enemies any rightful charges against us. Christ's honor is at stake in our lives, ministries, and churches, and when we are dishonored justly, so is Christ. Though David's life brought God great honor, he dishonored Him when he sinned against God and Uriah. The prophet Nathan said, "By this deed thou hast given great occasion to the enemies of the LORD to blaspheme [speak disrespectfully or abusively of God]" (2 Sam. 12:14). It was a rare exception to an otherwise exceptionally God-honoring life.

Like David, we profess a close relationship with the Lord. Shouldn't our practice agree with the truths we profess and preach? Besides, if there is anything holding us back from being all God wants us to be, we should want to know it now, while there's time to correct it—that is, if we hope to become uncommon overcomers instead of common hypocrites! We must not complain when sinners or Christians note discrepancies between our spiritual talk and unspiritual walk. Our faithful faultfinders may not mean to, but they are helping us.

It's time we see our merciless criticisms as good evils—adverse things that God uses for good ends in our souls. The Lord declared through Isaiah that He "creates" and uses not only good but also "evil," or adverse, situations: "*I make peace, and create evil*; I, the Lord, do all these things" (Isa. 45:7).[3] We must also carefully distinguish between cross criticisms and correction criticisms.

Armed with this overcoming perspective, we will find our thorny critics very useful. Their scrutiny will make us watch our step rightly, with the awareness that God also is scrutinizing us and that we don't want to fail Him. This holy pressure will force us to conquer our carelessness and constantly gird up the loins of our minds lest we dishonor Jesus. It will keep us stirred up to be at our best, to be incarnations of the title to Oswald Chambers' great devotional classic, *My Utmost for His Highest*. This spiritual attitude toward unspiritual complaints will release us to never again resist but evermore ride the currents of "Shimei's" cruel criticism all the way to the shores of spiritual maturity. In the end, instead of chafing us, merciless criticism will conform us to the image of the One who discerned and overcame far worse scrutiny long ago.

We'll also find surprising refreshment in the most unlikely situations.

Chapter Twelve

REFRESHING SPIRITUALITY

It may be that the LORD will look on mine affliction, and that the
LORD will requite me good for his cursing this day.

—2 SAMUEL 16:12

WHEN DAVID WAS forced to abandon his throne, it was a dark time for him. Very dark. (See 2 Samuel 15:1–18:33.) His own son Absalom had subtly slandered him and gradually stolen the hearts of the Jewish people. Finally, after thoroughly undermining David's authority, Absalom executed his coup, boldly possessing David's capital city, palace, throne, even his harem. Reeling from rejection, dishonor, and a wounded spirit, David retreated to the Judean wilderness—the same desolate landscape in which he had taken refuge from King Saul long ago. The chances of David, now much older, returning to power seemed small. Very small. Everyone was fascinated with the young, good-looking, ambitious, seemingly anointed Absalom. The new leader's popularity was growing by the hour: "The conspiracy was strong; for the people increased continually with Absalom" (2 Sam. 15:12). To any informed observer, the evidence was conclusive: David's day was done; God was finished with the son of Jesse. As David pondered the situation, his heart must have been heavy with grief. Very heavy. To say things looked bad is an understatement; they couldn't have looked worse.

SHIMEI'S REPROACH: SATAN'S BAIT

At this low point, a man named Shimei came along to add insult to injury—literally. (See 2 Samuel 16:5–14.) He bitterly reviled David and challenged him to retaliate: "He came forth, and cursed continuously as he came...*Come out, come out*, thou bloody man, and thou worthless fellow" (vv. 5, 7). He even threw rocks at David and his men to try to force their hand: "And he cast stones at David, and at all the servants of King David" (v. 6).

Shimei's words are rich with spiritual, albeit unpleasant, meaning. When Shimei repeatedly shouted, "Come out, come out," Satan was speaking through him, trying to bait David to abandon his place and peace in God's will. Let me explain.

The Hebrew word used here, *yatsa*, means "to go out, to come out or leave an area" with a straight course.[1] So Shimei was telling David, "Get out of Jerusalem!" But Satan's subtle, underlying message was, "Get out of your place in God's will, the kingship, the leadership of God's people." So both David's adversaries, natural and supernatural, wanted him "out" of the place of God's will, Jerusalem, and straightaway! For now David was forced to comply. He had no choice but to leave Jerusalem as long as the coup succeeded.

Additionally, *yatsa* conveys the figurative meaning of "[to] vent," or "give expression of anger."[2] So Shimei was also taunting David to vent his anger in response to all the hard words and rocks he was throwing David's way. Had David responded in kind, he would have lost his peace by entering headlong into a fight, a worldly, unspiritual, personal, me-versus-you fight! Thus through Shimei's layered words, Satan was tempting David to vent his justified indignation at Shimei and come out of his peace in God's will. Here David had a choice, and, true to his righteous character, he made the right one. Wisely he refused to respond to Shimei's fighting words, even when one of his loyal-but-unspiritual associates, Abishai, suggested he do so: "Why should this dead dog curse my lord, the king? Let me go over, I pray thee, and take off his head" (v. 9). If David had indeed "come out" of his peace and ordered Shimei's execution in the heat of rage, he would have repeated Adam's failure in the garden. Why?

In the beginning God told Adam not to eat of the tree of the knowledge of good and evil (Gen. 2:15–17). Satan, therefore, planned his strategy with one end—to entice Adam to eat of *that* tree. Why? Such an act would be rebellion against God and would break Adam's fellowship with his Creator. Then God's holy justice would have to be satisfied: Adam would have to be put out of his place of blessing in God's will—beautiful, fruitful, peaceful Eden. When Adam disobeyed, that's exactly what followed; he was expelled from his place of blessing: "Therefore the LORD God sent him forth from the garden of Eden...so he drove out the man" (Gen. 3:23–24). Thus, by making the wrong choice in temptation, Adam unwisely "came out" of his place and peace in God's will.

Shimei didn't realize the significance of the words he was speaking. He was just a bitter, angry Benjamite raging as he roamed. Evidently he had never gotten over David becoming king years earlier. In Shimei's demented and prejudiced mind, King Saul, also a Benjamite, was still the better man and David the usurper. Clearly he considered David's present distress to be God's just judgment upon him for having "rebelled" against Saul. Spiritually blind, Shimei mistook Absalom's diabolical insurrection for God's divine intervention: "The LORD hath returned upon thee all the blood of the house of Saul, in whose stead thou hast reigned; and the LORD hath delivered the kingdom into the hand of Absalom, thy son; and behold, thou art taken in thy mischief, because thou art a bloody man" (2 Sam. 16:8).

Satan, who inspired Shimei's vicious venting, knew well the implications of his provocative words. He longed for David to take the bait and, by venting his rage, "come out" of God's plan and peace. At issue was how David would respond: would he resist Shimei's reviling or, as we discussed in the previous chapter, ride them?

Through Shimei Satan was saying:

Come out, come out of your peace and place in God's will and retaliate. Resist this adversity and adversary God has permitted. You don't have to take this kind of abuse from anyone. Don't submit; fight this thing! Silence Shimei! *Come out* of that attitude of acceptance you're in, and contend. Sure, God wants you to accept this injustice and quietly move on, but you don't have to wear that "yoke of bondage." *Come out!* Rebel!

It was Eden all over again, Satan trying his best to prompt God's man to defy God's will and put himself out of the place of blessing. And I'm sure that, for a moment, David thought about doing just that! But a wiser man with a humbler heart, David refused to go the way of Adam. Why? He had a better idea, a refreshingly spiritual idea born of the Spirit of God. Here is how David's inspiration came.

DAVID'S REVELATION AND RESPONSE

After hearing Shimei's words and Abishai's proposed response—"Take off his head!"—David pondered his options. With God's law written on his heart, David knew God said, "To me belongeth vengeance" (Deut. 32:35), and that if he fought for himself, God would not fight for him; that if he took vengeance, God couldn't. He also knew the proverb that preached patient trust in divine justice, not hasty human hatred: "Say not thou, I will recompense evil; but wait on the LORD, and he shall save thee" (Prov. 20:22).

Furthermore, David remembered how he chose to handle all the injustice he suffered from King Saul. After prayer and soul searching, he chose to not retaliate against the backslidden king but instead commit all judgment to God. God responded to David's faith by removing Saul in His time and way. If he took matters into his own hands now concerning Shimei, he would take them out of God's hands. This he would not do!

Additionally, David remembered what he had learned when he dealt with Nabal. He could still hear Abigail's wise counsel ringing in his ears, pleading with him not to avenge himself with his own hand (1 Sam. 25:26) but to instead let God "sling out" his enemies (v. 29).[3]

Mindful of these lessons, David made a simple decision to handle Shimei exactly as he had Saul and Nabal. He would again trust God and wait for His justice. Turning to Abishai, he ordered him to sheath his sword: "Let him [Shimei] alone" (2 Sam. 16:11).

God's response was immediate and inspirational. Only moments after David spoke to Abishai, God spoke to David. Like a flash of light in a dark cave, the Truth illuminated David's heavy heart with a luminous thought, which he promptly spoke aloud: "It may be that the LORD will look on mine affliction, and that the LORD will requite me good for his cursing this day" (v. 12); or, "It may be that the LORD will see my distress and repay me with good for the cursing I am receiving today" (NIV). Why did God give David this saving insight? He had obeyed God's will in restraining Abishai. The moment David said, "Let him alone," the Spirit spoke to his heart, "It may be..."

Succinctly, David's revelation was this: special blessings would be his because he endured Shimei's severe reproach. If Shimei hadn't cursed him, God wouldn't have granted special blessings. But now, because of Shimei's new attack, new divine favors would come David's way. God would now turn Shimei's cursings into blessings, just as He had Balaam's centuries earlier: "The LORD thy God turned the curse into a blessing unto thee" (Deut. 23:5). True to His Word, God would "cause" all things to work together for the good of His obedient servant (Rom. 8:28, NAS).

David's faith was that *uncommon reproach (or opposition) overcome brings uncommon rewards to the overcomer.* The measure of extra blessing received is equal to the measure of extra persecution endured. Joseph endured extraordinary persecution: "The archers have harassed him, and shot at him, and hated him" (Gen. 49:23). Accordingly, God gave Joseph extraordinary blessings. As Jacob prophesied, "The blessings of your father have surpassed the blessings of my ancestors...may they be on the head of Joseph" (v. 26, NAS). Shimei's curses were certainly extraordinary; David didn't face such abuse every day. So David acquiesced in his extraordinary distress, believing it would bring him extraordinary delights.

This was the powerful spiritual boost that propelled David to overcome the worst Shimei could throw at him. It comforted, strengthened, cheered, and kept him: "Understanding shall keep thee" (Prov. 2:11). It gave him spiritual, or soul, *rest*—the "power to keep himself calm" and undisturbed in the middle of disturbing adversity (Ps. 94:13, AMP). Thus, in a very hot situation, David stayed very cool.

May I offer a conjecture? Though he never said it, David may well have said or thought:

> Shimei, I am glad you came out to curse me today. Your denunciation is a blessing, your condemnation a lift in spirit. Because of your extra belligerence, God will give me extra blessings—good things that would not have been mine unless you had come against me. *Thank you* for helping me by your very attempt to hinder me. Because you bitterly hated me, God will sweetly favor me; your indignities will release more of His honors. Truly, "ye thought evil against me; but God meant it unto good" (Gen. 50:20).

THE REFRESHING RESULT

As the scene closes, Shimei is vexed and thoroughly discontented: "Shimei went along on the hillside opposite him, and cursed as he went, and threw stones at him, and cast dust" (2 Sam. 16:13). He was an emotional wreck. Naturally, we would expect him to be as relieved and peaceful as a spent volcano. But not so; not Shimei. He was more wretched than ever. Why?

As discussed in chapter 7, evil people do not rest "unless they cause some to fall" (Prov. 4:16). Shimei had not succeeded in causing David to stumble. The satanic strategy executed through him to move David from his place and peace in God's will had failed. David still had his peace and was on course to return to his place. But the evil attitudes Shimei held toward David remained unsatisfied. Shimei's sin could find no "whipping boy," therefore he had no rest: "There is no peace, saith my God, to the wicked" (Isa. 57:21).

On the other hand, David and his men were thoroughly refreshed by the whole affair. They "refreshed themselves there" (2 Sam. 16:14). What a miracle of grace! We would expect him to be bristling with anger after the flood of false accusations that had just been directed at him, but he was supernaturally held by God's peace, the "peace of God, which passeth all understanding" (Phil. 4:7). And that resulted from his simple choice to be spiritually minded toward his affliction. Paul reminds us that this perspective is always the difference between victory and defeat: "For to be carnally minded is death, but *to be spiritually minded is life and peace*" (Rom. 8:6). Wisely, David acknowledged the kind heavenly Arranger of circumstances behind his cruel earthly afflicter: "*The* LORD hath said unto him, Curse David…*the* LORD hath bidden him" (2 Sam. 16:10–11). Philosophically, he also used his God-given faculty of reason: Shimei's reviling was not nearly as bad as Absalom's—his own son's!—rebellion. "Behold, my son, who came forth of my own body, seeketh my life: *how much more*, now, may this Benjamite do it? Let him alone" (v. 11). This spiritual, scriptural perspective gave David and his men not only "life and peace" but also surprising physical refreshment.

Shortly after this incident Absalom was killed, and David returned to Jerusalem, vindicated and triumphant. On his way, whom should he run into but *Shimei*! (See 2 Samuel 19:16–23.) He was the first man to greet David after he crossed the Jordan. Fearful now, Shimei humbly fell before David, confessed how evil he had been, and begged forgiveness. David must have been very glad then that he had not executed Shimei—which would have prevented his repentance! David's faith was confirmed; as he had hoped, God had done His wondrous work in Shimei's conscience. David's bitterest living enemy was now broken, penitent, and willing to make things right. And David wrote, "It is God who avengeth me, and subdueth the peoples under me" (Ps. 18:47).

WILL YOU BE REFRESHED?

Fellow disciple, have you been falsely accused of late by some "Shimei"? Have you been grossly misrepresented, mercilessly reviled, and challenged to fight back? Let David's experience save you from a great snare.

Choose to be spiritually minded toward your afflicter. Do not allow your enemies, natural and supernatural, to draw you out of your place and peace in God's will. If you allow yourself to be drawn into carnal retaliation, either in act or desire, your peace will spread its wings and fly away, and you'll abandon your secure, blessed, productive "Eden"—the circumstances God designed for you and placed you in for your spiritual growth in this season of your life. So obey Paul's inspired injunction, "Recompense to no man evil for evil," accusation for accusation, insult for insult (Rom. 12:17). When you must respond to verbally abusive adversaries, pray for grace, and then reply calmly, firmly, and as briefly as possible. Jesus instructed us, "Let your communication be Yea, yea; Nay, nay" (Matt. 5:37). Why the need for brevity? Too much talk may stir anger in us, or it may start or extend a heated argument, "for whatever is more than these cometh of evil" (v. 37); or "If you say more than yes or no, it is from the Evil One" (NCV). And just then, remember David's refreshing revelation!

If you had never been reproached for righteousness' sake, there would be no reward. Now, fresh rewards are reserved for you! So "rejoice ye in this day!"

> Blessed are ye, when men shall hate you, and when they shall separate you from their company, and shall reproach you, and cast out your name as evil, for the Son of man's sake. *Rejoice ye in that day,* and leap for joy; for, behold, your reward is great in heaven.
>
> —LUKE 6:22–23

And take your persecution patiently:

> For this is thankworthy, if a man for conscience toward God endure grief, suffering wrongfully... *[But] if,* when ye do well and suffer for

it, *ye take it patiently*, this is acceptable [pleasing and meritorious] with God.

—1 Peter 2:19–20

Then do what David did: fear not, stand still, and let God fight for you, while you remain very careful to obey His Word and guidance in all matters. Why? To please Him; that will prompt Him to defend you, as He did David: "When a man's ways please the Lord, he maketh even his enemies to be at peace with him" (Prov. 16:7).

Keep this up, and nothing will touch you. You'll have calm in the midst of chaos. You'll retain your peace. And you'll stand firm in your place in God's will, immovable as Mount Zion: "They that trust in the Lord shall be as mount Zion, which cannot be removed, but abideth for ever" (Ps. 125:1). Your "Shimei" may be up one day and down the next, delightful one minute and demonic the next, but you will be "steadfast, unmovable, always abounding in the work of the Lord" (1 Cor. 15:58). Why? David's revelation will refresh and refit you daily. And the more "Shimei" reviles you, the more the Father will refresh you.

This is good news from the "far country" of heaven: "As cold waters to a thirsty soul, so is good news from a far country" (Prov. 25:25). Drink, and let it cool your chaffed spirit today.

And look up, relief is coming!

Chapter Thirteen

WHEN RELIEF IS ON THE WAY

Then the disciples, every man according to his ability, determined to send relief unto the brethren who dwelt in Judea; which also they did, and sent it to the elders by the hands of Barnabas and Saul. Now about that time Herod, the king, stretched forth his hands to vex certain of the church.

—ACTS 11:29–30; 12:1

B EFORE RELIEF ARRIVES, however, problems often pop up, seemingly out of nowhere!

This pattern occurs so often in overcomers' lives that we may encapsulate it in a spiritual law: *unusually strong vexation sometimes indicates that unusual relief from God is approaching.* We see an excellent example of this in Acts 11:27 and 12:4.

There we find the Judean brethren in trouble. A great famine was approaching, and many of them were already living near or in poverty. So God, in His mercy, sent the prophet Agabus to the large and growing church in Antioch, the Roman capital of Syria and third largest city in the Roman world with a population of about half a million people.[1] In that young, thriving, zealous congregation, Agabus advised the believers through prophecy of the coming plight of their Judean brothers and sisters: "And in these days came prophets from Jerusalem unto Antioch. And there stood up one of them, named Agabus, and signified by the Spirit that there should be great famine throughout all the [Roman] world, which came to pass in the days of Claudius Caesar" (Acts 11:27–28).

The Christians in Antioch were deeply moved by this timely prophecy and felt compelled to help the Judean church in a material way. Realizing famine conditions would drive up the price of all food substances at market, they acted proactively, sending money ahead of time to meet this anticipated need: "Then the disciples, every man according to his ability, *determined to send relief* unto the brethren who dwelt in Judea; which also they did, and sent it to the elders by the hands of Barnabas and Saul" (vv. 29–30). Thus, in a time of great need, God did not forget His faithful ones in Judea.[2] "Relief," in this case money for buying high-priced grain, was on its way.

But while the "relief" was coming, something else was stirring. The Judean church came under a direct and brutal satanic attack through wicked King Herod Agrippa I: "Now about that time Herod, the king, stretched forth his hands to vex certain of the church" (Acts 12:1). "About that time" may be paraphrased as, "meanwhile." Thus we see that *as God's relief was on its way through Barnabas and Saul, Satan, through Herod, was vexing those who were about to receive it.* And in no small way! Satan tried to decapitate the local church!

Without warning, Herod lashed out and "killed James, the brother of John, with the sword" (v. 2). Not content with executing one church leader to delight his subjects, the Christian-hating Jews, Herod moved quickly to remove another—this time, *the* single most influential apostle Peter: "And because he saw it pleased the Jews, he proceeded further to take Peter also.... And when he had apprehended him, he put him in prison... intending after Easter to bring him forth to the people [for public execution]" (vv. 3–4). Well aware of Peter's previous miraculous escape (Acts 5:19–21), Herod placed the famous fisherman-turned-preacher under the highest security of the day: "He... delivered him to four quaternions [four-man squads] of soldiers to keep him" (Acts 12:4). With this, Herod's "blitzkrieg"[3] subsided.

Dizzied by it all, the Judean church still had no idea that "relief" was on the way. All they knew was that Satan had come in on them "like a flood" (Isa. 59:19) and left them stunned, treading water, and barely holding things together! And pondering their strange situation.

Surely the remaining leaders sat down, prayed, and reviewed the chronology of the whirlwind from nowhere. First, the apostle James, one of Jesus' original, handpicked special messengers, was suddenly arrested and *decapitated*, executed by sword! Second, Peter, their most dynamic, famous, and fruitful leader, was arrested and held for execution without cause. Considering James' grisly end, Peter's prospects didn't look too good. But their biggest question was: *Why?* Why had Herod erupted in fury against the Judean church? They had coexisted peacefully with the Jews in Jerusalem and its environs for nearly a decade.[4] Why the vicious attack at this time?

Though shrouded, the explanation was simple. Satan saw God's relief approaching and sought to crush the spirits of the Judean saints before it arrived. Limited by God's limitless power, he could not stop the blessing. But he could, and did, do his diabolical worst to spoil it. And God stood by, for the moment, and let him do it. This brings us to another why—why did God permit this?

Knowing "relief" was coming, God deliberately permitted Herod's devilry for several reasons:

1. To test the faith and loyalty of the Judean church by letting them suffer severe injustice for righteousness' sake (Matt. 5:10–12)

2. To permit James to win a martyr's "crown of life" (Rev. 2:10)

3. To enable James to "be with Christ" early, "which is far better" (Phil. 1:23), and obtain a "better resurrection" in eternity (Heb. 11:35)

4. To fulfill Jesus' prophecy that James would experience His "cup" of sufferings and "baptism" of death (Matt. 20:23)

5. To let Peter also suffer for righteousness' sake, so the Spirit could "rest" on him afresh and he could "glorify" God yet again (1 Pet. 4:12–14, 16)

6. To give Peter an opportunity of showing us the amazing, overcoming faith that can rest in God under the most extreme conditions (Acts 12:6)

7. To exercise, and thus grow, the church in persistent, overcoming prayer while facing a perplexing and apparently impossible problem (Acts 12:5)

8. To fulfill Jesus' prophecy foretelling Peter's martyrdom—but not until he was "old" (John 21:18)

9. To honor Jesus' great name (over Herod!) by working yet another miracle in Jerusalem (Acts 12:11, 18–19)

10. To set up wicked King Herod for his approaching day of divine judgment; by executing James, the Lord's anointed, Herod ensured and hastened his own execution (Acts 12:20–23)

And there's one more reason.

Our loving, wise Father permitted this cruel, strange scenario to give Christians an example for the ages—to teach us the enemy often attacks *us* just before divine help arrives to relieve us!

We see this principle in David's Ziklag experience.

WHEN DAVID'S "RELIEF" WAS ON THE WAY—ZIKLAG!

For many years David waited patiently for God to deliver him from evil King Saul and his relentless, oppressive persecution. Only then could David ascend to the throne of Israel as prophesied by Samuel. David realized that King Saul's judgment meant personal deliverance for him and his men and the beginning of a time of blessing for all Israel. But when the long-awaited day of liberation finally drew near, Satan tried to crush David with discouragement. Just as God was executing Saul's sentence of judgment upon Mount Gilboa (1 Sam. 31:1–6), the Ziklag drama unfolded, during which the Amalekites suddenly swooped down on the village where David and his men lived, burning their homes, stealing their flocks, and kidnapping their wives and children (1 Sam. 30:1–31). So we see that *while God was using the Philistines to judge Saul, Satan was using the Amalekites to vex David.*

So strong, so personal, so surprising was the Amalekites' blitzkrieg that David almost went under. Overwhelmed but not overcome, David dug deep in his soul and "encouraged himself in the LORD his God" (1 Sam. 30:6) and, by faith, held on to the Rock that was higher than him. Then, his faith restored, he pursued the Amalekites and "recovered all" they had stolen from him and his men (vv. 9, 18–19).

On the third day after David and his men returned to the burnt-out ruins of Ziklag, word came of Saul's death (2 Sam. 1:1–4). Like a flash of light, David realized what had really happened to him at Ziklag. His great distress and Saul's death had occurred *simultaneously.* Ziklag was no mere coincidence; though *by* men, it was not *of* men. The Amalekites performed the raid, but Satan planned and inspired it.[5] Ziklag was his well-timed blow, intended to crush David precisely when God was ready to relieve him from the rigors of his distressing wilderness trials. Thus *Satan vexed David to the breaking point just as God's relief was finally at hand.* And David wrote, "Thou hast thrust hard at me that I might fall, but the LORD helped me" (Ps. 118:13).[6]

The same Lord who helped David has provided help for us too when relief is on the way.

Countermeasures We May Take

Our adversary, the devil, still works against us as he did the Judean Christians and David, vexing us just when God's help is near. Why?

As stated earlier, he knows he can't unilaterally stop our blessing. If we continue to believe and obey God, the devil can't keep the omnipotent One's answers to our prayers from breaking through. But the spiritual "thief" can steal something else from us and God. As Jesus taught, "*The thief* cometh not but *to steal*" (John 10:10). Specifically, the devil hopes to steal our joy by vexing and troubling us to the point that we neither appreciate nor enjoy God's blessings when they arrive. And by doing so, he hopes to keep us from thanking, praising, and worshiping God for His help as we should. Thus the "thief" plots to steal our joy and God's praise. This is one of his "devices" against us: "For we are not ignorant of *his devices* ['evil schemes,' NLT]" (2 Cor. 2:11). But God has plans and devices too.

To prevent Satan from robbing us of our joy and His praise, God has given us three effective countermeasures. When the enemy comes in like a flood, overwhelming us with sudden troubles or needling us with persistent, pesky vexations, three simple responses will keep us from being overcome—and ready to fully enjoy our deliverances and worship our Deliverer. Let's review them.

Believe this principle!

We are greatly helped by merely believing the principle we're discussing in this chapter. When we realize that the Scriptures teach that satanic vexation often precedes divine blessing, we're immediately relieved—if we make the simple choice to believe this biblical pattern. And we're put at a distinct advantage, because discovering our enemy's strategy is winning half the battle.

From then on, every sudden onslaught of resistance through satanically influenced people becomes a joyful announcement of imminent relief from on high. The more we meditate on this, the more we believe it, because "faith comes from hearing...the word of Christ" (Rom. 10:17, ESV); and the more we believe it, the more we go free from the power of vexation. Believing God's truth imparts immediate internal liberation. Jesus put it this way: "The truth shall make you free...free indeed" (John

8:32, 36). This confidence in God's ways holds us still when everything around us suddenly goes crazy. It cools us in the heat of trial, strengthens us in the depths of weakness, and refills us when drained to the danger point. The moment we consider this truth sympathetically, faith imparts "rest"—cessation from all agitation, chafing, or anxiety—to our weary souls. The writer to the Hebrews notes this crucial Bible meditation-faith-rest link: "For we who have *believed* [God and the promises and patterns of His Word] do enter into *rest*" (Heb. 4:3).

Give thanks!

Giving thanks to God also counters the stress and strain of Satan's "blitzkriegs"—not necessarily thanking God for the vexation, but "in" it: "*In* every thing give thanks; for this is the will of God in Christ Jesus concerning you" (1 Thess. 5:18). (See chapter 1 for more on the attitude of acceptance.) This is most reasonable.

It's only logical that if we believe that resistance is often relief's harbinger, then we should start thanking the Lord for His imminent help the moment we recognize exceptional resistance. This exercises our faith in God's faithfulness, because we are thanking God before seeing His help arrive, based solely upon our confidence in the utter reliability of His character and ways. This also honors God when we offer Him the "sacrifice of praise...that is, the fruit of our lips giving thanks to his name" (Heb. 13:15) while trouble still swirls around us. It also pleases Him immensely.[7] And that helps us immensely, because thanking and praising God acceptably reconnects us with the Spirit, who refills and refreshes us with God's supernatural life and love, soothing our chafed spirit. And the more we thank Him, the better we feel. According to the biblical adage, "Give, and it shall be given unto you" (Luke 6:38), the one that gives praise is given peace.

Pray...more!

Prayer is another redemptive remedy. When stressed, increased prayer heals our incensed spirits. This is why Jesus taught, "Men ought always to pray, and not to faint" (Luke 18:1).

We see this exemplified by the Jerusalem saints, who overcame Herod's vicious assault by increasing their praying. The entire time Peter was in prison, they held a nonstop prayer meeting: "Peter, therefore, was kept in prison; but *prayer was made without ceasing* by the church unto God for him" (Acts 12:5). Thus by obeying the inspired apostolic direction, "Pray without ceasing" (1 Thess. 5:17), they vanquished their diabolical vexer and his plan to cripple their confidence in God by arresting and threatening their "senior pastor."[8]

Through James also the Holy Spirit prescribes increased prayer as a cure for the "afflicted," or distressed or troubled,[9] heart: "Is any among you *afflicted*? Let him *pray*" (James 5:13).

Jesus further taught that increased prayer would help make us strong, alert, and worthy in these perilous days before His appearing. When international unrest, national distress, ecclesiastical impotency, political strife, and personal stress rise to unprecedented levels, Jesus says, "Watch ye, therefore, and *pray always*, that ye may be accounted worthy to escape all these things that shall come to pass, and to stand before the Son of man" (Luke 21:36).

The psalmist David habitually turned to increased prayer when tribulation or persecution suddenly poured in. At Ziklag, after reviving his faith, David's first positive act in response to the Amalekite raid was to call for the ephod and "inquire of the LORD" (1 Sam. 30:8). Of his response to this and other crises, David wrote, "But I give myself [constantly or consistently] unto prayer" (Ps. 109:4). When Satan cast burdens on David, David cast them on God by praying "evening, and morning, and at noon" (Ps. 55:17). Therefore he counsels us to do the same: "Cast *thy* burden upon the LORD, and he shall sustain *thee*; he shall never suffer the righteous to be moved" (v. 22). Why is prayer so beneficial to tried saints?

In a word, this is due to *the reviving effects of God's presence.* Again, arising from his personal experience, David worships God and informs us, "In thy presence is fullness of joy" (Ps. 16:11). In prayer, the presence is more important than the petition. We should, of course, petition our Father for our every need, spiritual and worldly (Phil. 4:6–7). But soaking is more important than seeking answers. The Lord creates needs in our lives not only for us to seek and see His help but also to prod, even force, us to spend quality time in His presence. (If He didn't, sadly, some would never draw near!) Once we are there, He saturates our permeable souls afresh with His enlivening Spirit. The longer we soak in our heavenly Father's presence, the stronger we become (provided we're walking in the light). A vital catharsis, prayer enables us to safely and privately release to God thoughts and emotions we can't wisely share with others: "*Pour out your heart before him.* God is a [therapeutic, restorative] refuge for us. Selah" (Ps. 62:8). By such petitions and His presence, our Father supernaturally restores our souls in a way we can often sense or feel. Again, David testified, "He restoreth my soul" (Ps. 23:3). As we interface with the Immortal, God's Spirit refills ours, His mind sharpens ours, and His will molds ours. As we sit, stand, or lie in His awesome atmosphere, the Creator re-creates the core of His creature. After such times in His presence, we emerge thoroughly refreshed and ready to readdress the race set before us.

So the next time the enemy comes in on you like a flood, and you feel tempted to rebel or faint, don't! Don't stop doing God's will or charge Him with folly. Instead, remember and practice the three simple countermeasures discussed above. And review the reasons God permitted Herod's devilry against the early church and see if any of those insights bear on your situation. But mostly, remain confident that, although you can't see, hear, or touch it yet, some form of "relief" is on the way.

It may be a manifest answer to one of your petitions, long-awaited and greatly needed. It may be a great blessing you never expected, something "exceedingly abundantly above" anything you've ever dreamed or asked (Eph. 3:19). It may be financial aid, arriving when you could not go any further without it. It may be the repentance or removal of a cruel oppressor in your life, when further oppression would be the end of you. It may be the full physical or psychological recovery of a loved one, when their prolonged illness has taxed your faith and endurance to the limit. Or it may be any other timely blessing that lifts the burden from your shoulders.

If you hold this hope and practice these principles, no matter how many furious "Herods" or swarming "Amalekites" overwhelm you, they'll not overcome you! You'll stand firm till God's relief arrives.

And, if you will, you may choose to keep loving and serving your Blesser, even if His blessings *never* arrive! Others have.

"SANS BLESSINGS" SAINTS

> Then Satan answered the LORD, and said, Doth Job fear God for nothing?
>
> —JOB 1:9

I NDEED, SCRIPTURE TELLS of souls who persevered in close fellowship with God and faithful service to Him without any manifest blessings! We call them "sans blessings" saints.

Sans is a French word meaning "without, in the absence of," or "lacking."[1] During long periods of affliction or reproach, these supremely abandoned ones had nothing whatsoever to show for their godliness. All along they enjoyed God's richest internal compensations—His presence, voice, guidance, peace, and joy; anointings of His Spirit, insights from His Word, and understanding of His plans; and the abiding sense that, despite contradictory appearances, all was well—yet they had little or no outward evidence of His favor! Believers who serve the Blesser for His blessings are common, but "sans blessings" saints are rare. Very rare! Job is the greatest among them.

JOB: SERVING GOD FOR "NOTHING"

Job's strangest, hardest, longest trial began with Satan's insulting accusation, "Doth Job fear God for *nothing*?" (Job 1:9). Thereafter, this toxic allegation—that Job feared and served the Lord, not out of love and respect for the Most High, but only for the worldly rewards and favors he received from Him!—became God's top objective in testing Job. In short, He hoped Job would prove Satan wrong...and silence his slander against God and His servants!

Aiming at this goal, God set about to use Satan's hellish plot to serve His heavenly purpose. He let the "accuser" suddenly reduce Job, cut him back materially, and strip away his exterior blessings until, as Satan envisioned, Job was left with "nothing." Only Job's spiritual and physical life were to be left untouched, while everything else—possessions, relationships, ministry, friends—was fair game: "He is in thine hand; but *save his life*" (Job 2:6). Why? This was the only way God could see if Job would be as loyal and devoted without blessings as he had been with them.

During the days of his prosperity, Job was an outstanding man of God. Protected by God's angelic "hedge" (Job 1:10),[2] Job flourished spiritually, personally, materially, and ministerially. Spiritually, God personally testified that he was "perfect," or spiritually mature, and peerless: "There is *none like him* in the earth...perfect...upright...feareth God...shunneth evil" (v. 8). This meant he had no consistent faults or besetting sins, and that all the suffering that followed was, at least initially, as God declared, "without cause" (Job 2:3). Personally, Job was blessed with a wife and "seven sons and three daughters" (Job 1:2). With a lovely female "vine" and *ten* thriving "olive plants" round about his table (Ps. 128:3), his family life was as rich and full as anyone's. Materially, Job was "the greatest [wealthiest] of all the men of the east" (Job 1:3), possessing many thousands of sheep, camels, oxen, and donkeys, making him, comparatively speaking, the "Bill Gates" of his day. Ministerially, he had a teaching and counseling ministry that was both wide and effective. Eliphaz testified, "Thou hast *instructed many*, and thou hast strengthened the weak hands. *Thy words have upheld* him that was falling, and *thou hast strengthened* the feeble knees" (Job 4:3–4). Thus surrounded by God's evident favor, Job was the living embodiment of godly humanity, mature in devotion, fruitful in family life, influential in ministry, and overflowing with worldly blessings. But this ideal life was about to change.

Now the issue was this: *Would Job be the same man when stripped*

of all his possessions, relationships, ministry, respect, and even his health?
Would he continue to thrive spiritually? Would his love for God be
undiminished and his service unchanged? This was what God sought to
find out. Satan wagered that the bitter injustice of undeserved adversity
would end Job's walk and work with God. God believed, and staked His
honor on it, that it wouldn't.

Satan cited Job's abundant blessings as proof that his motives were
wrong: "Thou hast blessed the work of his hands, and his substance
is increased in the land" (Job 1:10). Satan's perspective and plan were
simple: if Job's manifold outer blessings were removed, his inner spiritual life would collapse; if his prosperity were broken off, he would break
off relations with his Prosperer: "But put forth thine hand now, and
touch [adversely] all that he hath, and *[offended,] he will curse thee to thy
face [and walk away]*" (v. 11). It was a serious charge requiring a prompt
response.

So the Lord quickly accepted Satan's cruel challenge, authorizing
the colossal contest but placing distinct limits on what Satan could do.
First, He didn't permit the enemy to touch Job's person, only his people
and property: "And the LORD said unto Satan, Behold, all that he hath is
in thy power; *only upon himself put not forth thine hand*" (v. 12). Later,
He let the enemy afflict Job with sickness but not kill him: "Behold, he is
in thine hand; *but save his life*" (Job 2:6). Having obtained divine permission to, at last, pass through Job's "hedge" of protection, Satan wasted no
time launching his assault: "So Satan went forth from the presence of the
LORD" (Job 1:12). And the test was on.

For an undisclosed amount of time,[3] Job suffered intensely (Job
1:13–42:9). Every outward token of divine approval was systematically
stripped away. Children, possessions, health, friends, respect, spousal
support, ministry—*everything* was taken from him—except his personal
relationship with God. And heaven offered no explanation. His entire
being was shot through with mental, emotional, and physical pain. In
indescribable agony, he cried out to God, contended with his callous

critics, questioned, and complained. But never, not once, did Job renounce his faith and abandon God. Through it all he trusted that God had the answers he did not have and would reveal them in His time and way. As his now-famous faith was being forged by God's final blows on His anvil of adversity, he cried out the essential theme of his test and teaching: *"Though he slay me, yet will I trust in him"* (Job 13:15). Thus the end the devil hoped for never materialized. Though severely shaken, confused, pained, grieved, and oppressed, the man Job stood true to God until He turned his captivity (Job 42:10). So the "father of lies" was proven just that—a liar!—and God and His servant were vindicated.

Job's epic endurance established forever the fact that he would serve God for "nothing." This was no longer a prospect but a reality. It was on the record now that, when stripped of all that he had, and that "without cause" (Job 2:3), he still maintained his walk with and service to God. Observing this after Job's first assault (Job 1), God personally testified, "And *still he holdeth fast his integrity*, although thou movedst me against him, to destroy him *without cause*" (Job 2:3).

Job's victory proved more than his personal integrity. Satan's insult implied that not only Job but also all of God's servants serve Him only for what He gives them, specifically material or other worldly benefits. Job's loyal endurance "sans blessings" proves forever that, although the undevoted majority may serve God for His favors, there exists a devoted minority who will cleave to Him and do His will, even for "nothing."

These true servants, God's overcomers, serve Him for Himself: "And his servants shall serve *him*" (Rev. 22:3). Irrespective of identifiable blessings or lack of them, they "cling unto the Lord" with "purpose of heart" (Acts 11:23). Neither poverty nor prosperity moves them from their dominant affectionate fascination with God. Their human contentment is deeply rooted in knowing that they are pleasing to the heavenly

Father. They have learned and inherited this motivational drive from Jesus, who said, "I do always those things that *please him*" (John 8:29). Their abiding joy lies not in external things but in their private fellowship with their Lord. Their sense of purpose is focused like a laser on faithfully executing the duties He has assigned them in their current field of service, large or small. Knowing that it is *His* will makes their task satisfying. Again, they have adopted this from Jesus, who said, "My food [soul satisfaction and source of life strength] is to do the will of him that sent me, and to finish his work" (John 4:34). Though worldly thinking people consider them worthless, these "sans blessings" saints are priceless to God.

Lesser servants of God—"Demas" types—come and go with God's outward tokens of favor. When blessings abound, they abound. When success and prosperity appear, they appear. While prosperous, they are happy and reasonably dedicated. But as soon as adverse conditions arise, their spirit wavers, love cools, and dedication slackens. Within a short period, sometimes only days, they forsake their God-given duties, ministries, churches, and leaders, just as Demas did. Paul described Demas' disappointing demise in his second letter to Timothy: "For Demas hath forsaken me, having loved this present world" (2 Tim. 4:10). Like Demas, these offended Christian opportunists wander off to resume their old life, walk in their old ways, seek their old goals, and serve their old idols, futilely seeking life among spiritually dead people and interests. Thus, spiritually speaking, they do what Job refused to do: "Curse God, and die" (Job 2:9). Their actions prove they serve God not for what He wants but for what they want. And when they don't get it, they walk away.

OTHER "SANS BLESSINGS" SAINTS

While Job was the "superstar" of abandoned God-servers, he wasn't the only one. Scripture tells of others with the stuff of Job in their hearts.

By the brook Cherith, Elijah was reduced to bread, flesh, water, and the humble company of a few birds for several months. Yet he remained content and in such close fellowship with Jehovah that he detected His voice the instant He spoke, ordering him to Zarephath (1 Kings 17:2–7). Joseph had his earthly father's protective favor and provision stripped away while he was a slave and prisoner in Egypt. But he continued to serve his heavenly Father faithfully, first in Potiphar's house, then in his prison (Gen. 37, 39–40). Moses, blessed with the comfort and wealth of Egypt, was drastically reduced and humbled when constrained to live the lifestyle of a desert shepherd[4] for forty years. Yet in that humble setting, he kept the vision and "endured, as seeing him who is invisible" (Heb. 11:27). Christian fellowship and ministry were stripped away from the apostle John when he was exiled on the lonely, windswept isle of Patmos. Yet he remained in close fellowship with his favorite Friend, and, in his isolation, he ministered to Him "in the Spirit" every Lord's day (Rev. 1:9-10).

"Sans blessings," all these continued to thrive in their spiritual life. They lacked rewards but not the Rewarder of "them that diligently seek him" (Heb. 11:6). They continued to adore and abide in Him when they were "abased" (Phil. 4:12). They consistently chose to remain content with His inner blessings even when He cut them back to life's barest essentials. Like Paul, they could be satisfied, if necessary, with bread, water, and the clothes on their backs. And through Paul's writings, Christ, the Head of the church and real Author of the epistles, calls us to the same extraordinary commitment: "Having food and raiment let us be therewith content" (1 Tim. 6:8).

GOD RESERVES HIS BEST BLESSINGS FOR "SANS BLESSINGS" SAINTS

God tested Job severely, but not forever. There came an end to his endurance: "And *the* LORD *turned the captivity of Job*, when he prayed for his friends" (Job 42:10). This turning of the captivity signified the end not only of Job's exterior hardships but also of his interior refinement. Let me explain.

As stated earlier, previous or ongoing sins did not cause Job's sufferings. Undeniably God declared he was "upright" and "perfect" in his walk with Him and he suffered "without cause." Why, then, did Job repent at the end of his long trial? "I abhor myself, and *repent* in dust and ashes" (Job 42:6).

Though Job's spiritual excellence remained intact through Satan's major assaults on his possessions, children, health, and spousal support, the sin of pride subsequently arose in his heart. When Job's friends, who after seven days assumed God was judging him for secret sin, turned and began to heap misjudgment and condemnation on him, Job yielded to pride by adamantly defending himself[5] and complaining.[6] His heated, personal quarrel was driven by a proud attempt to prove: (1) not that God was still good, but that he, Job, was still righteous; and (2) that his friends were wrong and he was right. Though Job's latter point was true, his spirit was wrong in asserting it, because he debated solely for his honor, not God's: "Only by pride cometh contention" (Prov. 13:10). And all his complaints, though justified from a mere human standpoint, were indirect slurs against God, who controlled his circumstances and could have prevented or ended his sufferings. Additionally, Job became personally offended with his three friends for betraying him in his lowest hour. This pride that arose during Job's trial, and all the strife, complaints, and hard feelings it produced in him, became his sin (sinful *reaction* to adversity) and necessitated his rebuke from God (Job 38–41), his repentance before Him (Job 40:3–5; 42:6), and his willingness to show mercy to his adversarial "friends" (v. 10).

With this "dross," Job's latent sin, now exposed and confessed in the "Refiner's fire," Job was a better man with a purer heart and ready to resume his life and ministry—as a husband, father, friend, teacher, and counselor—with greater spiritual power than before.[7] So we see God stripped away Job's blessings not only to disprove Satan's audacious accusation but also to purify his purest man and make him *purer* in heart and *better* in service.

When Job, proven in faith and purified in heart, reached the end of his trial, to his utter amazement, he found even greater blessings, specifically "twice as much" as he had before: "The LORD gave Job *twice as much as he had before.*...So the LORD blessed the latter end of Job *more than his beginning*" (Job 42:10, 12). This shows that *God saves His greatest blessings for those who serve Him without blessings.* Why? Those who walk closely with God with no portion can be trusted with His "double portion." Isaiah promises this: "Instead of shame and dishonor, you will enjoy *a double share of honor.* You will possess *a double portion of prosperity* in your land, and everlasting joy will be yours" (Isa. 61:7, NLT). When we serve God faithfully with an empty fold, He can safely grant us His "hundredfold" (Mark 10:30).

The experiences of Isaac and the apostles confirm this.

ISAAC'S "HUNDREDFOLD"

The only Bible character specifically said to have received a "hundredfold" earthly blessing is Isaac:

> Then Isaac sowed in that land, and received in the same year *an hundredfold*: and the LORD blessed him. And the man became great, and went forward, and grew until he became very great; for he had possession of flocks, and possession of herds, and great store of servants.
>
> —GENESIS 26:12–14

Yet we must note that before Isaac received this tremendous blessing from God, he first proved his willingness to serve God without blessings, even unto death.

On Mount Moriah, Isaac offered neither objection nor resistance to Abraham as Abraham moved steadily to put him to death (Gen. 22:1–10). In ultimate submission and trust, Isaac laid down his life to do the will of his earthly and heavenly fathers. (His amazing submission foreshadows Jesus' sacrifice at Calvary to do His Father's will.) Therefore Isaac had laid down *everything*—all the worldly blessings of Abraham's vast estate,

125

his by right, and his potential future wife, family, friends, vocation, and ministry—before he received the hundredfold blessing of God.

THE APOSTLES

The poor, young, spiritual apostles watched attentively as a rich, young, worldly ruler came seeking Jesus yet received no promises of worldly blessing from Him.

Instead the Master gave His eager candidate for discipleship a very different assurance, that, if he would sell out on Earth, he would qualify for treasure "in heaven." "Sell whatever thou hast, and give to the poor, and thou shalt have *treasure in heaven*; and come, take up the cross, and follow me" (Mark 10:21). These weren't terms of salvation. They were the high costs paid by every abandoned follower of the Blesser. Unwilling to lay down his blessings or his life to be Christ's "disciple"—a deeply serious, irrevocably committed, self-disciplined student-follower—this blessings-driven believer "went away grieved" (v. 22). And the Blesser was more grieved than he was.

Yet, to the apostles, Jesus promised something very different, "an hundredfold now in this time, houses, and brethren, and sisters, and mothers, and children, and lands, with persecutions,[8] and in the age to come eternal life" (Mark 10:30). Why the different pledge? Unlike the rich, young, worldly ruler, the apostles had already "left all" to follow the Master. Speaking for them all, Peter testified, "*Lo, we have left all, and have followed thee*" (v. 28). Homes, lands, wives, children, relatives, friends, businesses, careers—at the Master's call to discipleship, the apostles laid aside all these blessed things. The Gospels memorialize their great sacrifice: "And when they had brought their boats to land, *they forsook all, and followed him*" (Luke 5:11). The apostles paid the price the rich young ruler refused. They accepted the cross he rejected. They cast away the possessions to which he clung. They served Jesus "sans blessings," and he did so "for blessings." So they qualified for God's best blessings and he did not.

The God who tested Job, Isaac, and the apostles must also test us. Our adversary, the devil, who spoke against them, has also reproached us. Of this generation of materialistically laden Christians he has said, "Will *they* serve you for *nothing*?" To answer this new serious charge, God must in different ways and degrees test us in His crucible of reduction. In these last days of the Church Age, all believers will pass through some kind of testing similar to Job's. The details of our trials—the severity, duration, costs, and rewards—will vary, but the substance will be the same. All of us must be put to this test (if we haven't previously experienced it) so God may know where we really stand, whom we really serve, what we really seek. Also, as in Job's case, God will use these fiery trials to expose and purge our latent sins and faults, especially faulty reactions to adversity, so we may emerge not only proven but purified and more powerful in service.

All heaven knows we will sing God's praises while we are prosperous, popular, successful, and influential. Who wouldn't? *But will we be the same ardent worshipers when evidence of divine approval is partially or wholly stripped away for a season?* If the Lord should permit Satan to break through our "hedge" and steal possessions, relationships, reputation, and even health from us, will we still cling to God and, in our distress, be "in the Spirit" every Lord's day? Will persecution mean the end of our fellowship with God or the beginning of a new, lasting depth of sainthood? Will we draw back to carnal Christianity or "go on" to spiritual "perfection" (Heb. 6:1)? Will we curse God and die or trust Him and live? Will we prove Satan right or wrong? Silence or amplify his malicious mouth?

Today God earnestly seeks answers to these profound questions. He's searching His worldwide congregation for "sans blessings" saints. Pay the price to be one. Serve Him, if necessary, for "nothing."

And don't be surprised if some of your friends misunderstand your trials, as Job's friends did his.

Chapter Fifteen

WHERE TO TURN WHEN
OTHERS TURN AWAY

To him that is afflicted, pity should be shown from his friend,
but...my brethren [friends] have dealt deceitfully.

—JOB 6:14–15

IN JOB'S SEVEREST hour of trial, his closest friends took a surprising
turn. Just when he assumed they would understand and support
him, they judged and abandoned him. This was the third major blow
that Satan dealt Job. The first two (Job 1, 2) failed to shake him out of his
superb spiritual walk. This one hit its mark.

JOB'S WRONG TURN

How amazing it was that Job overcame the bitter loss of his children
and property by retaining a sweet spirit! "Job arose...and worshiped,
and said...The LORD gave, and the LORD hath taken away; *blessed be the
name of the LORD*" (Job 1:20–21). Even more amazing was the fact that he
endured the additional loss of his health with a steadfast spirit! "What?
Shall we receive good at the hand of God, and *shall we not receive evil
[accept adversity also from God's hand]*?" (Job 2:10).

But then a small crack appeared in Job's amazingly sustained spiritual reaction. Suffering intensely on all sides with no escape or end in
sight, Job began complaining: "*After this Job* opened his [formerly closed
and peaceful] mouth, and *cursed his day*" (Job 3:1). This prompted his
three friends, beginning with Eliphaz, to start finding fault. When
their sweet, silent support turned to loud, bitter opposition, that was it.
Job's consummate composure quickly unraveled. And while he never

renounced his faith, as Satan had hoped, Job did complain against his cruel circumstances (and, thus, their Creator) profusely and argue adamantly with his friends-turned-judges from then on. Not until God's eventual rebuke did Job regain his spiritual attitude.

Clearly, Job had hoped his friends would be sympathetic. After all, he had lost everything! Even his best friend, his wife, no longer believed God approved of him: "*Then said his wife* unto him, Dost thou still retain thine integrity? *Curse God, and die*" (Job 2:9). By thus advising apostasy, she spoke for Satan, as his very mouthpiece (Job 1:11; 2:5). So when his friends arrived, his heart breathed fresh hope—maybe things would start getting better now. After all, "a friend loveth at all times, and a brother is born for adversity" (Prov. 17:17). But things got worse, much worse! After his best friends lovingly and silently shared Job's grief for "seven days and seven nights" (Job 2:13), they morphed into his worst foes! It was a bitter disappointment. Wildly thirsty for help, he had desperately anticipated drinking refreshment from the brook of friendship (Job 6:14–21) only to discover the brook was dry. All human support had failed. Only God could save him now.

But Job couldn't drink from the "fountain of living waters" (Jer. 2:13) either! Unlike Job's other disappointments, this one was entirely his fault. Why? He had developed an offended spirit. Job was huffed and irritated with the Almighty over the surprising turn his friends had taken. When others turned away, he foolishly and unjustly blamed God for their turning and sullenly and stubbornly refused to look up for new inspiration. Thus, loathing the Lord who still loved him, Job turned away from his only remaining Spring of help.

Jesus warned us of this very danger:

> When affliction or trouble or persecution comes on account of the Word, at once he is caused to stumble [he is repelled and begins to distrust and desert Him Whom he ought to trust and obey] and he falls away.
>
> —MATTHEW 13:21, AMP

This, Job's wrong turn *away* from the Lord, caused the near-catastrophic collapse of his previously consistent composure. Had it not been for the compassionate correction of Him whose "mercy endureth forever" (Ps. 136:1), Job would have remained spiritually defeated.

By contrast, David learned where to turn when others turned away.

DAVID'S CORRECT TURN

Before King Saul forced him to flee for his life into the wilderness of Judah, David was loved and respected by all Israel.

The son of Jesse was widely known as a faithful son, a dedicated shepherd, a man of deep faith, a courageous warrior, a captain in the army, a skilled musician, a man of exemplary integrity and wisdom, son-in-law to King Saul, and his likely successor. The anonymous man who originally recommended David's services to Saul described him as "a Bethlehemite, who is skillful in playing, and a mighty, valiant man, and a man of war, and prudent in matters, and an agreeable person, and the LORD is with him" (1 Sam. 16:18). What a sparkling résumé! And after David defeated the Philistine gladiatorial champion and brute terrorist, Goliath, and routed the army he led, all Israel shared the same admiration for David: "*All Israel and Judah loved David*, because he went out and came in before them...so that *his name was much esteemed*" (1 Sam. 18:16, 30). David was a youthful, living legend, a young man whom thousands hoped would build a prosperous future not only for his family but also for their nation. Every Israelite was a friend to David, and he was one to them. Leaders and people alike constantly complimented his outstanding developing character. The godly priest Ahimelech testified before King Saul: "Who is so faithful among all thy servants as David, who is the king's son-in-law, and goeth at thy bidding, and is honorable in thine house?" (1 Sam. 22:14). Saul's slander campaign, however, changed all this.

Moved by his envy of David, which he chose to suppress instead of confess, Saul circulated a variety of vicious lies about David.

Most prominently, he reported that David and his men, at Jonathan's instigation and with his cooperation, were plotting to overthrow him: "Then Saul said unto his servants who stood about him...My son hath made a league with the son of Jesse...my son hath stirred up my servant against me, to lie in wait, as at this day" (1 Sam. 22:7–9). This, he claimed, was the reason he was forced to go out and hunt down Goliath's famed conqueror, who, married to the king's daughter, posed a very real threat to usurp the kingship. Or so the story went.

As ridiculous as this rumor was, it nevertheless gained strength as time passed. The longer God waited to vindicate David, the more villainous he looked—and the more Saul relished playing the victim. Duped by appearances, the people drank in every lie the king's administration poured out. After all, if God was with David, they surmised, why didn't He intervene and help him? Judging only by what they could see, the people assumed Saul had told the truth. After all, he was the king, divinely chosen, a prophet, a successful general, a tall, regal-looking fellow,[1] and of unimpeachable reputation. (His demonic fits and bitter envy of David's fame were apparently court secrets.) Soon the people forgot all that David had been and done. As the years passed, so did David's former reputation. After about ten years, the whole nation had lost all faith in the son of Jesse. The Scriptures tell this sad tale.

David and his men bravely and selflessly risked their lives to deliver the Israeli border town of Keilah from a Philistine attack (1 Sam. 23:1–13). His reward? Immediately afterward, the men of Keilah, suspecting or convinced David and his men were fugitives, were ready to deliver them into Saul's hands. Warned of this treachery by God, David and his men escaped. The Keilahites' unfaithfulness telegraphed their, and most Israelites', real opinion: God had abandoned David. It was a bitter disappointment to the future king, but not the last.

Sharing the flawed but popular opinion of the Keilahites, the men of Ziph also turned against David. When he and his men came to Ziph, the Ziphites went straight to Saul to inform him of David's presence and conspired to deliver him to the king at the first opportunity (1 Sam. 23:14–25). When Saul came seeking him, David narrowly escaped his grasp. If God had not intervened providentially by permitting the Philistines to divert Saul's forces (vv. 27–29), the Ziphites' treachery would have spelled David's end. Though not terminated, David was again abandoned by human helpers.

Sometime later, David's growing nomadic company, now six hundred strong, lacked food. So he sent messengers to Nabal, a wealthy sheepherder, asking him for provisions (1 Sam. 25:2–39). Since his men had at various times protected Nabal's herds without charge, David assumed Nabal would now respond in kind and spare him and his men a little food. But not so, not now, not Nabal. Instead, Nabal hastily rejected David's humble request and added a haughty insult. His rude retort revealed that his opinion of David had also changed drastically. Clearly a convert to Saul's "gospel," Nabal's reply accused David of being just another worthless insubordinate plotting insurrection against his just and compassionate master, the king: "Who is David? And who is the son of Jesse? There are many servants nowadays who break away, every man from his master" (v. 10). In the proverbial "dunghill" of utter public rejection, David surely felt he was at rock bottom.

But he would go lower still. At Ziklag, the unthinkable, the unimaginable, the unspeakable happened: David's own men turned on him! (See 1 Samuel 30:1–6.) Deeply grieved by the shocking kidnapping and possible killing of their wives and children, David's men "lifted up their voice and wept, until they had no more power to weep," their stunned souls deeply "grieved, every man for his sons and for his daughters" (vv. 4, 6). Their grief quickly turned to self-pity and their self-pity to anger at God—who had without explanation allowed the unthinkable. This anger at God naturally turned toward God's nearest representative—yes, David! When "the people spoke of stoning him" (v. 6), David reached the lowest moment in his long, low, laborious wilderness tribulation period.

It was his "midnight hour," a horrible spiritual "death pit" from which resurrection seemed impossible. Great adversity had besieged him, and all his friends were estranged from him. Now, with not one shred of human support, David was in precisely the same position Job was in. But note carefully David's opposite reaction.

When others turned away, David turned hard to God: "David encouraged himself in the LORD his God" (v. 6). When he looked around and saw no favor, no help, no way out, no hope, David looked up with all the energy his soul could muster. He later recorded the moment for posterity in a psalm:

> When my spirit was overwhelmed within me, then thou knewest my path....I looked on my right hand, and beheld, but there was *no man* that would know me [favorably]. [Human] refuge failed me; *no man* cared for my soul. *[So] I cried unto thee, O LORD.* I said, *Thou art my* [only unfailing] *refuge*.
>
> —PSALMS 142:3–5

Thus, in his lowest hour, David turned not away from but *to* the Lord. At least four quality choices enabled him to make this crucial spiritual turn and escape the pit of offense into which Job fell. Let's recall them.

DAVID'S QUALITY CHOICES

Choice one

David chose, no matter how severe his affliction, *not* to be offended with God for permitting it. He had already discovered the utter, unchanging love and faithfulness of God's character. So he trusted God was still very good, though circumstances were very hard and prospects very bad.

This decision gave him "great peace" even in the midst of great problems: "*Great peace* have they who love thy law, and *nothing shall offend them*" (Ps. 119:165). As Jesus later taught, this determination to never be offended with God at anything made David "blessed." *"Blessed is he, whosoever shall not [or refuses to] be offended in me"* (Luke 7:23). "Blessed" here refers to two things: *blessedness,* or a blessed state; and *blessings,* or the receiving of blessings. So David was specially favored by God in his soul, though he was still disfavored by many; and he qualified to receive new blessings, human benefits, and delights, both during and at the end of his trial.

Girded with this blessedness of soul and life, David didn't unravel as Job did. Rather than complain and contend his way into a depressing downward spiritual spiral, he held fast to God—though for the time he lost everyone and everything else.

Choice two

David chose *not* to fret at the cowardly, unfaithful "evildoers" who, knowing his good character firsthand, still refused to help him in his hour of need because of his sinking reputation. He recorded this choice in an epic poem, Psalms 37, that instructs us how to react to wrongdoers: *"Fret not thyself* because of *evildoers"* (v. 1). Neither would he fret at King Saul, the influential liar whose false-but-prosperous "wicked devices" had caused David's loss of reputation and public favor: *"Fret not thyself* because of *him who prospereth* in his [evil] way, because of the man *who bringeth wicked devices to pass"* (v. 7). Rather than senselessly self-destruct through anger or self-pity, David chose wisely to trust and delight in, and commit his anxieties to, God—and not lightly but fully, with decisiveness, finality, and thanksgiving: *"Trust* in the LORD... *delight* thyself also in the LORD... *commit* thy way unto the LORD... and he shall bring it to pass" (vv. 3–5).

This choice to trust God rather than fret kept David's soul free from the inner agitation and vexation that churned Job into a state of confused uselessness. Still and quiet, David's soul remained "online," detecting and following God's "still, small" voice despite all the voices raised against him.

Choice three

In obedience to the Forgiver of his sins, David chose to forgive all who sinned against him, especially his own men who had so stunningly turned against him at Ziklag.

Unknowingly, he was complying with a command yet to be given by a Savior yet to be sacrificed for the sins of all. That One taught, *"Forgive,* if ye have anything against any, that your Father also, who is in heaven, may forgive you your trespasses. But if ye do not forgive, neither will your Father, who is in heaven, forgive your trespasses" (Mark 11:25–26). In His greatest sermon, that One instructed us to pray, "Forgive us our debts, *as we forgive* our debtors" (Matt. 6:12), thus revealing that to get forgiveness, we must give it.

This choice to forgive kept Satan from finding "place" in, or access to, David's soul and embittering him (Eph. 4:26–27). So David kept worshiping and fellowshiping with God sweetly, despite the bitterness of his test.

Choice four

When tried to tears in the temporary realm of the "things which are seen," David chose to focus on the eternal realm of the "things which are not seen" (2 Cor. 4:18).

He looked away from all his falling favor and faithless friends to his unfailingly faithful heavenly Friend, remembering and discovering anew that "there is a friend who sticketh closer than a brother" (Prov. 18:24). In doing so he anticipated by nearly three thousand years the Christian epigram, "Look around you, be distressed. Look within you, be depressed. Look at Jesus, be at rest."[2] This enabled him to tap into the unlimited grace of God, who said, "My grace is sufficient for thee" (2 Cor. 12:9). Then he not only survived but also progressed. Empowered by God's all-sufficient grace, he rose, pursued, and "recovered all" he had lost (1 Sam. 30:18). Though simple, this last decision was dynamic.

Refocusing on the faithful One kept him flying faithfully when others nosedived into faithlessness. As the eyes of David's soul "zoomed in" on Jesus, his soul soared upward with faith like an eagle "mounting up" on a mighty updraft. Thus powered by the Spirit and lifted by faith above the grasp of the "things which are seen," he glided home to victory.

Study well and learn deeply these lessons from Job's error and David's triumph. When fallible humanity lives up to its name, make the right choices and turn to, not from, your infallible Friend and Fountain of living waters. No matter how offensive your circumstances, refuse to be offended with your Christ. Then you'll discover for yourself, fully and forever, the fabulous faithfulness of God. When human support fails, His will prevail. When brotherly grace is insufficient, His will be all sufficient—even in your lowest "Ziklag" moment.

The writer to the Hebrews urges you to do so:

> For he hath said, *I will never leave thee*, nor forsake thee. So that we may boldly say, *The Lord is my helper*, and I will not fear what man shall do [or fail to do] unto me.
>
> —HEBREWS 13:5–6

Whether Paul or Peter, this sacred author realized that we meet trouble not only out of God's will but also in it.

TROUBLE IN THE CENTER OF HIS WILL

> …tribulation or persecution ariseth because of the Word…
> —MATTHEW 13:21

U NLIKE THE WISE writer to the Hebrews, when we meet trouble, we often assume it has arisen because God is angry with us. Sometime, somewhere, somehow we disobeyed the Lord, and trouble's visit proves He's displeased with us. The Bible supports this often correct notion.

For example, Jonah's rebellion landed him in a fish's (or whale's) belly, Jacob's procrastination led to tragedy at Shechem, Judah's persisting idol worship caused a Babylonian invasion, and Lot's quest for gain and power in Sodom led to the loss of everything he had gained. So when we meet roadblocks, perplexities, silences, rejection, abandonment, reproach, sickness, or losses, God's wrath at our wrongs must be the reason. Right? Not so fast. The Bible also reveals other causes of trouble.

Repeatedly it teaches that God's perfect will always includes a measure of trouble. Adversity is not random force but rather reformative force, God's age-old instrument with which He tests His children and builds our characters. Consider these biblical examples.

TROUBLE IN GOD'S WILL

Isaac

God expressly led Isaac to settle in Gerar: "And the LORD appeared unto him, and said, Go not down into Egypt; dwell in the land which I shall tell thee of. *Sojourn in this land* [Gerar]" (Gen. 26:2–3). So Isaac submitted and obeyed divine guidance: "And Isaac dwelt in Gerar" (v. 6). Surely he felt secure in obeying God's perfect will.

Yet soon afterward, he ran into unexpected, unwanted, and unwarranted trouble. Stirred by their envy of God's blessing on Isaac's farming and ranching enterprises, the Philistines abruptly rose up and ran him out of town one day: "And [the] Abimelech [or Philistine ruler], said unto Isaac, *Go from us*" (v. 16). A peace-loving man, Isaac meekly complied with their wishes, but even his relocation didn't satisfy them, and they continued thinking and acting adversarially. Philistine herdsmen repeatedly attacked Isaac's shepherds claiming rights and seeking access to wells that Abraham had opened originally and Isaac's servants had recently reopened (vv. 15, 17–25). Isaac must have thought, "Whew!" as he pondered how strangely and quickly his beautiful, secure obedience to the Almighty had turned into an insecure, ugly situation.

Thus he learned a lasting lesson in Life University—even prompt obedience to God's perfect guidance sometimes leads to strife and division—and left it as a legacy for us.

Joseph

A good and dutiful boy, young Joseph aimed only to obey and please his father, Jacob, and his God.

But suddenly, and without cause or warning, Joseph found himself sold as a common slave—by his own brothers (Gen. 37:1–36)! And as he went further in this, God's chosen way, it only got worse. After a few years of peace and promotion to a higher position, Joseph found himself falsely accused, unfairly tried and convicted, and cruelly imprisoned, all because he steadily *refused* to disobey and "sin against God" (Gen. 39:9). Strangely, the more Joseph obeyed, the deeper and wider his troubles became! Stranger still, the more Joseph plunged into adversity, the closer God drew near: "But the LORD was with Joseph, and showed him mercy, and gave him favor in the sight of the keeper of the prison" (v. 21).

Though contrary to all logic, the trend Joseph perceived in his life-mirror was undeniable: not only rebellion but also righteousness brings trouble!

Moses

During a stunningly supernatural visitation, Jehovah told Moses where he was to go, what he was to do, and why. He was to go to Egypt and lead God's people from Egyptian slavery to the Promised Land, because God was answering their desperate cries for deliverance.

But Moses' glorious return quickly turned inglorious when, upon arrival, instead of decreasing, the Hebrews' sufferings *increased*! When Moses presented God's demands to Pharaoh,[1] the proud monarch defied them and, furious, made the Hebrew slaves' backbreaking labors harder! Instead of marching toward liberty, the chosen liberator and libertines found themselves stumbling toward death! Puzzled to prayer, Moses reported his perplexity to his mission Planner: "And Moses returned unto the LORD, and said, Lord, wherefore hast thou so badly treated this people? Why is it that thou hast sent me? For since I came to Pharaoh to speak in thy name, he hath done evil to this people; neither hast thou delivered thy people at all" (Exod. 5:22–23). God didn't deny this troublesome trend, nor did Moses immediately escape it.

Later, the Spirit of God explicitly ordered Moses to lead the long columns of freed Israelites to the scene of their harrowing Red Sea experience. He could have chosen an easier, safer route, but instead "the LORD spoke unto Moses, saying, Speak unto the children of Israel, that they turn and encamp before Pi-hahiroth, between Migdol and the sea, over against Baal-zephon; before it *shall ye encamp by the sea*" (Exod. 14:1–2). They and their leader dutifully obeyed the voice from heaven, but again it looked like certain death for them all—until the Almighty supernaturally and spectacularly intervened.

By this point, Moses was sure of one thing: sin-free living doesn't mean a trouble-free life.

The Israelites

The pattern the Israelites discovered during the Exodus persisted in their wilderness tests.

Not their leaders' impulsive whims but their Lord's intelligent word led the Israelites into a divinely arranged and preplanned time of testing in the wilderness. Yet there, in the center of God's will, they faced a wide array of difficulties and dangers. When recollecting that trouble-filled season, Moses said, "[The Lord] who led thee through that great and terrible wilderness, wherein were fiery serpents, and scorpions, and drought, where there was no water" (Deut. 8:15).

Again, the pattern was unmistakable: though divinely led, they still encountered difficulties. Neither the passing of time nor a change in leadership altered this persisting, perplexing pattern.

When Moses passed, and the time came for Israel's new leader, Joshua, to lead God's people across the Jordan to take possession of the Promised Land, the ultimate trouble—war—lay in the middle of the divinely marked pathway. How unreasonable it all seemed: God was commanding, Joshua was leading, and Israel was obeying, but still war had to be faced.

Jesus' temptation

After filling Jesus of Nazareth, the Holy Spirit immediately gave Him clear guidance. But instead of leading God's supremely obedient Son to abundant blessing and bliss, He directed Him instead to a head-on confrontation with the devil himself.

As Luke describes it, "Jesus, being full of the Holy Spirit, returned from the Jordan, and was *led by the Spirit* into the wilderness, being forty days *tested by the devil*" (Luke 4:1–2). As unreasonable as this seemed, it was for a good reason. Before the heavenly Father would commission His Son for His ministerial and redemptive work, Jesus had to meet and overcome the ultimate troubler, and on his own wilderness "turf." Our Captain's personal testing had to be finished and complete so He could produce a finished and complete work of salvation for us. The writer to the Hebrews noted, "For it became him...to make the captain of their salvation perfect through sufferings" (Heb. 2:10).

So not only the redeemed but also the Redeemer found trouble in the center of God's will!

The apostles

After dramatically releasing the apostles from incarceration, an angel of the Lord issued new orders to the Lord's special messengers: "Go, stand and speak in the temple to the people all the words of this life" (Acts 5:20). True to their characters, these godly leaders obeyed immediately, bravely returning to the very place where the Sanhedrin's guard had arrested them before, the area of the temple courts known as "Solomon's porch" or colonnade: "And when they heard that, they entered into the temple early in the morning, and taught" (v. 21). Surely good would follow such intrepid submission.

But again evil waylaid them. Instead of leading yet another successful meeting with miraculous conversions and healings (vv. 12-16), they ran into more opposition from the corrupt religious leaders. The temple guards reappeared, rearrested them, retried them before the high priest, and they narrowly escaped execution!

I wonder if they wondered, "Wow, what will happen the *next* time we obey one of the Lord's angels?"

Paul and Silas

After strongly forbidding Paul's ministry team to go to Asia Minor and Bithynia (Acts 16:6–8), the Spirit of God gave Paul a vision in which He urgently called them to Macedonia.

> And a vision appeared to Paul in the night; there stood a man of Macedonia, beseeching him, and saying, Come over into Macedonia, and help us.
>
> —ACTS 16:9

Everyone on Paul's ministry team agreed and quickly prepared to sail to Macedonia. Luke speaks for them all: "And after he [Paul] had seen the vision, immediately we endeavored to go into Macedonia…" Everyone was sure this initiative was divinely inspired: "…assuredly gathering that the Lord had called us to preach the gospel unto them" (v. 10). What did their obedience bring? Did all Macedonia turn to the Lord, as Lydda and Sharon had when the Lord led Peter to minister there (Acts 9:35)?

Negative. Once in Philippi, Paul and company experienced no glorious citywide favor, stunning signs, or mass conversions. They managed only to gain favor with one woman, Lydia, and her family and quietly founded a small church in her house (Acts 16:11–15). Did things begin to prosper soon after this? Double negative. After "many days" (v. 18) of unnoticed ministry, Paul achieved a notable victory, bravely exorcising a demon from a young fortune-teller—for which he and Silas were promptly arraigned, illegally condemned without a hearing, illegally and viciously flogged,[2] jailed in a filthy, dark "inner prison," and bound in painful stocks (vv. 16–24).

With all these woes befalling him in God's perfect will, again I wonder if Paul dreamed of having a few days *out* of it. But not Paul! He was set to finish his course, already confident that, *when the way grows harder, God's grace grows stronger!* (See 2 Cor. 12:7–10.)

Years later, in Jerusalem, the Lord appeared to Paul and told him plainly that it was imperative for him to minister in Rome in the coming days: "And the night following the Lord stood by him, and said, Be of good cheer, Paul; for as thou hast testified of me in Jerusalem, *so must thou bear witness also at Rome*" (Acts 23:11). Paul's heart must have leaped for joy when he heard his next "pulpit" would be Rome! The world's capital! Teeming with unsaved millions! And home to a young, spiritually hungry church! But Paul's road to Rome was not rosy.

Indeed, God's perfectly planned path was a strange, hazardous, "long and winding road." Paul encountered unjust court hearings, death plots, a lengthy imprisonment, a turbulent voyage in a hurricane-churned sea, a violent shipwreck, a deadly snake bite, and initial rejection on his island of refuge (Acts 23:12–28:6)!

Most troubled of men, the apostle Paul often found *nothing but trouble* in the center of God's will!

A single thread of truth runs through the illustrations above: God's servants frequently experience trouble not because they've disobeyed but because they've obeyed Him! All those cited met vexation, frustration, roadblocks, enemies, abuse, temptations, or injustice while pursuing the very paths to which God called them. So, obviously, the presence of trouble doesn't always prove one has disobeyed God's Word or guidance. To the contrary, mature disciples of Christ often see trouble as *divine confirmation*, God's subtle way of reassuring spiritually minded ones they are indeed doing His will. Why? They understand the basic nature of loving and living by God's Word in a Word-hating world.

All Christians, but especially earnest Word-seekers and Word-bearers, are in a lifelong spiritual war. In conventional war, stiff resistance arises when combatants pursue or approach targets particularly valuable to their enemies. Spiritual conflict is the same.

Our enemy, Satan, is the prince of darkness,[3] and his kingdom, the kingdom of darkness. His realm's most prized possession is spiritual darkness, namely, unbelief in or ignorance of spiritual light. That light is the knowledge[4] of the one true God, His Savior Son, and His comprehensive plan of salvation—including the rebirth, sanctification, edification, examination, transformation, and, ultimately, the translation, of penitent sinners by grace through faith. Always Satan and his agents, the "[demonic] rulers of the darkness of this world" (Eph. 6:12), feverishly seek to increase and preserve spiritual darkness. Specifically, their mission is to promote the darkness of sin, unbelief, and error in the world and in the church in order to preserve the world's darkness and dim the church's light so it doesn't illuminate the world as Jesus intended when He appointed it the "light of the world" (Matt. 5:14).

Of this invisible but incessant satanic work, particularly among the unredeemed, or "lost," Paul writes:

> If our gospel be hidden, it is hidden to them that are lost. In whom the *god of this age* hath blinded the minds of them who believe not, *lest the light* of the glorious gospel of Christ, who is the image of God, *should shine unto them.*
>
> —2 CORINTHIANS 4:3–4

Consequently, the "rulers of darkness" attack, hinder, and dispel all forms and carriers of spiritual light. That light is contained exclusively in God's Word, the Bible, and conveyed to the church and the world through believing, obedient Christian disciples. Narrow minded as it sounds to unbelievers, it is nevertheless true that the Bible, rightly divided, and not any other religious writing, doctrine, or revelation, is the only light that dispels Satan's darkness in sin-darkened, spiritually ignorant, or heretically taught souls and illuminates them with truth, thus ending Satan's rule over them.

The principal combatants in this ongoing war—the "rulers of the darkness of this world" (Eph. 6:12) and light-bearers[5]—are in perpetual conflict. As predictable as gravity or clockwork, the "rulers of darkness" attack light-bearers every time their prayers, actions, or ministries invade or disrupt the kingdom of darkness and diminish its control of the world or influence in churches and individuals. How? They prompt people subject to Satan's influence (sinners, also carnal [immature or disobedient] Christians) to oppose, intimidate, frustrate, hinder, hate, harass, wrong, tempt, or bait light-bearers. Why? By provoking them to sin, discouragement, or unbelief, they want to stop their *light progress* or *light growth*; that is, halt their progress or growth in discovering spiritual knowledge, obeying it, or sharing it with others.

Specifically, here are the rules of spiritual battle: Whenever believers study God's Word rightly divided (correctly interpreted), they are receiving light and dispelling darkness in their souls and becoming *light-receiving* light-bearers. Also, they're becoming potential examples and ministers of the light. So they become a target. Whenever believers begin consistently obeying God's Word in their daily lives, the light is growing, and darkness diminishing, in their souls, and they are becoming *life-witness* light-bearers, disciples whose daily lives shine and show Jesus to others. Also, their ability to minister the light with authority is growing. So they become a more desirable target. Whenever believers share God's Word regularly and effectively with others—in conversation, counsel, evangelism, preaching, or teaching—they become *ministry* light-bearers, whose Spirit-inspired sharing of God's Word, like powerful spiritual lasers, beacons, and spotlights, dispels darkness in other souls and diminishes Satan's influence. These are Satan's most desirable targets.

These rules explain what Jesus meant when He said, "Tribulation or persecution ariseth *because of the word*" (Matt. 13:21). Whenever we believe, study, obey, or minister Word-light, we meet resistance—vexatious "tribulation," dogged "persecution," or alluring temptation sent by the prince of darkness, stirred by his demonic "rulers of darkness," and carried out through people who, at the moment, are subject to his complete control or subtle influences. We must understand and accept these rules of spiritual battle, especially in the gross darkness of these last days...unless we don't want to grow.

If we're *not* making light progress, we meet no such resistance. Our "adversary, the devil" (1 Pet. 5:8) doesn't bother with us when we're spiritually delinquent, distracted, deceived, disbelieving, or disobedient. He likes us as we are and is quite content to leave us alone...for the present. While no light growth means no trouble from the "rulers of darkness" "because of the Word," taking this easier road has serious consequences. It means not pleasing Jesus, not winning His approval for service (2 Tim. 2:15), not spreading the light to bless others, not building Christ's kingdom, and not glorifying God. Translation? *Total spiritual failure* as a Christian!

So if you are hard pressed of late by the prince of darkness and his demonic and human servants, and are tempted strongly to turn from obedience to escape his pressure, let me remind you: *disobedience will cost you far more later than obedience will cost you now!* Everybody meets trouble—the good, the bad, the wise, and the foolish. (See Matthew 7:24–27.) The wise Christian pays his spiritual "dues" up front, willingly obeying God and taking the consequences now, trusting the Lord to deliver and reward him in His time and way. Foolish Christians compromise their way out of trouble for the moment, only to pay much higher dues later on—and without any reward.

Abraham and Lot typify the wise and foolish Christian respectively.

ABRAHAM, THE WISE BELIEVER

Initially, Abraham paid a high cost to obey the call of God—separation from family and homeland, hardship in travel, uncertainty of when God would fulfill His promise, baffling contradictory appearances, and unrealized hopes during many years of waiting. But in his later years Abraham experienced fruitfulness, blessing, joy, and honor. Again, the writer to the Hebrews teaches, "And so, after he [Abraham] had patiently endured, he obtained the promise" (Heb. 6:15). Abraham finally received the coveted "end of the Lord" (James 5:11), his son of promise, Isaac, because he obeyed all the way through to the end of his testing process. His guiding principle was *obey God, whatever the cost!*

Although he was rarely completely trouble-free, this pioneering light-bearer kept himself in God's will, the place of immediate soul peace and eventual highest blessing. Can you see the light of his example shining through the pages of the Bible? Will you walk in this light?

LOT, THE FOOLISH BELIEVER

On the other hand, Abraham's redeemed but worldly nephew, Lot, assiduously avoided trouble and hardship. He consistently took the path of least resistance by choosing self-will, not God's will, in every issue. The opposite of Abraham's guiding principle, Lot's motto was *regardless of what God wants, avoid the cost!* Or, in the language of Gethsemane, "My will, not Thine, be done."

For years, this inverted rule of life appeared to work fine for Lot. He was a prosperous and powerful[6] man in the wicked but prosperous Sodomite society. But his day of reckoning finally came, and in one swift stroke of divine judgment, Lot's false prosperity and empty power was stripped away...and never restored. In the end, this believer[7] who compromised God's righteousness to gain everything lost everything and was left with nothing—no authority, reputation, possessions, wife, sons-in-law, honor, or testimony! And his belated sufferings did not win him rewards or honors, as Abraham's had. Though saved "as by fire" by God's grace and Abraham's intercessions, Lot's life works were a tragic total loss. Thus, he perfectly foreshadows the saved but unrewardable Christian at the judgment seat of Christ: "If any man's work shall be burned, he shall suffer loss; but he himself shall be *saved, yet as by fire*" (1 Cor. 3:15). Lot's was a dark, disappointing biography.

By contrast, every wise Christian will see this light: Lot is an example not to follow!

Remember, then, that trouble comes not just when you disobey God, but also when you're walking in the center of His perfect will. This is because you're a light-bearer—seeking, obeying, or sharing the light of God's Word and growing or progressing steadily in this light-bearing—and the "rulers of the darkness of this world" hope to hinder or harass you to the point you turn from the light and depart from God's will to seek relief. But that relief is ruinous.

Like Abraham before you, be wise! Never exchange light-bearing for relief-seeking. Be willing to pay any cost—lose, suffer, forgo, wait, be misunderstood and mocked, be lonely and grieved—but stay in God's will and sustain your light-growth! Then, whatever your difficulties,

God's grace will be sufficient. You will be amply consoled by His present peace and the joyous assurance that you're fulfilling your calling as a believer. That's the ultimate spiritual victory.

And the best victories are hard-fought victories.

Chapter Seventeen

VICTORY THE HARD WAY

And there came against Gibeah 10,000 chosen men out of all Israel,
and the battle was hard.

—JUDGES 20:34, AMP

A HARD-FOUGHT VICTORY IS just what the Israelites experienced in their brief but bloody civil war in the days of the judges (Judges 19–20). It was a most unusual way of winning.

Typically Israel routed her enemies as soon as the battle was joined. As long as her people were living in God's will, God smote, slew, and prevailed over their opposition, whether feeble or formidable. In short order, the chosen nation was delivered and her unelected enemies vanquished. This was the norm for Abraham's seed in the day of battle.

But in Israel's conflict with its own tribe of Benjamin, victory came very differently. Neither quick nor easy, this triumph was hard-fought, costly, and slow in coming. God let His righteous ones suffer before they celebrated. He permitted them first to fall and then strengthened them to stand. They knew sorrow and grief before they felt joy and elation. They tasted two stunning defeats before savoring success on the "third day" (Judg. 20:30). This is victory the hard way—victory through the midst of defeat.

What preceded and produced this peculiar military precedent?

A SAD, STRANGE STORY

Judges 19, along with the opening verses of Judges 20, describes the backdrop for Israel's civil war. It's not your typical Bible story.

It tells of a certain Levite who, while staying overnight in the city of Gibeah with his concubine, found the home in which he was lodged surrounded by a mob of rowdy, sexually perverted men who demanded that his host, an old man, surrender not his concubine but him so they could sodomize him in the public square. Their brazenness reveals that there was no public restraint of lawlessness, specifically aggressive homosexuality, among God's very own covenant people. They had fallen so far into sin that they now had a society shockingly similar to that of Sodom long ago. (See Genesis 19.[1]) To escape the danger, the Levite appeased these rabid rapists by giving them his concubine to do with her what they would. After abusing her all evening, they left her dead on the doorstep. It was a sad story.

Then sad became strange. After discovering her, the Levite took her lifeless body and returned home to Mount Ephraim. Once there, he surgically dismembered it into twelve parts and sent one part to each of the twelve tribes of Israel, apparently to stir their outrage at the crime in Gibeah. Mission accomplished. Shocked beyond words, all the tribes except Benjamin gathered in Mizpah, solemnly vowing to make full inquiry of the matter. After learning the lurid and horrific details from the Levite, the eleven tribes decided action had to be taken and the criminals executed. But when they called the host tribe of Benjamin to turn over the bisexual rapists, the men of Benjamin refused and united instead to fight the other tribes. It was a strange scene indeed. God's people were out of control and slipping off into the abyss of complete anarchy and irrecoverable national self-destruction.

At first reading, this sad, strange incident and the shockingly lethal civil war that followed may suggest that God, angry at His people's apostasy, simply stepped back and let them devour themselves as just punishment for their widespread iniquities, self-willed living, and failure to worship as He ordained in their law. And had He done so, He would have been justified. Though redeemed, the Jews as a people were living far from God and His order. Emphasizing the absence of strong, central, righteous authority among God's people, the Book of Judges twice notes sadly, "Every man did that which was right in his own eyes" (Judg. 17:6: 21:25). Unbelief, idolatry, and sin abounded, and faith, righteous living, and true worship were in short supply.

Yet this general substandard spiritual condition was not the reason eleven of their tribes suffered overwhelming casualties twice at the hands of the tribe of Benjamin. Generally, and in the specific issue at hand, the eleven were far more righteous than their deceived brethren who were so ungodly and spiritually blind they defended depraved, defiant sodomites and rapists.[2] As for God, He certainly didn't have to ask the angels which of the two warring factions He should support. The issue was not clouded. God's sentiments were strong and His will clear. His response to the united tribes' request for counsel, instructing them that "Judah shall go up first" (Judg. 20:18), along with the absence of any censure of their actions, proved that He was behind them 100 percent in their effort to purge the moral cancer growing in Benjamin—and quickly, before it took the life of their nation. Reason dictated they would win a quick, overwhelming victory.

But reason was about to be surprised.

A Sadder, Stranger War

When the heavy-hearted eleven tribes gathered at Mizpah, they immediately asked God's direction and help in the stern but unavoidable duty that lay before them. Their cause was just and their mission clear. They sought not to conquer and spoil but to correct and redeem. They warred, but only to preserve justice, peace, and liberty. They killed, but only to save lives. Thus minded, they marched off to battle, confident the Lord of hosts would cause them to win.

But though their ideals and objectives were high, "the battle was hard" (Judg. 20:34, AMP). For two consecutive days, the united tribes attacked the stubborn Benjamites only to be defeated. Severely defeated! Routed! The first day they lost 22,000 men; the second, 18,000! This was baffling, a complete mystery to reason and faith. The sinful had defeated the righteous and the ungodly the godly. Morality had been smitten by immorality and sanctification by sinfulness. And God seemed to be playing mind games with them, saying one thing but doing another. As sad and strange as the death and dismemberment of the Levite's concubine was, this war, thus far, was sadder and stranger. It gave them pause.

Introspecting, the Israelites reexamined themselves and their situation: They were entirely in God's will in this matter. Heaven wanted Gibeah's criminals brought to justice. They were in complete unity: "The congregation was *gathered together as one man*, from Dan even to Beersheba...*knit together as one man*" (Judg. 20:1, 11). They were in faith. Their law and history gave them complete confidence that they would prevail, and no cowards were in their war camp to weaken this resolve. They were under the Lord's direct leading. Again, His two attack orders (vv. 18, 23), without any countermands, made that clear enough. They were sanctified. There was neither overconfidence nor secret sins in their midst, as was the case when Joshua attacked Ai the first time (Josh. 7). So Scripture, reason, and history agreed: they should have had a mighty victory when the first swords clashed. Instead, they were defeated not once but *twice*. Why?

God was taking them into new spiritual territory, up to a whole new level of faith in God and knowledge of His ways. He was teaching them, educating them, training them in His hard way. Let's see how this severe schooling unfolded.

Both days the united tribes experienced fierce combat, suffered traumatic casualties, regrouped, and then asked counsel of the Lord *again*. After two costly defeats, their mission was still not accomplished. So this forced them to gather up their faith and courage and attack one more time. As never before, this generation of Israelites had to *persevere*.

This required that they exercise their faith in Jehovah to the very limit—and beyond. They had to ignore the two fresh defeats they had seen. Thus they did what Paul urged us to do when faced with baffling contradictions to God's promises, namely, look beyond visible natural facts to the invisible spiritual realities behind them: "While we look not at the things which are seen, but at the things which are not seen; for the things which are seen are temporal, but the things which are not seen are eternal" (2 Cor. 4:18). Cruel contradictions forced them to brush aside their own baffled sense of justice and harassing doubts about God's faithfulness and to flatly *refuse* to be offended with God or overwhelmed by the discouraging "things seen." In going to battle the third day, the eleven tribes had to ignore not only this perplexity but also their deep pain at their previous days' losses and step out in blind faith on the basic goodness, utter faithfulness, and naked Word of God.

And they do this, because He had spoken. Until this third day, God did not promise them the specific time of victory. On the two previous days, He told the eleven tribes only to go, giving assurance of His support but no specific promise of an immediate victory; they hoped for that, but He had not guaranteed it. But now, on the eve of the third day, when Phinehas the priest asked Him about fighting "again," He revealed the specific time of victory: "Shall I yet again go out to battle against the children of Benjamin, my brother, or shall I cease? And the LORD said, Go up; for *tomorrow* I will deliver them into thine hand" (Judg. 20:28). This time God bound Himself: "tomorrow" was the day!

So, like Abraham before them, the shaken but steadfast eleven tribes "staggered not at the promise of God through unbelief," but were "strong in faith" (Rom. 4:20) despite staggeringly contradictory facts. On the third day, they marched off to battle again, this time confident things would be different. Despite the two previous unforeseen, unwarranted, and unexplained defeats, they would fight today and win! And win they did: "And the LORD smote Benjamin before Israel" (Judg. 20:35).

With this win under their belts, the eleven tribes now had a stronger faith than before. Now they not only believed, they also *knew* that no matter how many contradictions, delays, or defeats intervene, God always performs every promise He makes in His time and way. Every time! Period! They also had a new understanding of God's ways. Never again would they try to anticipate exactly *how* or *when* God would give victory, other than saying it would be *His* way and time! They grasped now that His plans and ways of operating were truly altogether higher and different from theirs. (See Isaiah 55:8–9.)

But a deeper faith and broader knowledge of God's mysterious ways were not the only reasons God led them to victory the hard way.

The Hard Way Is Jesus' Way

Our Lord Jesus also walked in this hard way in the days of His flesh.

The Father could have taken His beloved Son straight to heavenly glory without any suffering, had He chosen to do so, though this would have meant no redemption for the human race. But He did not. He let Jesus suffer—to save us. For two long, sad, strange days, the powers of evil prevailed over the Son of goodness in Joseph of Arimathea's tomb. Then, as with the hard-pressed eleven tribes of Israel, victory—O sweetest of victories!—came for Jesus, mankind, and all creation on "the third day" (Matt. 16:21).

Thus through the humiliation of the cross, Jesus obtained the honor of the resurrection and the goal of redemption. He tasted defeat for two days before He savored victory. The Father let Him fall before He revived Him to stand. The Captain of our salvation was first conquered, then He conquered. Thus He "learned...obedience," not by quick, easy victories in the wars of life, but "by the things which he suffered" (Heb. 5:8). So the hard way is Jesus' way.

It's apparent, then, that the Father took the Israelites the hard way to conform them, however briefly, to the character image of His Son. That's not all that's apparent.

The Hard Way Is Our Way

As with Israel and Jesus, the Father can give us quick, easy victories in every trial if He so desires. And often He does just that. But not always.

There will come a day in every Christian's life when the heavenly Father leads His adopted child into the hard way. Why?

As already stated, He wants to take us into new spiritual territory, up to a whole new level of faith and knowledge of His unique ways. And He uses our hard-way experiences to reshape and remake our characters into the image of His Son, which is the common predestination of all Christians: "For whom he did foreknow, he also did *predestinate to be conformed to the image of his Son*" (Rom. 8:29). But there's more.

Our endurance of defeat(s) humbles us, and we need this sobering of our viewpoint so we won't be moved by the uplifting exhilaration of victory. So God uses defeat to prepare us psychologically and emotionally for success: "Before honor is humility" (Prov. 18:12). Enduring defeat also creates compassion in us for others who suffer defeats, failures, losses, or delays. We then can empathize with their disappointment and disillusionment and minister to them with new power, passing along to them in their defeats the insights that kept us in ours. (See 2 Corinthians 1:3–4.) No matter how naturally kind or broadminded we are, we simply cannot understand what it's like to suffer stunning defeats until we've experienced them ourselves. Enduring defeats also proves God's grace is indeed "sufficient" (2 Cor. 12:9) for us at all times. If God brings us through these bafflingly dark, low times, His grace is truly enough to keep any Christian through any and every adversity. It further proves that, as discussed previously,[3] we love God supremely and will serve Him with a victorious spirit even if, in defeat, our blessings are stripped away.

Finally, the Father takes us the hard way to prepare us to live with Jesus and the saints forever. How can we truly fellowship with the crucified Christ if we've never known defeats in the way of righteousness? How would we "no-cost" Christians feel if we were seated at the heavenly marriage supper of the Lamb, or permitted to live in New Jerusalem, directly beside Christian confessors,[4] martyrs, or others who walked humbly and faithfully in the hard way? We could not have joy in such a scenario. To prevent this, God lets us suffer to make us like the King of kings and His loyal subjects, all of whom bear His image in their souls through sufferings. Thus, as the apostle Paul taught, we go the hard way, "that ye may be counted worthy of the kingdom of God, for which ye also suffer" (2 Thess. 1:5).

The sad, strange story of Israel's apostasy and the even sadder, stranger story of its civil war prove this: *even in doing God's will we may suffer stunning temporary defeats.* When they come, we must not misunderstand God's dealings with us and succumb to anger, reasoning, unbelief, and discouragement. Rather, we must do what the united tribes of Israel did after their painful defeats: not retreat, but regroup; not cease praying, but inquire again of the Lord; and, once reassured, banish fear and bravely return to the scene of our previous defeats to obey God *again!* We've suffered setbacks, it's true, but God is still with us. We'd much rather win our conflicts outright from the start, but we'll win our victories through the midst of defeat, if necessary. Since our God has assured and reassured us, we have only to *persevere*—keep walking forward in the midst of trouble—and He will soon show Himself for us and against our unjust, deceived "Benjamites."

Sharing this very conviction, David wrote:

> Though I *walk* [going forward, persevering] in the *midst of trouble,* thou wilt revive me; thou shalt stretch forth thine hand against the wrath of mine enemies, and thy right hand shall save me.
> —PSALMS 138:7

Approximately a decade of walking "in the midst of [the] trouble" of defeat, courtesy of deceived, unjust King Saul, qualified David as a veteran of the hard way. Will you become one too? If so, it won't happen quickly.

In this instant age, we've become spoiled. Everything we want, we obtain quickly. Improved technologies, communications, and travel have virtually eliminated the waiting process from many of our common daily tasks. I enjoy modern conveniences as much as anyone, and I don't condemn us for using these blessings but merely state the facts. There is a downside to the creed of speed we should pause and ponder.

When we come to God, most of us bring with us this deep-seated worldly haste. Foolishly, we frenetically and insatiably demand instant gratification in the things of God. We want our prayers answered, and now! We want our visions to materialize, and pronto! We want spiritual growth, and quickly! We want spiritual insight and power, and suddenly! We want our churches revived, today, and our nations converted, tomorrow! But the Eternal, unhasting and unchanging in His ways, does not cater to impatient imploring, nor does He succumb to impetuous importunity. If we are to know Him, love Him, walk with Him, receive from Him, and bear fruit unto Him, we must learn to wait patiently. If we persistently believe and obey, God will always give us victory, as promised, but not always when we want it. Not always on the first day of spiritual "battle." Or the second. Indeed, satisfaction may not come until the "third day."

Let's face some facts. Many Christians today are "one and done" warriors. We fight the Lord's battles with conviction, faith, and zeal—but only once. If God doesn't appear quickly, our resolve is quashed. We're done. Finished. Ready for another lord and life. For this and other reasons, few Christians today will submit to the hard way. Jesus said:

> *Hard is the way*, which leadeth unto [full, rich, overcoming, spiritual] life, and *[comparatively] few* there be that find it.
> —MATTHEW 7:14

But you can be one of the few that find full-orbed, spiritually rich, deeply satisfying victory in Jesus by patiently submitting to His hard way, when He so leads.

When your time comes, pay the price God asks—and bear the fruit He wants.

Chapter Eighteen

THE PRICE OF FRUITFULNESS

In this is my Father glorified, that ye bear much fruit....If the world
hate you, ye know that it hated me before it hated you.

—JOHN 15:8, 18

I
T'S ALL ABOUT fruit-bearing"—this epigram encapsulates Jesus'
message to us in John 15, a chapter in which He uses the word *fruit*
eight times in just a few verses (vv. 2, 4, 5, 8, 16). Truly, producing
fruit for God's eternal kingdom is the great end toward which every
messenger and means of grace point. Jesus pointed this out.

The divine Vine called Christians "branches" in Him (v. 5), and
branches are made to bear fruit. He ordered us to "abide" in close union
with Him and to let His "Words abide" in us by meditation and obedience (vv. 7–8), so we may bear fruit. If we won't abide, eventually His
fruit-loving, fruit-seeking Father will "take away" (vv. 2, 6) our place of
ministry in the Vine because we're not bearing fruit. If we abide, the Father
will periodically "purge" (v. 2) or prune us through humbling, refining
trials so we may bear "more fruit." As we abide, we should pray spontaneously and steadily for everyone we contact, "ask[ing] what ye will"
(v. 7) so that not only in our lives but also in others we may bear fruit.
And when that "fruit"—drawn, convicted, converted souls—appears, we
should continue praying, so our "fruit" should not wither but "remain" (v.
16). The Father sends some "branches" on missions, domestic or foreign,
and others into ministries so they may "go and bring forth fruit" (v. 16).
Above all else, the Vine commanded us to "love one another, as I have
loved you" (v. 12) so we may bear the choicest fruit, love. He challenged us
to fully obey Him, doing "whatever" He commands, so we may bear the

rarest fruit, friendship with God: "Ye are my *friends*, if ye do whatever I command you" (v. 14). By consistently abiding and obeying, we bear the chiefest fruit, "glory," or honor, for God and His eternal kingdom: "In this is my Father *glorified*, that ye bear *much fruit*" (v. 8).

Let's consider this kingdom "fruit" more specifically.

THE FRUIT OF THE KINGDOM

In Christian living and ministry, kingdom "fruit" is twofold: the *fruit of the Spirit* and the *fruit of souls*.

The fruit of the Spirit

The apostle Paul details the "fruit of the Spirit" for us in his epistle to the Galatians: "The fruit of the Spirit is *love, joy, peace, long-suffering, gentleness, goodness, faith, meekness, self-control*" (Gal. 5:22–23). These fruit are the specific manifestations of Jesus' life produced in us as we yield to the Holy Spirit daily, thus keeping Him flowing into and through us. Together they define the elusive term *Christlikeness*. If Christ's amazingly beautiful character can be categorized, these terms would be the categories that comprise His wondrous being and describe His beautiful behavior. They also give us an accurate measure or standard of spiritual maturity. When these fruit are manifesting consistently in us, they mark us as being "perfect," or fully developed, spiritually adult, consistently Christlike Christians. When they are mostly or entirely absent, they betray spiritual immaturity or, in the case of mere professing Christians, the absence of spiritual rebirth.

By using the word *fruit*, the Lord draws an instructive analogy for us. The fruit of the Spirit is like the fruit of the earth. Whether found in vineyards, gardens, orchards, or farms, all earthly fruit is *beautiful, healthy, delicious, delightful, constantly changing*, and *honorable*. Let's follow through with these parallels.

Beautiful. Fruit is often beautiful to look at. Consequently we arrange it in baskets, bowls, and platters for display. To God, the fruit of the Spirit is the apex of beauty. It is the rare "beauty of the LORD our

God...upon us" (Ps. 90:17), Christ's lovely, gracious character traits manifested in God's Spirit-born, Spirit-taught, Spirit-molded children. The most exquisite works of this world's masters of art—Rembrandt, Michelangelo, Da Vinci—can't compare with the Re-creator's artful strokes and sculptures of divinity in dust. "This mystery" of "Christ in you, the hope of glory" (Col. 1:27), or the splendor of the divine love, peace, and joy of Jesus seen in a man or woman of dust, is Earth's consummate art. Whenever sinners, saints, or angels see it, they stop, gaze, and wonder at the rare fruit of "the beauty of the LORD our God...upon us"—and worship its Artist.

Healthy. The fruit of the Spirit is also healthy—or a sign of good spiritual health. When you see rich, full fruit hanging from a tree, you know it's a healthy tree. If a nearby tree's fruit is spotted, pitted, or discolored, you know it's diseased and suffering from a virus, fungus, blotch, pox, or rot. Jesus taught this truth: "Every good tree bringeth forth good fruit, but a corrupt tree bringeth forth bad fruit" (Matt. 7:17). To emphasize its certainty, He added, "A good tree *cannot* bring forth bad fruit, *neither can* a corrupt tree bring forth good fruit" (v. 18). So when God, friends, or enemies consistently see in us the Spirit's rich, full fruit—long-suffering, goodness, meekness, self-control—they may be sure of one thing: we're spiritually healthy "trees of righteousness, the planting of the LORD" (Isa. 61:3), or developing believers with no besetting sin diseases in our motives, attitudes, and habits.

Delicious. When mature, nature's fruit is delicious, sweet, and satisfying to our palates. One bite from a ripe watermelon, date, or strawberry sends signals from our taste buds via our nerves to our brain, which interprets them as *satisfaction*. Similarly, when sinners or saints interact with mature "branches" of Christ laden with ripe kindness, patience, and gentleness, it's a deliciously reassuring experience to their often discouraged, spiritually hungry souls. Starving for the fruit of real Christianity, they "taste and see" that, yes, "the LORD is good" (Ps. 34:8) and, yes, Christlike Christians do exist on planet Earth. With all life's bitter, disillusioning experiences and people, such a "taste" is a sweet, delicious surprise.

Delightful. Natural fruit gives growers pure delight. To dedicated gardeners and farmers, there's no greater joy than seeing their plants, vines, or trees bent over with harvest-ready fruit. Forget fame, fortune, or fans; give them *fruit!* The same is true of the Master and His ministers. Nothing delights Jesus like seeing the "produce" of His gracious nature and noble character growing in us daily, ready for harvest at His appearing. Nor is there anything more joyful for those who labor faithfully in the fields or vineyards of His church. One, the apostle John, described his delight at hearing of the Spirit's fruit in Gaius and his fellow Christians: "I have *no greater joy* than to hear that my children walk in truth" (3 John 4).

Constantly changing. Never static, fruit is a constantly changing life form, always growing and ripening...or spoiling. Similarly, the fruit of the Spirit is constantly changing. As Jesus said, if we abide, the Spirit's fruit grows, manifesting clearly and regularly (John 15:4–5). If we continue abiding and obeying under the hot "sun" of testing, the Spirit's fruit ripens or matures, as Christ's graces in us grow sweeter, stronger, and more consistent. But if we stop praying and learning and living God's Word, our fruit withers and spoils until, reverting to selfishness and sinfulness, we bear no resemblance to our Savior Vine.

Honorable. Natural fruit is honorable—or a means of honor to its plant, land, and grower. The vineyard owners, vineyards, and vines whose grapes make the best wine are renowned worldwide for their vintage. Similarly, whenever Christians, churches, or the body of Christ at large consistently bear the best spiritual fruit—"love, joy, peace, long-suffering, gentleness, goodness, faith, meekness, self-control"—we win more honor for our heavenly Vinedresser, the Vine, and His vineyard (kingdom). Why? The Spirit is producing in us a prodigious harvest of a prize-winning vintage. And we'll collect our "prizes" at the judgment seat of Christ.

More than our religious works, this *fruit of the Spirit* is the product of the Vine the Father seeks first. Why? It fits us to live blissfully with

Him and His Son in New Jerusalem forever. Without it, our ministry works, however prodigious or prestigious, won't please or honor Him.

The fruit of souls

The *fruit of souls* is the spiritual produce of *people ministered to*, or kingdom results produced in other souls by our ministries, whether by intercession, utterance, or charity.

Intercession ministry. Intercession begins, sustains, and perfects our ministry fruit. This is why Jesus mentioned it in the same breath in which He commissioned us to "go" out among men and women and "bring forth fruit" that would not fade but "remain," or endure eternally: "I have chosen you, and ordained you, that ye should go and bring forth fruit, and that *your fruit should remain*; that *whatever ye shall ask* of the Father in my name, he may give it you" (John 15:16). When we abide and "ask" (vv. 7–8), God draws unsaved souls to the Savior, beginning His work of grace in their lives. Once they are converted and baptized, and under Spirit-inspired Bible teaching and faithful pastoral care, if we continue "asking" God to sanctify and grow them, He does so. Thus His fruit in their souls is sustained and eventually perfected—they are brought into a consistently close walk with Jesus.

Utterance ministry. Utterance ministries—sharing the Word audibly or in print—are the most noticeable ways we bear fruit in souls. When we share the gospel in pulpits, conversations, or tracts, souls are netted, drawn, and saved from the sea of darkness to the shores of the kingdom of light. When we teach the Bible in public classes or private discussions or through books, radio, television, CDs, DVDs, or websites, saved souls are edified, educated, and established in their faith and walk with God. As pastors and counselors exhort growing disciples, their souls are corrected, purified, guided, and protected. The apostle Paul yearned to teach and counsel the Christians in Rome, "that I might have some fruit among you also" (Rom. 1:13). Thus, by the spoken and written word, utterance ministries bear lasting fruit in souls.

Charitable ministries. Charitable ministries help both redeemed and unredeemed souls by giving financial and practical help to those experiencing need or hardship (Acts 11:27–30). They also give hospitality to traveling ministers and laymen (3 John 5–6). Kind not only to the righteous but also the unrighteous, they help not only the church's needy but also the world's poor and afflicted ones, dispensing good things with the Good News. These free gifts of God's goodness lead many lost souls to repentance and the Redeemer (Rom. 2:4). Charitable ministries are "branches" growing out of the "mustard seed" tree of the church, on which not only native but also wild "birds of the air" may perch, if only briefly, and find rest, food, shelter, and the way to eternal life under Jesus' covering (Mark 4:30–32).[1] Their material gifts of grace do not come back void but bear the fruit of eternal salvation in many desolate and despairing souls.

The Father greatly desires this *fruit of souls* because it increases the quantity and quality of His personal eternal inheritance—the redeemed people who will populate New Jerusalem forever! They are His coveted "riches" in which He "glories." Paul prayed that our minds would be opened to comprehend just how much God's redeemed, transformed people mean to Him: "The eyes of your understanding being enlightened, that ye may know…the *riches* of the *glory* of *his inheritance in the saints*" (Eph. 1:18). To the Father and Son, these *souls ministered into Christlikeness* are the "precious fruit of the earth" (James 5:7) for which they patiently and passionately wait. The very best fruit of souls is produced by those who consistently manifest the fruit of the Spirit. By not only their ministering but also their modeling of Jesus, souls are brought to Christ *and* established in Christlikeness.

This high and holy ministry exacts a high and heavy price from those who conduct it. Kingdom fruit is expensive!

The Cost of Kingdom Fruitfulness

In chapter 16 we learned that light-bearers are opposed by the "rulers of the darkness of this world." The same is true of fruit-bearers. They too have their enemies.

As every productive vineyard, garden, or farm has its eager enemies—scavenging squirrels, ravenous raccoons, pecking birds, invading insects, and burrowing worms—so God's thriving Vineyard has its nemeses. As nature's fruit-bearing plants are frequently assaulted, fruit-bearing servants of God are often beset before and behind by the devil's trouble-making heavenly and earthly agents. But this is the unavoidable price of fruitfulness in a fruitless world.

Jesus' visit to Gerasa illustrates this.

Jesus in Gerasa

Luke 8:22–37 tells us Jesus left the relatively peaceful city of Capernaum to go on a fruit-bearing mission for His Father. A strongly bound demoniac living near the city of Gerasa needed liberating. To bear this kingdom fruit, Jesus had to endure trouble before and after His act of deliverance.

Before the Minister of deliverance arrived, He endured a terrific storm while crossing the Sea of Galilee (vv. 22–25). It was so perilous that some of His disciples, though experienced sailors, panicked for fear (v. 24). Next came the deliverance itself.

Ironically, this extraordinary exorcism was the easiest part of Jesus' work. In short order, Jesus interrogated the demoniac, expelled approximately six thousand[2] demons possessing him, and sent them into a nearby herd of two thousand pigs (Mark 5:13), which immediately "ran violently down a steep place into the lake, and were choked" (Luke 8:33). This man who before had been insane, naked, uncontrollable, and a vagrant immediately put on clothes and calmly sat down at Jesus' feet, rational, docile, and desiring to join Jesus' disciples (v. 38). Then the "storm" resumed, albeit in a different form.

The local residents immediately and unitedly gave Jesus a very rude reception: "*The whole multitude* of the country of the Gerasenes round about, *besought him to depart from them*" (v. 37). Why the rejection? Scholars conjecture two key reasons: economy and superstition. The locals, worldly minded Hellenists[3] in the Decapolis[4] region east of Jordan, were probably offended that Jesus had destroyed a large and valuable herd of swine without consulting their owner (but He, the real owner, had invoked His divine prerogatives for the greater good; see Psalms 24:1). Or these Greeks feared He was a magician with all-too-real and threatening supernatural powers. Or both of these factors may have prompted them.[5] Whatever their reasons, Jesus took their cold shoulder in stride. Why? He knew, and fully accepted, that trouble was the price of fruitfulness. To Him, accomplishing His Father's will—in this case, liberating a terribly troubled soul—meant much more than a trouble-free existence.

Furthermore, Jesus always saw things from a spiritual viewpoint. He saw and understood the natural factors but looked beyond them and analyzed people and events primarily by the spiritual factors involved. In this case, He recognized the ferocious storm on the Sea of Galilee as Satan's desperate onslaught against Him and His little band of deliverers. It was the collective effort of the supernatural demonic "power(s) of the air" (Eph. 2:2) initiating or exacerbating bad weather (Job 1:19) to try to stop the deliverance of one of their most prized captives, the "wild man" of Gerasa. To Jesus, such supernatural opposition was to be expected. It was part of His calling.

So, after expelling the demons, Jesus didn't let down His guard. Baptized by fire, He anticipated more heat. Fruit had been borne, the kingdom had been enlarged, the Father was pleased and honored, and Satan was furious about it all. Whatever natural factors turned the people against Him, I'm sure Jesus saw His rejection by the Gerasenes spiritually. Why? The Head of the church who through His apostle exhorted us to be "spiritually minded" (Rom. 8:6) would do no less. He surely recognized He was not "wrestling" merely with "flesh and blood," but rather with the demonic "rulers of the darkness of this world" (Eph. 6:12) who were expressing their displeasure through the locals, who, being unbelievers, were subject to their prompts. *Just as the raging storm was Satan's veiled attempt to dissuade Jesus before the deliverance, so the Gerasenes' rejection was his attempt to offend Him after it.*

But to Jesus, a veteran Fruit-bearer, this was nothing novel. He knew well the facts of kingdom fruitfulness. Let's consider them.

The Facts of Kingdom Fruitfulness

The facts of kingdom (or spiritual) fruitfulness are found in Jesus' teaching, in the Book of Acts, and on the battlefield.

In Jesus' teaching

Not surprisingly, Jesus taught the facts of kingdom fruitfulness He lived and labored in daily. In John 15, there is a natural progression of thought, an intentional order to the main subjects Jesus opened. The core subject matter shifts from abiding (vv. 1–7) to fruitfulness (vv. 8, 16–17) to persecution (vv. 18–21). This order has a subtle underlying message: *Abiding brings forth fruit, and fruit brings with it trouble.* Indeed, if we abide very close to Christ and His Word, we become fruitful in the fruit of the Spirit and the fruit of souls. Then, because God's Spirit is bearing fruit in and through us, we become a prime target for Satan's arrows of trouble. This is why Jesus also taught, as stated earlier, that whenever the Word is bearing fruit in and through us, "tribulation or persecution ariseth because of the word" (Matt. 13:21).

Not coincidentally, Jesus' teaching is enacted in the Book of Acts.

In the Book of Acts

If, doubting, despising, or despairing of these facts, we fancy we can bear "much fruit" without facing much frustration, we need to reread the Book of Acts. Slowly. Prayerfully. Completely.

That chronicle of the church's first thirty years is filled with steady fruitfulness accompanied by steady persecution. Though God gave the first

Christians sufficient grace to endure, He nevertheless let the opposition have at them. If we imagine we'll be dynamically fruitful for the kingdom, yet evade the enemy's backlash, we're dreaming an *un*inspired dream that won't be fulfilled. Why? The facts are all against it. The spirit of the devil is still set in fierce opposition to the Spirit of Christ. Darkness still hates the light. Truth is still scorned by iniquity. True Christianity and lukewarm or apostate Christianity still live at the opposite poles of the spiritual world. Workers of iniquity are just as bent on stopping fruitful disciples and ministers as the deceived Jewish religious leaders were on halting Peter, Stephen, and Paul. So if we're not experiencing periodic trouble from the enemy, we're not bearing kingdom fruit. It's as simple as that.

The history of human warfare teaches us another lesson that can't be shooed away by wishful thinking.

On the battlefield

For centuries conventional combat has dictated that soldiers can't be heroes without taking risks. If they stay far from the battlefield or hide deep inside fortifications, they'll be safe but militarily unfruitful. They'll never complete vital missions or take key ground from the enemy. To be fruitful, they must accept some degree of exposure to enemy fire.

Like foolish soldiers, many of us want awards without adversities and commendations without clashes. We dream of receiving the honorable distinction of being an "overcomer," yet we refuse to leave the fear-marked boundaries of lukewarm Christianity. With pseudo-bravery we profess we'll do *anything* God asks—unless it may in the remotest way cause us trouble. Devoted to no-risk living, we consistently take the path of least resistance and leave braver saints to stand fast against the enemy's onslaughts. Jesus' mind-set was just the opposite.

Not only at Gerasa but also throughout the Gospels we see the Good Soldier bearing kingdom fruit while under heavy enemy fire. As He healed the sick, expelled demons, evangelized sinners, announced the coming kingdom, and taught the Word, the "barrage" was ceaseless. His home synagogue rejected Him violently, the nation's religious leaders declared Him possessed, His brothers mocked Him, His friends tried to turn Him back, Herod threatened Him, many of His disciples went back, one apostle betrayed Him, the nation's highest jurists demanded—and got—His execution from the Roman governor, and all "without a cause" (John 15:25). Jesus paid this high price for one reason: to take His Father's kingdom objectives. Though wounded, tortured, and finally killed, He took them all and completed His mission.

At His debriefing, the Good Soldier reported to His Commander-in-Chief, "I have finished the work which thou gavest me to do" (John 17:4). For this outstanding service in the face of overwhelming fire, the Commander-in-Chief promoted Him to His current rank of "Lord of Hosts," or General of Heaven's Armies.

Jesus and the early Christians paid the price of fruitfulness. Will you? Will you pay the cost of being a fruitful "branch" on the Vine of the kingdom, thriving in the fruit of the Spirit and the fruit of souls? And will you accept the facts of the spiritual battlefield and fulfill your mission orders, enduring hardness "as a good soldier of Jesus Christ" (2 Tim. 2:3)? There is no middle ground here. Every soldier either faces combat or cowers.

Cowards spend all their thought, time, and energy trying to avoid inevitable confrontations. Throughout the history of human conflict, cowards have never won a battle, much less a war. They never will. Nor will God use them in His ongoing conflict with the spirit of this world.

That sacred commission is reserved for His courageous ones.

Chapter Nineteen

WE MUST BE COURAGEOUS

Arise; for this matter belongeth unto thee...be of good courage, and do it.

—EZRA 10:4

H OWEVER WE MAY deny or downplay it, it takes courage to obey God. And the further we go in obedience, the more courage it takes. Biblical discipleship is not for the faint of heart.

Looking around us in the church today, bold talk is plentiful, but brave living is rare. We're blessed with unprecedented amounts of biblical knowledge, inspiring examples from Christian history, material resources aplenty, wondrous technological advances, and open doors for ministry worldwide, yet we're still coming short of God's purpose. We're wandering in the wilderness of lukewarm Christianity when we should have occupied the promised land of spiritual maturity long ago. Why? We lack the moral courage to act on all the knowledge God has given us—or, more precisely, to fully do God's Word.

Courage is "the attitude of facing and dealing with anything recognized as dangerous, difficult, or painful, instead of withdrawing from it."[1] This defines not only *courage* but also its primary antonym, *cowardice*, which is simply the opposite. It's the attitude of withdrawing from anything recognized as dangerous, difficult, or painful instead of facing and dealing with it.[2] So, what the courageous soul faces and deals with, the coward considers and flees from. One stands fast, while the other runs fast. One withstands, while the other withdraws. Solomon memorialized this in his proverb, "The wicked flee when no man pursueth, but the righteous are bold as a lion" (Prov. 28:1).

A common misconception is that courageous folks have no fears, that they are made of different human "stuff." We imagine they don't feel the hesitancy, the quivering, the internal turmoil the rest of us feel. But this is not true—at least, not initially. Courageous souls do have fears like everyone else, but at some point they learn to no longer yield to them.

Courageous Christians learn that whenever God speaks to their hearts—clearly, scripturally, and with His confirming sustained peace—they must overrule fear and obey, acting upon their courageous instincts. Cowardly Christians hesitate, and hesitate, and hesitate...until their fears have smothered all their braver inclinations.

In a word, they fail because they never learn to press through their fears.

Pressing Through Fear

Christian bravery doesn't just happen. It results when a believer determines, with God's help, to press through his or her paralyzing fears. Two examples, one biblical and another historical, help illustrate this.

David's courage

David, who became a man of great courage, stated that he had great fears at one time in his life. Through God, however, he overcame them all. The son of Jesse described his deliverance in memorable words: "I sought the Lord, and he heard me, and delivered me from *all my fears*" (Ps. 34:4). Exactly how did David overcome his fears?

Was it merely by praying, "Lord, please take away my fears"? Well, he did pray: "I sought the Lord." But it didn't end there. David also did his part in the practical, down-to-earth sense by refusing to tolerate fear anymore, by confessing his faith, and by doing everything God challenged him to do. Only by this brave practical cooperation did he gain the first cautious victories over his fears. Then, gradually, he grew more confident, first slaying a lion, then a bear, when they threatened Jesse's sheep (1 Sam. 17:34–37). Established in this initial courage, David moved on to greater challenges: first, the imposing Philistine gladiator, Goliath, and later, the large, heavily armed, battle-hardened Philistine armies. Thus, not overnight but over time, David grew to become a man of great courage.

God wants us to do the same. He wants to deliver us from our fears, establish us in trust in Him, and then increase our confidence until we're as bold as David. He did this in the brave Jews who fought in the Maccabean revolt, of whom Daniel wrote, "The people who know their God shall be strong, and carry out great exploits" (Dan. 11:32, NKJV). He can do it in us too. But our road to deliverance is the same as David's. Like him, we must face our fears in the name of the Lord. No man can gain the upper hand over fear unless he's willing to go face-to-face with the people, situations, or issues that have intimidated him and, with God's help, overcome them. Jacob had to face Esau...Samuel had to deliver God's message of judgment to Eli...Peter had to receive Gentile Christians in the presence of the Judaizers. There was no other way for these individuals to "stand fast...in the liberty" with which Christ had set them free (Gal. 5:1). When fear visited, they had to stop panicking and press through.

Ulysses S. Grant

Many prominent historical figures have reached heights of greatness from small, timid, trembling beginnings. As Bildad exhorted Job, "Though thy beginning was small, yet thy latter end should greatly increase" (Job 8:7).

Ulysses S. Grant, who became a bold, successful military leader, grew to valor from a very shaky start. After graduating from the United States Military Academy and participating in the Mexican-American War, Grant, disillusioned by the unjustness of the war, left the military service for civilian life. He experienced a series of failures at various occupations and settled into obscurity as an employee at his father's leather shop in Galena, Illinois. Then the Civil War broke out. After being denied a commission in the regular U.S. Army, Grant obtained one with the Illinois Volunteers[3] and began doing something Union officers of the period found difficult—winning battles against the Rebels. These initial victories, which demonstrated his resourcefulness, resolve, and relentlessness as a military leader, and which climaxed with his most notable, the conquering of Vicksburg, brought him to the attention of Abraham Lincoln. Desperately in need of a commander with Grant's skills and boldness, Lincoln soon placed him over all Union armies.

Grant later wrote that, when leading his first attack against Confederate forces during the early years of the war, he realized he lacked "the moral courage to halt and consider what to do." Upon finding the enemy camp abandoned, he realized that the Confederate commanding officer "had been as much afraid of me as I had been of him." After this, he "never experienced trepidation upon confronting any enemy, though I always felt more or less anxiety."[4]

Evidently Grant learned to *press through* his anxious feelings rather than surrender to them. This apparently minor correction in his attitude made a major difference in the man—and the war and this nation. The timid, green officer of the Illinois Volunteers began to grow more confident and victorious. And his confidence and victories kept growing until he became an intrepid, proven general, the only to bring the legendary Confederate General Robert E. Lee to surrender, and the first to receive this nation's then newly created and highest military rank, General of the Army of the United States.[5]

Without Courage...

Thank God loss of courage doesn't cause loss of salvation. But the cowardly Christian, though saved, will never soar to the heights of a David or Grant. Without courage we are left sad and sinking in the unsatisfying pit of timid Christianity, without revival, deliverance, fulfillments, or breakthroughs.

No revival!

Without courage there can be no revival. Ezra's experience demonstrates this.

When Ezra, the scribe, returned to Jerusalem, he found the Jews spiritually backslidden (Ezra 9–10). Jerusalem's post-exile temple and walls had been reconstructed, but its inhabitants' souls needed reviving. So God called Ezra to act courageously on Earth so He could send revival from heaven: *"Arise*; for this matter belongeth unto thee…*be of good courage*, and *do it"* (Ezra 10:4). If God's people were to have new life, Ezra had to lead them down a new path, one marked by a painful process of divinely required divorce. For years the Jews had ignored God's prohibition, duly recorded in His law, against intermarriage with the Gentiles. So now, to position themselves for fresh showers of divine blessing and to preserve the spiritual and ethnic purity necessary for the coming of Messiah, God ordered the unequally yoked Jewish men to "put away," or divorce, their foreign wives and children.

As sensitive as he was scholarly, Ezra realized that this would cause bitter domestic upheaval and possibly rebellion. It could mean violent opposition and persecution for the reform movement, its leaders, and him! But after reviewing these fearful possibilities, Ezra overruled them, put God's will before his own comfort and safety, and proceeded to deal with the nation's sin.

With these necessary corrections made, the moral foundation for national revival was in place. Then God could, and did, send spiritual refreshment in response to His now-righteous remnant's prayers.

No deliverance!

Without courage, there can be no deliverance. This is evident in the story of Esther.

Haman's wicked decree demanded and dated his much-anticipated extermination of all Jews in the Persian Empire "upon the thirteenth day of the twelfth month" (Esther 3:13). But before that holocaustic hour arrived, God called upon Esther to act bravely.

Through Mordecai's message, God charged Queen Esther to intercede before King Ahasuerus (Xerxes) for her people's rescue from Haman's genocide (Esther 3–7). When Esther initially hedged with cowardly intent to save herself, Mordecai shot back a response warning her of the dire consequences of cowardice in a crisis hour. Only after she complied with this call to courage did God give Esther the favor that saved her and her people from annihilation.

Esther possessed many admirable qualities—beauty, grace, knowledge, discretion, kindness, obedience, humility, and faithfulness—but none of these brought her people release from ruin. Her courage alone did so. It not only brought her and her nation through the crisis, but it also ensured the coming of the Savior and the success of His salvation.[6] It was not Esther's stunning physical beauty but her attitude of facing and dealing with things recognized as difficult, dangerous, or painful, rather than withdrawing from them, that God immortalized in her words, "So will I go in unto the king...and if I perish, I perish" (Esther 4:16).

No promises fulfilled!

Without courage, there can be no fulfillment of divine promises. Israel's Canaan conquest showcases this.

By Moses' hand, Jehovah led His people out of Egyptian bondage with wonderful promises of a new, rich, fruitful land filled with excellent vineyards, orchards, wells, cities, and houses, all soon to be theirs. But there was one condition—one very big condition. They had to *take* the land He had given. Canaan would not fall into their hands like ripe figs off a tree. They would have to do battle with the fearsome Canaanite "giants," the sons of Anak (Num. 13:33), who inhabited the land. "Giants" is translated from the Hebrew *nepilim* (nef-eel'), meaning a "feller,"[7] or one who is *cruel, fierce, dreadful, or savage.* Any war would mean difficulty, danger, pain, and loss, but especially one against such "giants."

Redeemed but not resolute, and seeing big men but not their bigger God, the men of Moses' generation shrank from this challenge and, sadly, never entered in. Their firm refusal to be courageous, which climaxed with the national referendum at Kadesh-barnea (Num. 13–14), ensured their grave markers would bear the epitaph "coward" when they contentedly died in fear, never having enjoyed the blessings God so lovingly planned, provided, and promised them. He had *given* everything they could ever need or dream of, but they *took* nothing. And because they took nothing, they received nothing. Theirs was a tragically unfulfilled generation.

But their children's generation was delightfully different. Following Joshua's exhortation and example, they overcame their fears and forged courageous characters. Not once or twice but *three times* in the opening verses of the Book of Joshua God exhorts Joshua and, through him, the people to be "courageous":

> Be strong and of good *courage*; for unto this people shalt thou divide for an inheritance the land which I swore unto their fathers to give them.
>
> —JOSHUA 1:6

> Only be thou strong and very courageous.
>
> —JOSHUA 1:7

> Have not I commanded thee? Be strong and of good *courage*; be not afraid, neither be thou dismayed; for the LORD thy God is with thee wherever thou goest.
>
> —JOSHUA 1:9

This repetitive challenge heavily underscored the fact that they had to be courageous if they were to receive God's fulfillments. Unlike their fathers' generation, Joshua and his men accepted God's challenge. In faith, they waged war with the more experienced and numerically and militarily superior Canaanites and won. Even with God's help, this was no easy thing. They endured a series of frightfully deadly conflicts, at times suffering painful losses (Josh. 7:5), but in the end they prevailed over the "giants" their fathers had feared. Thus God fulfilled His promise not only because of His faithful character but also because of their firm courage. He gave Canaan, again, and this time they bravely reached and took it!

No breakthroughs!

Without courage we cannot break through the barriers that confront us periodically in the way of righteousness. We see this in the reconstruction of the Jewish temple during the post-exilic period.

After Cyrus' decree liberated the Jews from Babylonian captivity in 538 B.C., many returned to Jerusalem, where they erected an altar and began reconstructing their temple. But after completing the foundation in 536 B.C., the local Samaritan population protested to the reigning Persian monarch, Artaxerxes, and his favorable response authorized the Samaritans to "make them [the Jews] cease by force and power" (Ezra 4:23). Thus, strangely stymied in their inspired attempt to do God's express will for their time—reestablish biblically ordered temple worship—the Jews stepped back and, discouraged, stopped working altogether on the project: "Then ceased the work of the house of God" (v. 24). For over fifteen long years, this high-priority project was laid low and its workers sunk even lower as they lost interest in God and His house and reverted to living for their own "house[s]" (Hag. 1:9), or self-interest. Meanwhile something else was rising.

That imposing psychological obstacle was the mountain of seemingly invincible opposition posed by the Samaritans, who seemed to have all the influence and authority on their side. But God was still on His throne, and, in His time (520 B.C.[8]), He sent the prophets Haggai and Zechariah to stir the people to action. They called the sleeping remnant to awake, to abandon their low, self-interested, self-serving lives, and rise to new heights. Those holy highlands were the pursuit of God's will, specifically, their generation's prime project: rebuilding God's temple. To do this, however, they would have to break through the stubborn Samaritan opposition, which would surely resurface the moment they returned to God's will. To bolster their faith, God promised not only to bless their reconstruction efforts (Hag. 1:7–8) but also to *move the mountain* that blocked their way to the completion of His temple: "Who art thou, *O great mountain*? Before Zerubbabel [the Jews' governor] *thou shalt become [as flat as] a plain*" (Zech. 4:7).

As anticipated, when the Jews resumed reconstruction, the Samaritans resumed obstruction, this time trying to intimidate the Jews by writing the new Persian king, Darius, questioning the Jews' authority to pursue their reconstruction project. But this time their plan backfired. God turned Darius' heart to strongly support the rebuilding of the Jewish temple and ordered the Samaritan governor, Tatnai, to do the same—or be executed (Ezra 6:6–12)!

This was the breakthrough the weary Jews needed! And they received it only because they were willing, again, to face resistance from their enemies to do God's will.

FACING OR FOLDING UNDER THE FEAR OF MAN

When we stand before Christ, not the indomitable temerity of sinners but the inexcusable timidity of the saints will be found to have been most damaging to God's cause. It will have caused as much hindrance, harm, and heartache as the combined efforts of demons, sinners, workers of iniquity, impostors, heretics, and false prophets.

One of our most paralyzing fears is the fear of people, specifically of their reproach—everything from mild criticism to strong condemnation to vicious revilings. God has commanded us, "*Fear not* the reproach of men, *neither be afraid* of their revilings" (Isa. 51:7). Yet honest self-reflection will reveal we are far too often terrorized, mildly or monstrously, by recurring imaginations of how others may react if we dare obey God in certain matters. What will they say? What will they do? Will they criticize us? Turn against us? Turn others against us? Will our family oppose us? Our neighbors avoid us? Other Christians misjudge us? Will we be mocked as fools or maligned as cultists as our reputation freefalls? Quiet but persistent thoughts like these harass all Christians in varying degrees.

They are our real enemies, the "giants" that keep us from our

fulfillments, the mountainous "Samaritans" that block our progress toward spiritual maturity. These invisible, insidious demons feed
our fears, quench our courage, halt our obedience, and spoil our joy.
We must press through these reasonings and courageously take them
captive—or be captivated by them. There are only two choices here, fear
and be snared or trust and be safe: "The fear of man bringeth a *snare
[trap]*; but whoso [courageously] putteth his trust in the LORD shall be
safe [preserved, delivered]" (Prov. 29:25).

This brutal battle for our minds is our pivotal "Kadesh-barnea." It's
the Canaanites versus the Israelites all over again. We defeat these fears
or they defeat us. We put them out of the "land" of our minds, or they
prevent us from having God's promised peace, the "peace of God, which
passeth all understanding" (Phil. 4:7). We cast them down—"Casting
down imaginations" (2 Cor. 10:5)—or they cast us down in discouragement, despair, and defeat.

Still very human, we're all prone to attacks of timidity. But, thank
God, with Christ and His Spirit within, we can all "be *strong* in the Lord
and in the power of His might" (Eph. 6:10). "Strong" is translated from
the Greek *endynamoō*, meaning "enabled, empowered."[9] To be "enabled"
or "empowered" with courage, we must do two things: (1) no longer deny
but now face our fears, and (2) no longer slump under but now rise above
our fears by stirring the Spirit within us: "*Stir up* the gift of God, which
is in thee" (2 Tim. 1:6). How? By using five keys to fearlessness we'll
discuss later in this chapter.

Will you slump or stir? Will you face your fears or fold under them?

RELIANCE ON GRIT OR GOD?

Stubbornly independent, the natural man of valor relies on his own
strength. His foundation is creature-trust, not Creator-trust; self-reliance,
not Spirit-reliance. By his own grunts, growls, and guts he grinds through
his problems on his own power. When taken aback, he emboldens his
soul by remembering his wisdom, strength, and past victories. Thus his

pride prods him ever forward. Even when scared, he dares not admit to fear, lest others hear and mock. Thus girded by his grit, he faces his fears with mere human firmness.

Fundamentally dissimilar, God's bold ones rely on their God, not their grit; their Father, not their flesh. When weak, worn, or wobbly, they draw strength by remembering, not their wisdom, but God's; not their strength, but God's; not their faithfulness, but God's; not their grace, but God's; not their resources, but God's; not their past successes, but God's. Frankly, they'd love to flee difficulty for the sake of their comfort, but, firmly, God's love constrains them to face it for the sake of His name. Nehemiah was so constrained by love for the name: "Should such a [God-representing] man [of God] as I flee?" (Neh. 6:11). Thus, the Savior's soldiers may quiver, but they'll *not* cower. No sir! Why? "That he [they] may please him who hath chosen him [them] to be a soldier" (2 Tim. 2:4). Also, so their rewards, temporally and eternally, may be "full" (2 John 8).

So they look to the Rock that is higher than they are—and grow rocky, resilient, and redoubtable: "*They looked unto him*, and were *radiant, and* their faces were *not ashamed* [with fear]" (Ps. 34:5). So, trusting not their grit but their God, they stand unmoved and unmovable: "They that trust in the LORD shall be as Mount Zion, which cannot be removed, but abideth forever" (Ps. 125:1).

FIVE KEYS TO FEARLESSNESS

Here are five simple but dynamic keys for converting cowardice into courage. If practiced consistently, they'll make us consistently fearless.

Face your fears.

When God orders you to do something difficult and fear begins working on your mind, recognize it for what it is. Don't deny it; declare it—quickly, and to God. Don't repress it; express it—quickly, and to God. This humble confession of truth (reality) is the first step toward freedom. And God, who "resists the proud, but gives grace to the humble" (James 4:6, NKJV), requires it to forgive and cleanse sin: "If we confess our sins, he is faithful and just to forgive us our sins, and to cleanse us from all unrighteousness" (1 John 1:9). And fear is sin, an unbelieving refusal to trust God to help us.

Recall God's Word.

Remember what God says about fear. For instance, "God hath *not* given us the spirit of fear, but of power, and of love, and of a sound mind" (2 Tim. 1:7); or "He that feareth is not made perfect in love [loving trust in God]" (1 John 4:18). Only God's Word nourishes faith, and only faith overpowers fear. So soak in the scriptures that bring God's assurance, peace, and strength straight home to your heart regarding your specific fear-problem.

Reject fear-thoughts!

Take yourself firmly in hand and "act like men, be strong" (1 Cor. 16:13, ESV). Determine to terminate your timidity. If God doesn't give us fear, it must come from Satan. Refuse it, and him! "Perfect love *casteth out* fear" (1 John 4:18). Stop entertaining fearful thoughts, which are Satan's "terrorists." "Fear involves *torment*" (1 John 4:18, NKJV). Start complying with God's repeated biblical command, "Fear not!" Jesus purged the Jews' temple of Satan's moneychangers; rid yours of his "terrorists." Don't let them hold the courts of your heart hostage ever again!

Confess your faith.

Say to yourself what you believe and what you intend to do with God's help: "I'm not going to be held back by fear any more. I can conquer these fears 'through Christ, who strengtheneth me.' Fear will not be my lord!" Ground your declarations in God's promises: "*He hath said*, I will never leave thee, nor forsake thee. *So that we may boldly say*, The Lord is my helper, and I will not fear what man shall do unto me" (Heb. 13:5–6). This was the key to David's victory over Goliath (1 Sam. 17:45–47), and we find it frequently in his psalms (Ps. 27:1–3). Confessing our faith releases God's salvation in and to us in our present circumstances: "With the mouth he confesses, *resulting in salvation*" (Rom. 10:10, NAS).

Speaking words of agreement with divine truth stimulates, activates, and maximizes our faith, thus reestablishing us in peaceful reliance on God. So, "let the redeemed of the LORD *say so*" (Ps. 107:2).

Act!

It has been correctly said, "Put your faith in the facts, and the feeling will follow." The facts are that God is always strong whether we're weak or strong. So whether you feel puny or powerful, *act* on what God has shown you, trusting Him for strength, and you'll feel stronger afterward. Don't expect to feel bold before you act boldly. Act first (whether by energetic action or patient, dutiful, worshipful waiting), and God, seeing your courage, will refill you spontaneously with His Spirit, who will impart a new, enhanced sense of confidence in God and freedom from fear: "Be of good courage, and he shall strengthen your heart" (Ps. 27:14). "And no one will take away your joy" (John 16:22, NIV).

Here's good news: *all born-again, Spirit-baptized believers can be equally courageous because of the equally bold One inside us.* The intrepid nature of Jesus, our bold "Joshua," our brave Commander, the valiant Lord of Hosts, is in us to help us do His good pleasure. If we will just accept every challenge He sends and practice the keys to fearlessness, we can't fail. Human willingness plus divine ability is unconquerable.

But know this. If after God shows you what to do, you hold back, fear will gain the upper hand. The more you worry, the more you hesitate; the more you hesitate, the more your fear grows, until it smothers your initiative and leaves you weak, defeated, and ashamed—and your Commander grieved: "If any man draw back [from the courageous obedience of faith], my soul shall have no pleasure in him" (Heb. 10:38). So rise and act courageously...unless God says, "Wait."

Courage doesn't always imply vigorous action. It takes just as much courage to wait for God as it does to work for Him, sometimes more! To keep patiently enduring reproach, hoping against hope, doing unnoticed, unappreciated work, alone and lonely, until God performs His promise requires the highest kind of courage. In such times, vigorous action may be false courage, a doubt-inspired, self-reliant effort to help God fulfill His promise or plan that only weakens our trust and rest in God and delays His help. God needs courageous waiters as well as courageous workers.

So when the "giants" of fear stand before you, overrule them before they overrule your courage. Rely on God, not grit. Face, don't fold under, the fear of man. Press through, and take every deliverance, breakthrough, fulfillment, and revival God gives you.

Then, when He leads you to take a stand, nothing and no one will move you.

GOD EMPOWERS THOSE
WHO TAKE A STAND

A long time, therefore, abode they speaking boldly in the Lord,
who gave testimony...and granted signs and wonders to be done
by their hands.

—ACTS 14:3

COURAGEOUS BELIEVERS ARE divinely empowered every time
they take firm stands for God in the necessary conflicts of
Christian life.

If we run from the devil's every threat, we remain fearful, weak,
and defeated. If, however, when vital spiritual or moral issues arise we
take the right stand and hold our position without reacting wrongly,
we'll find that as we stand, God strengthens us.

STRENGTHENED AS THEY STOOD FIRM

Let's study three examples of courageous ones God strengthened after
they took firm stands for Him. We'll consider Paul and Barnabas, King
Jehoshaphat, and King Hezekiah.

Paul and Barnabas

When Paul and Barnabas first visited the Galatian city of Iconium
(Acts 14:1–6), God blessed their evangelistic efforts there, and many souls
came into the kingdom of God: "In Iconium...they...so spoke, that a
great multitude, both of the Jews and also of the Greeks believed" (v. 1).
But the prince of darkness didn't take this invasion of the Light lightly.

Incensed, he stirred up serious trouble for the brethren through

Christ-rejecting Jews: "But the unbelieving Jews stirred up the Gentiles, and made their minds evil affected against the brethren" (v. 2). With more townspeople turning against them daily, Paul and Barnabas had a crucial decision to make: Should they move on to friendlier territory or stay and continue God's work in Iconium? Courageously, Paul chose the latter option. It wasn't easy to carry on his work in an environment filled with suspicion, condemnation, and hostility, but Paul knew the enemy's tactics. Earlier in his ministry he had learned never to yield to satanic threats. So rather than search for a more preacher-friendly atmosphere, Paul and Barnabas took their stand in Iconium: "A long time, therefore, abode they speaking boldly in the Lord" (v. 3).

The Lord's response is most notable. Paul and Barnabas' resoluteness pleased Him so much that He granted a special anointing of spiritual power: "*The Lord*, who gave testimony unto the word of his grace, and *granted signs and wonders to be done by their hands*" (v. 3). So we see that the Lord empowered the apostles *after*, not before, they took a stand for Him in Iconium. The Lord didn't give Paul a conscious influx of fresh spiritual power that inspired him to stay on in a very difficult place. No, Paul and Barnabas' courageous choice came *first*—then the Lord strengthened them.

Later, these two missionaries extraordinaire left Iconium, but in God's will and time, not their own, and prompted by necessity, not timidity. Luke writes, "And when there was an assault made both of the Gentiles, and also of the Jews with their rulers, to use them despitefully, and to stone them, they were aware of it, and fled unto Lystra and Derbe...and there they preached the gospel" (vv. 5–7). Here the apostles "fled," or left quickly seeking refuge,[1] but with purpose, not panic; with calm trust, not chaotic terror. When the opposition became violent, they realized the locals, who had now heard the gospel a "long [lit. *adequate*[2]] time," had hardened their hearts against the Word. So nothing further could be done for the moment as far as public evangelism was concerned. Jesus had instructed the first light-bearers, "whosoever shall not receive you, nor hear your words…depart" and "when they persecute you in this city, flee into another" (Matt. 10:14, 23). So Paul and Barnabas took their adamant rejection as a sign it was God's time to move on and prudently followed Jesus' instructions. Not only knowledgeable but also wise, they recognized there is a time to take a stand and a time to move on, and this was the latter.

If, however, they had left earlier because of the initial change in atmosphere, they would have been failing the Lord, since there was still much work for them to do there. But after they bravely took their stand, received empowerment, and went on to complete their mission, the time came when God, satisfied, released them from their hard duty. His sovereign hand didn't permit the Jews to plan their violent attack until His servants' work was faithfully finished. As with Job, the plot to assault the apostles, though satanic, came forth "from the presence of the LORD" (Job 1:12; 2:7).

Jehoshaphat

One day godly King Jehoshaphat suddenly found Jerusalem surrounded by the hostile armies of his previously peaceful neighboring nations (2 Chron. 20:1–30). Shocked, he was initially very shaken: "And Jehoshaphat feared" (v. 3).

But after "set[ting] himself to seek the LORD" (v. 3), he returned very stimulated. Indeed, after emerging from the secret place, he was filled with heavenly determination, not to take flight from Jerusalem but to take a stand for Jehovah! Equally refilled with heavenly direction, he immediately made a number of Spirit-led decisions: calling the people to fast and pray, summoning them to Jerusalem, leading them in congregational prayer in the temple courts, listening to and interpreting God's prophetic response through Jahaziel, praising and worshiping God spontaneously for His response, overseeing military preparations, appointing singers to lead Judah's soldiers into battle with worship, and exhorting the frightened congregation to fully believe in God and His prophetic promise to rescue them (vv. 3–21).

Not surprisingly, God's prophetic response confirmed and commended the brave stand Jehoshaphat had personally taken, and it called the whole nation to take their stand with him: "*Set yourselves, stand ye still,* and see the salvation of the LORD" (2 Chron. 20:17). As Jehoshaphat and all Judah stood firm in faith in God's unfailing faithfulness, God strengthened, delivered, and rewarded them with a great victory.

Hezekiah

When the proud, cruel, undefeated armies of Assyria marched arrogantly into Judah and surrounded Jerusalem, King Hezekiah found himself in trouble—deadly trouble, to be exact! (2 Chron. 32:1–22).

The imminence and immensity of this terrible situation must have sent fearful alternatives racing through Hezekiah's mind. He could flee for his life, as Zedekiah did years later during a Babylonian siege. He could sue for peace, offering the Assyrian king, Sennacherib, riches or whatever tribute he desired, as other kings did, and as Hezekiah himself had done previously.[3] Or he could hastily dispatch a messenger to hire the armies of Egypt or another regional power. But this brave heart who trusted God more than any other Judean king[4] chose none of these options.

To the contrary, in deadly trouble Hezekiah took a determined stand. He trusted God alone to deliver him from the dreaded power of Sennacherib's hordes. Whether or not inspired by Jehoshaphat's earlier example, Hezekiah nevertheless sprang to action with similar zeal. Calmed and energized by the power of the God whom he trusted, he quickly bolstered the city's defenses, mas   terfully rerouted the main water supply to aid his people only and not their besiegers,[5] and preached faith to the people, encouraging them to trust God's power and angels rather than fear the fierceness and numbers of Sennacherib's warriors. All who heard him were comforted and cheered and stirred to stand firmly with him: "And the people rested themselves upon the words of Hezekiah" (2 Chron. 32:8).

Ever the Evaluator, God tested His people's stand. For days He allowed the Assyrians to remain encamped outside the city walls in plain sight and let Sennacherib's military spokesman, the Rabshakeh, shout blasphemous reproaches, revilings, threats, and mockery in their hearing and native Hebrew tongue (vv. 9–19). He wanted to see, would the people maintain their faithful stand with their faithful king? Or would they call for a compromise? Or panic and run for their lives? Like their leader, these brave hearts held firm, relying on their utterly reliable God. So in the end, God saved them, thus showing us He always stands with those who stand with Him.

WHEN THE GOING GETS TOUGH

Another worldly saying of merit is, "When the going gets tough, the tough get going." God apparently agrees with this because He frequently arranges tough places for His servants to live or work in. Why? He wants to see who will get going doing His will and who will get "gone."

Not all of His children react as Paul and Barnabas, Jehoshaphat, and Hezekiah did. When the going gets tough, they clear out. Like Gideon's original recruits, many of the Savior's soldiers abscond when they should adamantly stand. Why? They have no intention of taking an unpopular, risky, or distressful stand for Christ and His righteousness. So when the going gets tough, they get gone, abandoning their churches, ministries, duties, gifts, callings, spouses, or children. How will we respond when God challenges us to take a stand for and with Him?

Some of us have never been strengthened and upheld by God because we've consistently refused to take stands for Him when and where we should have. When things became uncomfortable, we conveniently made an exit. That's not God's way. If He should call us away from a difficult setting, as He did Paul in Iconium, by all means we should move on. But many times the "call" we hear is not that of our spiritual godliness but of our ungodly selfishness. Consequently, instead of standing, we spurt out of the place God wants us in and miss all He wants to do in and for us there—infuse us with new strength, open His Word more deeply, reveal His presence more sweetly, teach us His ways more convincingly, work through us more powerfully, reveal His plan for our generation more fully, and fill us with more peace, joy, and praise!

It's time we stop running and start taking stands. We need to believe in something and stand for something. It's time we become uncompromising in our loyalty to Jesus' teachings; call evil, evil and good, good; speak out for what's right and against what's wrong. The Lord wants strong saints who dare to be different, different from the world that doesn't know God and lukewarm Christians who dare not be different. But we must not misunderstand.

To take a stand is not to start a fight. God wants us to be bold, but not bellicose; to stand, but not strive; to be immovable, but not insolent. "Taking a stand" means simply to *assume and hold the correct position and testimony in a moral or spiritual controversy and refuse to be moved by the various pressures our antagonists bring to bear on us.* The Spirit exhorts us to "put on the whole armor of God" and "be strong in the Lord" and "stand" against Satan's various tricks aimed at stumbling us (Eph. 6:10–11), but He does not tell us to verbally, legally, or physically "attack" our human opponents or plot their downfall. When God leads us to the right stand and we take it, yes, our antagonists will fight against us in every conceivable way. We must then carefully do two things: (1) hold the biblical stand we have taken for "his righteousness" (Matt. 6:33) without compromising or retracting our position, and (2) not be provoked into a wrong reaction, especially personal retaliation.

As stated previously,[6] God commands us, "Recompense to no man evil for evil" (Rom. 12:17). Ever mindful of this, Satan will try everything in his very large and full bag of tricks to get us to *resist evil with evil,* knowing any attempt to retaliate is a form of rebellion against God and disqualifies us from receiving His help. If we fight back in our old ways, God won't fight for us, and we'll fall; if we hold our position and let God fight for us, we'll stand. This completely God-dependent position, combined with steady prayer in the Spirit, is the key to ultimate victory. As we thus stand firm with Him, the Father says to us what He said to His Son, "Sit thou [resting, trusting in] at my right hand [my right-hand power], until I [intervene in judgment to] make thine enemies thy footstool" (Ps. 110:1).

THE EARLY CHURCH

For more key insights, let's look to the early church. The first Christians took stands frequently.

Only weeks after the church's birth, its witness drew opposition, as the powerful Jewish Sanhedrin, the highest court in Israel, attempted to quench its message of salvation through the resurrected Christ with a religious gag order. Specifically, it commanded the apostles "not to speak at all nor teach in the name of Jesus" (Acts 4:18) or be prepared to face much more serious punishment than the brief detainment they had already experienced. Immediately the early Christians were forced to make a crucial decision: submit and cease bearing light, or take a stand on the "lampstand" where Christ had placed them (Jerusalem) and let their light shine. Remarkably, they chose to keep shining! What followed was even more remarkable.

Rather than ask the Lord to take away the Sanhedrin's weighty threat, they prayed for more strength to stand strong under its weight! "And now, Lord, behold their threatenings; and grant unto thy servants, that with all boldness they may speak thy word, by stretching forth thine hand to heal; and that signs and wonders may be done by the name of thy holy child, Jesus" (vv. 29–30). Deeply pleased, the Lord answered immediately and inspirationally: "When they had prayed, the place was shaken where they were assembled together; and they were all filled with the Holy Spirit, and they spoke the word of God with boldness" (v. 31). But their struggle didn't end there.

When the disciples took their stand, the Jews promptly took a counterstand...and threw the apostles in jail, again! "Then the high priest rose up, and all they that were with him...and laid their hands on the apostles, and put them in the common [general or public] prison" (Acts 5:17–18). At this point, we might think Jesus, having seen such bravery from His young students, would have counseled them to step back and let things cool off a bit. To the contrary, the General of heaven's hosts sent His "standing army" stunning orders: take another stand! One of His angels released them and relayed the message, "Go, stand and speak in the temple to the people all the words of this life" (v. 20). Bravely and promptly, the apostles did so: "When they heard that, they entered into the temple early in the morning, and taught" (v. 21).

After this second "stand," the Lord again strengthened the apostles, this time by strong favor. When the Sanhedrin decided to kill them, the Lord prompted the highly respected Rabbi Gamaliel to advise the council to leave them be (vv. 33–40). When they agreed, the crisis passed. Again, we see the Lord stood with those who stood with Him.

TAKE THE RIGHT STAND

In the Book of Acts, the early church consistently took stands over the right issues. Wisely, they stood firm where God led them to do so, but not in other issues, realizing they couldn't fight every fight.

As a body they never took unified, sustained stands that were purely political, ethnic, social, or national in nature. Rather, their stands were over spiritual or moral issues pertaining to their lives, work, and mission for Christ. Adamantly they refused to compromise living or ministering Christ, sharing His teachings, following His guidance, or fulfilling the Great Commission He gave them. Whenever Satan's servants tried to bully them from these essential truths, values, duties, or ministries, they stood, with meek hearts but manly resolve, and continued their walk and work with Jesus. And every time He gave them sufficient grace to hold their position until He changed their trying circumstances.

Like these first Christians' stands, ours must be over the right issues. We must be led by the Holy Spirit and not merely by our personal reasoning, sentiments, preferences, scruples, or ideology. Skilled and experienced in the arts of deception and diversion, Satan always tries to get us to take the wrong stands, to wax adamant, but about purely political issues, nationalistic causes, social controversies, or any other causes outside the scope of the church's direct responsibilities. If we spend all our passion, prayer, energy, and thought on these issues, we may be ignoring the more spiritually and morally vital issues and controversies over which the Spirit wants us to take stands.

Paul tells us plainly we are not presently called to judge and correct unredeemed society, which will become "worse and worse" in these "last days" (2 Tim. 3:1, 13), but rather to oversee and rule the sin and truth issues within our own ranks:

> What have I to do to judge them also that are outside [the church]?
> Do not ye judge them that are within [the church]? But them that
> are outside [the church] God judgeth.
> —1 CORINTHIANS 5:12–13

Satan wants to reverse this, to get us to focus on *societal* sins and forget *church* sins. He knows our current "hot button" issues—abortion, homosexuality, the definition of marriage, the national debt, global warming, energy sources and usage, and so forth—and through conservative but unspiritual media personalities uses our 24-7 news cycle to relentlessly work us up into a proverbial lather about social sins, crimes, and outrages. As modern prophets, Christians need to *testify* against these things, and some of us are called to work against them, but they are not our primary battlegrounds. They are peripheral, not central issues to disciples having the true spiritual, biblical, kingdom mind-set. Why? They realize God's plan is to correct the church first, then society, not vice versa. Should we, then, ignore these societal debates?

Absolutely not. We should take stands in societal issues, but while realizing our most vital, Christ-pleasing, kingdom-building "stands" need to come on the issues, sins, and errors that most directly hinder the growth and maturity of *Christians* in particular and the *body of Christ* in general. Ongoing impenitent sins, errors, faults, frauds, and abuses in God's own house—these are the issues over which we should take Book of Acts-like stands, and in which, oddly, we are apathetic more often than ardent. We can't overemphasize this, as God is now moving to get us, the redeemed, into His order:

> For the time is come that judgment must begin at the house of God.
> —1 PETER 4:17

Since God's judgment—graciously but firmly enforced restoration of divine order—begins among the redeemed, not the unredeemed, stands on the moral, spiritual, and theological issues among us are paramount.

AVOID WRONG REACTIONS

As stated earlier in this chapter, after taking correct stands, we must be careful to not react wrongly toward our antagonists. Godly ends never justify ungodly means.

We must never resort to not only passionate retaliation but also the unethical, mean-spirited, petty, offensive, and un-Christlike methods we see so often and unconscionably employed in the political arena or other areas of worldly conflict—lying about enemies who slander us, planting spies among them, mocking them, refusing to cooperate with them when we should, refusing to give them credit when due, denying their rights, or working, wishing, or calling for their demise. All of this is shameful and worldly, and none of it is "his righteousness" (Matt. 6:33). We must practice the high standards we preach, no matter how low our detractors sink in opposing us. Then even if we presently have little influence, rank, or control, we have moral authority.

Resorting to any form of malicious mischief betrays spiritual immaturity and an unconscious lack of trust in God's ways, power, and ultimate justice. And it discredits our otherwise honorable stands.

So don't react wrongly to those whom you stand against. However unscrupulous they are, never abandon biblical ethics. If so, you'll render your stand ineffective...and fall flat on your face.

SPIRITUAL ROLE MODELS

Christians who take the right stands and hold them until Christ delivers them are not only overcomers but also spiritual role models. Hearing of their victories, other Christians are inspired to follow their examples. Thus their courageous stands become contagious, spreading from one disciple to another.

Or, in the inimitable words of Oswald Chambers:

> One strong moral man will form a nucleus around which others will gather; and spiritually, if we put on the armor of God and stand true to Him, a whole army of weak-kneed Christians will be strengthened.[7]

Repeatedly, Scripture illustrates Chambers' observation.

Moses' bold stand before Pharaoh encouraged his exhausted Hebrew brothers and sisters to stand through their long, laborious final days in Egypt's slime pits. David's remarkable stand against the imposing giant Goliath inspired Israel's other soldiers to rise and stand against the powerful Philistine armies. The apostle John's lonely stand on the rocky, volcanic isle of Patmos encouraged other suffering disciples in the churches of Asia Minor to stand firm and endure their sufferings for faithfully proclaiming "the word of God, and...the testimony of Jesus Christ" (Rev. 1:9). And Paul's unwavering stand in a Roman prison emboldened many to preach with a conviction they had never known before. He wrote, "Because I am in prison, most of the believers have become more bold in Christ and are not afraid to speak the word of God" (Phil. 1:14, NCV).

After these men took their stands, God empowered not only them but also many others through their examples.

So take your stands, whenever and wherever God leads you to them: "Having done all...*stand. Stand,* therefore, having your loins girded about with truth" (Eph. 6:13–14). And be sure your stand is the correct one. If it is, expect God to empower you. "Hold fast" your stand, wisely avoiding wrong reactions, as long as God requires: "*Stand fast,* therefore, in the liberty with which Christ hath made us free, and be not entangled again with the yoke of bondage" (Gal. 5:1). If God requires you to stand a long time, remember, the longer you maintain the right stand, the more He will empower, use, and mature you to "*stand perfect and complete* in all the will of God" (Col. 4:12). If you get weary, keep standing, remembering that your example will inspire many others to stand strong with and for the Lord: "*Then [after the apostles stood strong] stood there up one...*named Gamaliel" (Acts 5:34).

We need to know how to stand well now, because, like it or not, clashes are coming.

Chapter Twenty-One

WHEN THE CLASH COMES

If any man come to me, and hate not his father, and mother, and wife, and children, and brethren, and sisters, yea, and his own life also, he cannot be my disciple.

—LUKE 14:26

To TAKE AND hold the right stands, we must understand this: In every true disciple's life clashes occasionally occur between God's will and others' will for us; also between God's will and our will. At such times we must deliberately disregard every claim that competes against the Master's will. This is one of Christ's hard sayings.

It's hard because it is very difficult for our old nature to accept the new fact that, in Christ, we no longer belong to ourselves but to God: "What? Know ye not that...*ye are not your own? For ye are bought with a price*; therefore, glorify God [by doing His will] in your body and in your spirit, which are God's" (1 Cor. 6:19–20). This reminds us that when Jesus died for our sins, He redeemed us, or bought our freedom from slavery to sin and its cruel master, Satan. By accepting His salvation, we acknowledge that we no longer belong to Satan or to ourselves but to Christ. From now on, in Christ, we are God's fully blood-bought, redeemed love slaves, ready to do not what Satan demands or what we desire but what God wills. It's a lofty ideal, and one many Christians ignore.

But as serious disciples of Christ, we must no longer ignore but now implement this ideal in our practical living. Christ alone, not self or other people, must rule our life decisions, plans, actions, and reactions. We must allow Him free command of our every step without interference from well-meaning friends, relatives, or Christian brothers or sisters—or from our own willfulness or reasoning: "Lean not unto thine own understanding" (Prov. 3:5).

Understanding and accepting this hard saying is vital if we are to answer the call of God.

THE CALL OF GOD—AND CLASH OF MEN

The call of God

The call of God is strictly an individual matter. God calls each one of us to two closely connected ends: (1) a Person and (2) a path. Mark describes this twofold call of God.

The Person to whom He calls us is Himself, specifically in the person of His Son, Jesus. Jesus called His twelve disciples first to "be with him" (Mark 3:14), so they could get to know Him closely and fully and His teaching deeply and truly. Then, in His time, His plan was to "send them forth" (v. 14) to preach, teach, and minister in His name. Thus the first phase of God's call is to a *Person*—sustained, close fellowship with Jesus. The second is to a *plan*—the life path and life works He has predestined for us in Christ: "For we are...created...unto *good works, which God hath before ordained that we should walk in them*" (Eph. 2:10). While every believer is called to the same Person, we are all called to different paths.

At times the path He calls us to take seems reasonable to us and to others. So we take it readily, and others smile and give their nod of approval. But at other times the Spirit calls us to go in a way neither we nor they can understand. Why? Our natural minds can't understand and therefore don't accept the spiritual ways and divine methods of the Spirit of God: "The natural man receiveth not the things of the Spirit of God...neither can he know them, because they are spiritually discerned [understood only with the Spirit's help]" (1 Cor. 2:14). Our minds operate by human reason while the Spirit's mind is driven by the incomparably higher intelligence of divine wisdom. Through Isaiah, God says, "My thoughts are not your thoughts, neither are your ways my ways, saith the LORD. For as the heavens are *higher* than the earth, so are my ways *higher* than your ways, and my thoughts than your thoughts" (Isa. 55:8–9). So sometimes God's wise plans seem "foolishness" to mortals.

This fundamental disconnection, or breakdown in understanding, creates an awkward situation. The disciple cannot explain to other people the way the Lord is leading him. Why? He doesn't fully understand it himself. In such times the Lord requires us to trust and obey His call without a detailed explanation on His part. He calls us to walk by faith, not by reason alone, as we did before we were converted. We must now obey His initiatives without knowing what our obedience will lead to and how God will work out problems presently unresolved—and seemingly unresolvable! Jesus may whisper to our hearts what He told Peter, "What I do thou knowest not now, but thou shalt know hereafter" (John 13:7). If so, we must walk in the steps of the father of our faith, Abraham, who "by faith...obeyed; and he went out, *not knowing whither he went*" (Heb. 11:8).

At this crucial point, aware of our dilemma, Jesus faithfully draws near us. As we ask His help and meditate in the Scriptures, He speaks and assures us with biblical verses that in effect say, "Child, fear not. Take the path I set before you. I will go before you, strengthen you, give you wisdom and counsel, and open up My perfect plan before you as you take each step in obedient faith."

Inspired by this assurance, we take our first steps in obedience to His call. After we do so, the "clash" comes.

The clash of men

First, our family protests. Father says, "That's ridiculous. You're being fanatical; you must be deceived." Mother says, "Aren't you taking a big risk? That's such an uncertain prospect these days." Our spouse says, "Oh, that could never be God's will for you. You're just not suited for that." The children join in the clamor, "No, no, we want you home more, not less. Don't you love us?" Our siblings complain, "We don't see you much anymore. Where have you been keeping yourself? All that study and prayer, all those meetings, you're not taking that religion of yours too seriously, are you?" Even our spiritual siblings, brothers and sisters in Christ, may voice disapproval: "What's wrong with you? Why are you planning to do this? The Lord hasn't called any of us that way. Why you?" After all these external naysayers sound off, we hear the low but persistent rumblings of internal opposition.

Our self-life, previously quiet and unchallenged, begins raising objections: "If I answer this call, what will I do for money? Who will help with this task, that responsibility, this need? What will God do next? Where is He taking me?"

Thus far God has called, and other claims—outward and inward—have clashed with that call. The question, though difficult, is now clear: Will I be a true disciple of Christ? Not a converted Christian merely, but a committed Christian? Will I "forsake all and follow Him" as His original disciples did long ago?

Christ left aspiring disciples instructions for such moments in Luke 14:26–27.

Christ's instructions

When "great multitudes" followed Him, Jesus sensed it was time to separate the true disciples from the curious crowd.

> And he turned, and said unto them, If any man come to me, and *hate not* his father, and mother, and wife, and children, and brethren, and sisters, yea, and his own life also [or his life as his own], he cannot be my *disciple*. And whosoever doth not bear his [this] cross, and come after me [following my personal example], cannot be my *disciple*.
>
> —LUKE 14:25–27

Here He taught us that when the clash comes, specifically from our closest family members, we must "hate" all other claims, accept the clash as our personal cross, and follow on faithfully in the footsteps of our misunderstood, misjudged Master. Some clarification is needed here.

Did Jesus really mean we should *hate* our family or friends if they clash with the call of God in our lives? Certainly not! "Hate" is taken from the Greek *miseō*, which is a comparative term meaning "to detest," and "to love less."[1] Obviously Jesus was using the second meaning here. Any godly pastor or counselor will tell you that one huge obstacle to the Spirit's work of fully sanctifying and maturing Christians is that they too often do *hate*—loathe, detest, resent, condemn—one or more members of their immediate or extended families! These old, carnal attitudes must be confessed and forsaken before they can progress as a disciple and be conformed to Christ's character image. If Christians don't stop hating their parents, envying their siblings and cousins, resenting their aunts and uncles, condemning their children, and despising their in-laws, they cannot grow spiritually. For believers, wherever there is hatred, there is hindrance; specifically, spiritual darkness: "He that hateth his brother is in *darkness*, and walketh in *darkness*;" and blindness, "and…darkness hath *blinded* his eyes" (1 John 2:11).

But once these attitudes are confessed and corrected, and God calls, and the clash comes from family and friends, we then must "hate" them in that we *love them less* than we love Christ. Our greatest love is revealed in our choice to please; whomever we love most, we please first. One expositor states, "The stress here is on the *priority of love*….One's loyalty to Jesus must come before his loyalty to his family."[2] Jesus spelled out this "priority of love" plainly in His first full discourse to Word-bearers in Matthew 10:

> He that loveth father or mother *more than me*, is not worthy of me; and he that loveth son or daughter *more than me*, is not worthy of me.
>
> —MATTHEW 10:37

Thus Jesus calls us to make Him and His will the first priority of our love.

He calls us to please Him by doing His will as He pleased His Father by doing the Father's will: "I do always those things that please him" (John 8:29). Paul challenged the Galatians to ponder who it was they were seeking to please first, Christ or others: "For do I now seek [first] the favor of men, or of God? Or do I seek [first] to please men? For if I yet [first] pleased men, I should not be the servant of Christ [serving His pleasure first]" (Gal. 1:10). Thus Paul's challenge is linked spiritually to Christ's instructions. Both charge us to *always please Jesus first,* and by comparison love others less. When we do, our "clash" may escalate into a full-blown spiritual war!

In the same context, Matthew 10:34–39, Jesus openly foretold that some Christians' families would be divided, "a man at variance against his father, and the daughter against her mother, and the daughter-in-law against her mother-in-law" (v. 35). Here He only cites a general reason for this conflict: "for my sake" (v. 39). More specifically, the reasons are often our faith and the call of God. Disbelieving family members reject spiritually reborn Christians for their evangelical faith, changed lifestyle, and biblical standards of righteousness. And, as discussed above, non-Christian and Christian relatives may object when a disciple answers God's call to discipleship, service, ministry, or sacrifice. And sometimes the objections are unrelenting, the feelings strong, and the divisions deep, so much so that a state of spiritual war exists.

For this reason Jesus warned us not to be spiritually naïve or blind: "*Think not* that I am come to send peace on earth [as things are presently]" (v. 34). Then He used the symbol of a "sword" to signify division, conflict, and war: "I came not to send peace, but a *sword [war]*." Natural war is a violent conflict of wills resulting from failed diplomacy; spiritual war is a bitter spiritual division that results when a Christian's faith, calling, or biblical stand is not accepted by one or more of his (or her) family members. In the clash of spiritual war, a disciple's best friends (family members) become his worst enemies, as Jesus warned, "A man's foes shall be they of his own household" (v. 36). This war lasts until the disciple compromises, the resistors relent, or the Lord intervenes and converts them.

In Matthew 10, Jesus goes on to link this "sword" with our "crosses."

The topic He starts in verse 34 continues through verse 37 and is connected to verse 38 by the conjunction "and." "*And* he that taketh not *his cross* and followeth after me..." (v. 38). So, in this context, as in Luke 14:26–27, Jesus charges us to carry the "cross" of faithfully enduring the "sword" of spiritual war in our "households."

In the same context, He also informs us that any Christian refusing to do so is "not worthy" of Him? Why? As we'll discuss momentarily, Jesus put His love for His Father ahead of His love for His own family and friends. If we won't do the same, we're not worthy of Him.

Returning to Christ's instructions in Luke 14:26–27, one expositor noted, "We must love Christ supremely, even more than we love our own flesh and blood.... Our love for Christ must be so strong that all other love is like hatred in comparison."[3] Another states, "This saying does not justify malice or ill will toward one's family, but it means that devotion to family must take second place to one's devotion to Christ."[4] Another states, "In a clash of claims, Jesus must be first and everything and everyone else have a lesser claim."[5] While we understand, then, that "hate" here doesn't mean "detest," but rather "love less," others may not. When our clashes come, the people we have to displease may *feel* and *say* we literally *hate* them, when in fact we still love them deeply, but less than we love Jesus, whom we have chosen to please over their objections. Sorry for themselves and angry with us, they may then slander us to anyone who will listen. And someone will always listen and misjudge us! This inevitable misunderstanding and misjudgment are two more "nails" in our crosses. But that shouldn't stop us; we're following One with nail-pierced hands.

Of the calls, clashes, and crosses of God, the twentieth-century Assemblies of God Bible teacher Walter Beuttler said:

> No natural claim, no earthly possession, no kind of a relationship or attachment to things or persons, can be allowed to stand between us and the call of God, if we are indeed to "follow Him." Everything we are and possess and aspire to in the natural has to be subservient

and subordinated to the claim of the Master, "Take up thy cross, and follow me."[6]

—WALTER H. BEUTTLER

When faced with this painful choice, we may take comfort in remembering that the One who calls us to take up our crosses has taken up His before us. The infrequently taught truth is that when the Father called Jesus to leave Nazareth and launch His itinerant ministry, His family and friends clashed with the divine call. Mark tells us that "when his friends ['relatives,' or 'they from his home,' (WEY)] heard" of His newly launched ministry headquartered in Capernaum, "they went out to *lay hold on him*" (Mark 3:21); or "to take custody" (NAS); or, "to seize Him by force" (WEY). Thus they were prepared, if necessary, to use violence to take Him from His followers and return Him to His Nazarene home—and sanity!

Mark continues by revealing the surprising motive behind their bold move: "They said, He is *beside himself*" (v. 21); or, "He is *out of his mind*" (NIV, ESV, NKJV). Why did Jesus' family and friends fear He was insane, after knowing Him so closely for so many years? Mark also discloses this. The most respected religious leaders in the nation— "the scribes who came down from Jerusalem"—had declared He was possessed by a chief demon who enabled Him to exorcise lesser ones: "He hath Beelzebub, and by the prince of the demons casteth he out demons" (v. 22). These hard slander "nails" pierced Jesus' heart long before the Romans hammered their iron spikes through His hands.

This "clash," springing from the fundamental disconnection, or complete breakdown in understanding, between Jesus and His relatives, explains Jesus' reaction when they arrived where He was teaching. When told they were outside the house calling for Him, Jesus didn't stop teaching and go greet them. Instead He continued teaching, opportunely using "his brethren and his mother" outside to teach that, in conflicts of interest, our new spiritual family, the church, comes before our biological family (vv. 31–34). He did this because He knew their intentions.

If He had gone out to greet them, they may have tried to apprehend Him bodily, thus sparking resistance from His deeply devoted but not yet fully spiritual disciples. (Peter, James, and John had displayed quick, fiery tempers; see Luke 9:54; John 18:10.) Thus, in His dilemma, Jesus loved His heavenly Father and His will more than His earthly mother and brothers.

So when He says that, to be His disciples, we too must at times "hate" our family and friends, pick up our crosses, and follow His example, He knows what He's saying. He's done it. In all His clashes Jesus heeded the call, moving steadily forward while His mother misunderstood Him (Luke 2:50; 8:19–21), His brothers hated and mocked Him (John 7:1–9), His friends called Him insane (Mark 3:21), and the members of His home synagogue tried to kill Him (Luke 4:28–30). We'll never have a clash as painful as His. So when hurting, we should seek comfort from Him who "was in all points tempted like as we are" (Heb. 4:15).

That is, unless we defect and heed the clash instead of the call.

SOME HEED THE CLASH, NOT THE CALL

Though some very zealous believers may cringe at the thought, discipleship nevertheless remains optional for Christians. Jesus will never make us take up our crosses and follow Him.

He consistently stated the terms of discipleship prefaced with a conspicuous "if"—"IF any man come to me, and hate not..." (Luke 14:26). And He carefully stated noncompliance would mean forfeiture of discipleship and its rewards but never salvation, which is solely given by grace and not earned by the sacrifices of discipleship: "...he cannot be my *disciple*...cannot be my *disciple*" (vv. 26–27). When our clashes come, we may heed (yield to) the clash and "hate" Christ, loving Him less than we do others or ourselves. Many do so.

Despite their genuine conversion experiences, professions of faith, church attendance and/or membership, personal devotions, giving, and Bible studies, millions of born-again Christians "hate" the call to discipleship and the crosses it brings into their lives. The apostle Paul testified, "For many...are the enemies of [or at enmity with] the cross of Christ" (Phil. 3:18). With Christ's full permission, yet never His approval, we may ignore His claims and go back to a nominal, static, dead, fruitless, religious Christian lifestyle to keep unspiritual people, or our unspiritual self, happy. But if we do, we will never be genuine disciples. Saved? Yes, by God's grace and Jesus' blood. Committed, sold-out disciples? No! And for the rest of our lives we'll be haunted by the memory of our spiritual failure.

Many Christians today suffer painful flashbacks of their personal "Kadesh Barnea." As stated in chapter 19, it was at Kadesh Barnea that the Israelites, after their wondrous salvation from Egypt, took a long hard look at the costs of fully doing God's will, namely, waging war to possess the Promised Land. And after counting the costs, they turned back and wandered in the wilderness until they died. Our "Kadesh Barnea" is the time and place where we come to the very border of the purpose of God for our lives—full-fledged, sold-out, spiritually mature discipleship—and we look upon it, touch it, taste it. Then, with the call of God ringing in our ears, we turn back from what God is plainly impelling us to do, namely, courageously step out into the life plan He has for us. Why do we turn back?

While our reasons may be legion, we often simply fear the clash. Like the Pharisees of old, the opinions and praises of men mean more to us than the Lord's approval: "For they loved the praise of men more than the praise of God" (John 12:43). So to please them, we displease Him, and love them (or more accurately, *ourselves*, whom we don't want to distress by their disapproval) "more than" Him (Matt. 10:37). Such Christians grieve God's heart today as the Israelites did long ago: "Wherefore, I was *grieved* with that generation" (Heb. 3:10). And they grieve themselves too.

In Luke 14:28–35, Jesus foretells the sad end of believers who hear the call of God but refuse to pay the high costs of discipleship. The very people whose approval they so carefully sought will ultimately mock their evident hypocrisy: "This man began to build, and was not able to finish" (v. 30). They will surrender their beliefs to forge a false peace and unreal union (e.g., Jehoshaphat and Ahab) with the very enemies God called them to confront and overcome: "While the other is yet a great way off, he sendeth an embassy [messenger], and *desireth conditions of peace*" (v. 32). Compromised, fruitless, unfulfilled, and unhappy, they will be as useless to God as tasteless salt is to men, sad incarnations of Jesus' warning that potentially valuable Christians can become utterly worthless: "Salt is good; but if the salt have lost its savor...it is neither fit for the land, nor yet for the dunghill" (vv. 34–35). Why all this woe? They decided the costs of discipleship were too high.

They are high. Jesus ever heralded and never hid this fact. Not immediately and overwhelmingly, but methodically and thoroughly God will test disciples over every possession and relationship they have. By the end of their life courses, disciples have chosen Jesus over everything: "Whosoever he is of you that forsaketh not *all that he hath*, cannot be my disciple" (v. 33). When these crucial clashes come, remember this: though the immediate cost of obedience to God's call is great, the cost of disobedience will ultimately be much greater. Excuse me, but I believe I hear the sound of loud "Amens" being sung by a chorus of Lot, Achan, Samson, Demas, and others. Can you hear it too?

When the clash comes in our lives, there is no middle ground. We either heed the call or succumb to the clash.

When God calls you, respond. When He brings you to the border of Canaan, walk out into it. When He asks you to love Him more than family and friends, or self, do so. When spiritual war visits, endure it. It won't be easy, but it will be glorious. And God's sufficient grace will gird you every step of the way as you stay very close to your nail-pierced

Master and remember He and many other disciples have carried their crosses before you: "For consider him that endured such contradiction of sinners against himself" (Heb. 12:3).

Always heed the call, never the clash—even if the clash occurs in your marriage.

Chapter Twenty-Two

A MATRIMONIAL MESSAGE

Then Zipporah...said, Surely a bloody husband art thou to me.
—EXODUS 4:25

H EAVEN-SENT MARRIAGES ARE not always heavenly, but they always serve heavenly purposes. Moses' marriage illustrates this.

God sovereignly chose Zipporah to be Moses' wife and brought her to him providentially through the priest of Midian, Jethro: "And Moses was content to dwell with the man [Jethro[1]]; and he gave Moses Zipporah, his daughter" (Exod. 2:21). Whatever attractive personality traits Zipporah possessed, Exodus 4:24–26 reveals her unattractive ones—she was unruly, contentious, merciless, and without respect for Moses or his God! These grievous flaws must have made Moses wonder whether a place much farther below had arranged for his matrimonial mess. However, though his union with Zipporah was not the happily-ever-after kind, it was indeed ordained of God, and it served His supreme purpose.

To establish these truths, let's take a closer look at Exodus 4:24–26.

INSIGHTS FROM "A LODGING PLACE ON THE WAY"

First, let's note the facts in this story. His call to deliver his brethren renewed at long last, Moses was on his way to lead the grand Exodus, with wife and children in tow (Exod. 4:20). But suddenly, strangely, God interrupted His own plan.

Without warning, I AM THAT I AM visited His personally selected deliverer and "sought to kill him" (Exod. 4:24). Apparently He struck Moses with a deadly disease[2] to chasten him for continuing to neglect the most basic Hebrew covenantal duty, male circumcision. It seems Moses had neglected to perform this rite on his second son, Eliezer.[3] Faced with the terrifying prospect of her husband's imminent death, Zipporah very reluctantly—and reproachfully—complied with Moses' request to execute the surgical procedure. Moses then recovered and resumed his journey to Egypt—without Zipporah and their two sons. Apparently her disruptive outburst of incompatibility awoke Moses to the realization that her presence would cause unnecessary, perhaps unbearable, contention during the difficult days ahead. So heavily, but necessarily, he "sent her back" (Exod. 18:2).

Some may interpret these facts from "a lodging place on the way" (Exod. 4:24, NIV) as reflecting on this incident and moment only, but I believe they intimate much more. They are a revelation of Moses' private life. The events in this unspecified "lodging place" unveiled what his forty-year marriage to Zipporah was like, if not throughout, certainly by this time. Her contentious behavior in the roadside inn gives us a glimpse of her consistent behavior in Moses' home.

Let's identify and describe Zipporah's evident personality flaws.

She was unruly.

After circumcising Eliezer, Zipporah's tongue was as sharp as the "sharp stone" she used to perform the rite. Her belligerent words—"A *bloody* husband thou art, *because of the circumcision*" (Exod. 4:26)—betray her rebellious spirit, still unbowed despite her superficial compliance. A "meek and quiet spirit" (1 Pet. 3:4) she had not!

Specifically, she was still defying: (1) God's circumcision command, without which Abraham's children were cut off from His covenant (Gen. 17:9–14), and (2) her husband, who expressed his desire to obey it and who, in their patriarchal society, was her domestic authority. Her description of Moses as "bloody" is an enigmatic statement perhaps implying that, insensitive to others' suffering, he liked blood-letting, or worse, he and his God were sadists, secretly pleased by Eliezer's pain. Whatever her meaning, her manner, method, and message conveyed that she was *unruly*—unsubmissive to and uncooperative with authorities and therefore hard to govern or rule.

And if even in this high-pressure, life-and-death crisis she resisted authority, she likely did so previously in the unpressured atmosphere of Moses' home.

She was contentious.

While all scriptural evidence indicates that Moses was content and peace-loving, it tells us Zipporah was contentious—argumentative, quarrelsome, and disputatious. Contentious people love to continue bringing up controversial matters, even when no chance for agreement exists. Preferring not to stop but to spark arguments, they habitually "strive…about words to no profit" (2 Tim. 2:14).

Zipporah confirmed her strifeful nature when she repeated her reproach. She called Moses "a bloody husband" not once but twice: "Surely *a bloody husband* art thou to me…*a bloody husband* thou art" (Exodus 4:25–26). She spewed her first "bloody" after circumcising Eliezer but was apparently still dissatisfied. So she spat it out again. While this may have released her stress, it increased Moses'.

Moses surely empathized with the psalmist who wrote, "My soul hath long dwelt with him that hateth peace. I am for peace; but when I speak, they are for war [contention]" (Ps. 120:6–7). Wise King Solomon also lamented the inescapable unpleasantness of dwelling "with a brawling woman in a wide house" (Prov. 21:9). It appears that Moses could have written both of these sacred texts, since he apparently lived for years with an incarnation of the proverbial "contentious woman" (Prov. 27:15).

She disrespected Moses.

After delivering Moses, Zipporah dishonored him. After cutting off Eliezer's foreskin to save Moses' life, Zipporah "cast it at his feet" (Exod. 4:25). This disgusting gesture—tossing her son's bloody flesh at her bedridden husband—testifies she was utterly devoid of personal respect for her husband. This is confirmed by the absence of any apology, show of remorse, or attempt to reconcile after her dismaying display of spousal contempt. This audacious act, combined with her impenitence, tells me this wasn't the first time she had put Moses down. She was accustomed to belittling him.

Ironically, it was she who was little, not the magnanimous Moses. Zipporah's name means "a little bird,"[4] such as a sparrow, and intimates not only her feminine petiteness but, sadly, the smallness of her character and love. And of her spiritual perception; the husband she belittled was a spiritual giant!

She was merciless.

Zipporah's soul was without that sweet, gentle kindness that has historically typified and endeared the female gender to men. This daughter of Jethro had no mercy—at least none for her man! Still recovering from an unspecified deadly illness, Moses desperately needed peace and quiet. Prostrate in his sick bed, it was neither the time nor the place for an ugly marital spat. But compassionless as she was, Zipporah tried to ignite one anyway. After Moses' compliance with God's will, God mercifully "let him go" (Exod. 4:26). But not Zipporah! Mean-spirited, she kept after him with her tongue: "A bloody husband thou art" (v. 26). Though well-born, she redefined the adjectives "mean" and "low."

To strike a wounded man is a mark of the lowest sort of character. To strike a wounded husband is evidence of the lowest kind of wife. By her words here, Zipporah placed herself squarely in this lowest of ignominious categories. Instead of lovingly nursing her husband back to health, she cruelly increased his pain. When presented with a perfect opportunity to endear herself to him, she estranged herself; thus she reaped not reconciliation but removal.

She disrespected Moses' God.

By far the most serious charge against Zipporah is that she tried to turn Moses away from God.

Though not stated, it is implied that the subject of circumcision had been discussed in Moses' home before this pivotal crisis. Apparently Moses suggested it, Zipporah opposed it, and that ended that. When the "clash" (see last chapter) came in Moses' home over circumcision, he heeded the clash, not the call, opting to please his wife first instead of his God. Moses alone was to blame for yielding to his wife's ungodly counsel. God made that quite clear when He tried to kill not Zipporah but *Moses!* Nevertheless, by opposing Moses' desire to obey God before and after his discipline, Zipporah was openly campaigning for him to disobey God. Thus she did her best, consciously and culpably, to put a wedge between Moses and God. Why did she so strongly oppose Moses' God?

This too is not disclosed, leaving us to conjecture. Perhaps unbelief captivated her. She may easily have lost faith in Moses' God when for *forty* years He failed to renew Moses' call. Perhaps religious pride arose. She may have returned to her religious roots and, through family pride, chosen to revere the deity of her father—the well-respected "priest of Midian"—over the God of her then-undistinguished husband. While Zipporah's motivational "driver" remains unclear, the disrespect it produced is clear. Crystal clear.

Summary

Summing up, Moses' wife was no longer fulfilling her calling and had become a serious threat to his.

Originally given as Moses' helper, Zipporah had by this time become his hinderer. No longer assisting, she now only resisted him. Instead of being a joyful crown of honor on his head, she had become a shameful, painful thorn in his side. Since God had already informed Moses that Pharaoh would initially resist the Exodus (Exod. 4:21), Moses realized that his mission, though ultimately successful, would be a very difficult and contentious affair. With this in mind, he made a crucial decision: he would send Zipporah and his two sons back to Jethro for the duration of his mission. He had to publicly withstand a stubborn king, that much he knew, but privately contending with a stubborn wife was optional. So he exercised his option.

Since Zipporah was failing her calling and frustrating his, Moses "sent her back" (Exod. 18:2).

DESPITE THESE PROBLEMS, GOD'S PURPOSE WAS PERFORMED

While it's true, then, that Moses' heaven-sent marriage was far from heavenly, it is equally true that it ultimately served God's designated purpose in him. How?

Omniscient, God knew what Zipporah and her marriage to Moses would ultimately become. So why did He ordain her marriage to His handpicked leader? The primary reasons were obvious: to bless Moses and Zipporah with marital love and comfort during their initial, presumably blissful, "honeymoon" years, however long; and to bless them with two children, for further human companionship and fulfillment. But there was a greater reason: in learning to live with Zipporah, Moses was preparing himself to lead the children of Israel, who later proved to be every bit as unruly, contentious, merciless, and disrespectful to him and his God as Zipporah. Thus, forty years with Zipporah in the desert readied Moses for forty years with the Israelites in the desert.

And, except in the matter of Eliezer's belated circumcision, Moses did learn to consistently overcome Zipporah's difficult nature and vexatious behavior. If he had not, God would never have reappeared to send him back to Egypt to deliver His people (Exod. 3:1–12). God's release and immense blessing of Moses after Eliezer's circumcision proves that no other disobedience remained in his life.

During the long, difficult years that followed the Israelites' great "exit," they repeatedly tried Moses' faith, patience, and graciousness. They were so petulant, so small-hearted, so self-centered. Consistently they refused to trust God, complained about everything, resisted Moses' and Aaron's leadership, and stubbornly rebelled just as God was moving to bless them. Their unbelief was unbelievable, audacity amazing, and stubbornness stunning. They were the last word in vexatiousness. How was Moses able to respond as graciously and patiently as he did? How was he able to rise above their relentless provocations? Why did he constantly forgive and intercede for them instead of reject and revile them?[5] He had learned, practiced, and perfected all these graces during his years with Zipporah. She had often acted as the Israelites did, vexing him to tears, wearying him to exhaustion, and trying his faith and patience to the breaking point. In handling her difficult nature by faith, prayer, and obedience to God's guidance, Moses had unknowingly prepared himself to lead God's difficult people.

So his painful personal life was not a waste but a workshop. There God remade Moses after His will, shaping His "vessel unto honor" to serve His predestined plan. It was a classic cross experience, a death to self-will, that afterward led to a personal resurrection of fruitful service—and the joyous deliverance of an entire nation. Thus God's heavenly purpose of raising a strong, spiritually minded leader was performed after all, even in the midst of a less-than-heavenly marriage.

Like Moses' marriage, yours may be far from ideal. You may live with a small-hearted Zipporah or a mocking Michal (2 Sam. 6:12–23). Or you may be an Abigail married to a no-good Nabal (1 Sam. 25). Or your situation could conceivably be worse. Much worse! Whatever the difficulties of your home life, remember what God did in and through Moses despite his very difficult marriage. Let Him duplicate His purpose in your life. Moses' marriage was not easy, but it was fruitful. It offered little bliss, but it yielded plenty of blessing! Though Moses ultimately couldn't save it, God used it, as He did Joseph's life, to "save many people alive" (Gen. 50:20).

So, Mr. or Mrs. sad, sinking, Christian spouse's, look up! The God who worked wondrously in Moses is waiting to do the same in you. But your attitude—not your spouse's, but yours!—is the only key that will open the door to the divine purpose. The outstanding British pastor and theologian F. B. Meyer wrote:

> Never let the evil disposition of one mate hinder the devotion and grace of the other. Never let the difficulties of your home lead you to abdicate your throne. Do not step down to the level of your circumstances, but lift them to your own high calling in Christ.[6]

Here's the way your version of this great lesson will play out. If due to your persisting marital difficulties you rebel and stop walking with God, you will never be a mature, spiritually minded disciple of Christ or minister to His people. But if you see your difficulties from the spiritual viewpoint and obey God diligently, you will emerge from your "Midian" experience strong, merciful, spiritually minded, consistently unflappable, and ready for God's use. Ultimately God's purpose will prevail in your life. He will cause all things to work together to conform you to the image of his Son.

> We know that God *causes all things* to work together for good to those who love God…who are called according to His purpose…predestined to become *conformed* to the *image of his Son.*
>
> —ROMANS 8:28–29, NAS

Yes, He will heal all your wounds and use you, in the image of His Son, to heal others' wounds.

Chapter Twenty-Three

HE WOUNDS AND HE HEALS

See now that I, even I, am he...I wound, and I heal.
—DEUTERONOMY 32:39

A S IN MOSES' life, God often finds it necessary to wound souls in order to bring His kingdom purposes to pass. But if you or one of your loved ones is so chosen, take heart: the hand that wounds also heals. Through Moses God promised, "I wound, and I heal" (Deut. 32:39). We see His promise performed in Mary's life.

MARY—WOUNDED AND HEALED

On the day Mary and Joseph dedicated Jesus, Simeon informed Mary by the Spirit that she must experience deep personal sorrow in order that many might be given repentance and salvation. Specifically he told her that her soul (inner self) would be pierced (ripped through) with a large, long sword[1] (severely painful wounding) in an implied deadly or warlike conflict:

> Simeon blessed them, and said unto Mary, his mother... (Yea, a *sword* shall *pierce* through thy own *soul* also), that the thoughts of many hearts may be revealed.
> —LUKE 2:34–35

This "sword" period lasted from the beginning of Jesus' ministry until His post-resurrection appearances. During that interim, Mary's heart was repeatedly and poignantly pierced by misunderstanding, perplexity, and sorrow. When Jesus went forth to fulfill His "Father's business" (Luke 2:49)—His merciful, miraculous, masterful ministry

215

and sacrificial death—Mary simply could not understand the fast and furious frenzy of the religious war that engulfed her specially gifted Son. Consequently, for the time being, her soul became "collateral damage."

As unwanted as this was, it was unavoidable that Mary should become a casualty of spiritual war. To save the world, a sacrifice had to be made, and God sovereignly chose to lay it on Mary. If mankind was to be permanently healed, she had to be temporarily wounded. So her motherly love was slain so that God's fatherly love might adopt many children. Her family was divided so that God's family might be established and united. Her comfortable life was taken so that God could give comfort and life to all who believe.

As Jesus' mother, Mary was His *closest natural relative* at the time He began His ministry.[2] That it was she who suffered so greatly due to His fruitful but difficult ministry points up this principle: *those closely related to God's chosen servants must sometimes suffer greatly so that God's eternal fruit may be brought forth.* What exactly did Mary suffer? What caused her sorrows, her piercing "sword"?

Mary's wounding

In brief, Mary's sufferings sprang from Jesus' sufferings. She suffered as she watched Him suffer.

When we love someone, an intangible but real channel exists between us and that person through which all emotional impulses are shared. When they feel joy, we feel joy; when they hurt, we hurt. This empathy, or "vicarious experiencing of the feelings, thoughts, or attitudes of another,"[3] was the means by which Mary was psychologically "pierced." Everything that was done and said against Jesus, Mary felt and suffered along with Him. The psalmist's description of his empathy with God also describes Mary's empathetic link with Jesus: "The reproaches of those who reproached thee are fallen upon me" (Ps. 69:9). More than anyone else's before or after Him, Jesus' reproaches would be many and mean.

With the Spirit's hand heavy upon him, Simeon characterized Jesus' upcoming ministry as "a *sign* which shall be *spoken against*" (Luke 2:34).

And truly, Jesus' ministry was a sign, a work marked by many attesting miracles, that was spoken against. As His wondrous teachings, healings, deliverances, and prophecies increased, so did the rumors, misunderstandings, false representations, wild accusations, and enthusiastic and vicious denunciations. Some were caused by the people's ignorance or lack of spiritual understanding, as they misinterpreted His teachings and actions: "There was much murmuring among the people concerning him; for some said, He is a good man; others said, Nay, but he deceiveth the people" (John 7:12). Mostly, however, His deluge of derision was the direct result of the deliberate and spiteful slander campaign conducted against Him by the scribes and Pharisees, who envied His knowledge of God, spiritual power, and popularity with the people: "[The Pharisees] said...Give God the praise; we know that this man [Jesus] is a sinner" (John 9:24). Some scholars believe that the Jewish leaders also reproached Jesus as being an illegitimate child, when, "They said unto him, *We are not born of fornication* [as you are]; we have one Father, even God" (John 8:41).[4] Knowing Jesus' true character and the truth surrounding His scandalous birth, false reports such as these grieved Mary deeply. And Nazareth proved to be no comfort zone for the mother of the Messiah.

Jesus' two visits to Nazareth made it clear that He was dangerously unpopular in His hometown: "They [the Nazarenes] were offended at him" (Mark 6:3). Stirred to fury, the members of Jesus' home synagogue tried to assassinate Him: "All they in the synagogue...were filled with wrath, and rose up, and thrust him out of the city, and led him unto the brow of the hill on which their city was built, that they might cast him down headlong" (Luke 4:28–29). Wherever He looked in Nazareth, Jesus found no refuge, not even in His childhood home. His homecomings turned into heckle fests, merciless mocking sessions led by His unimpressed half-brothers, who laughed off His messianic claims and lampooned Him as a vain religious showman: "His brethren, therefore, said unto him, Depart from here, and go into Judea, that thy disciples also may see the works that thou doest. For there is no man that doeth anything in secret, and he himself seeketh to be known openly. If thou do these things, show thyself to the world. For neither did his brethren believe in him" (John 7:3–5). Although His "cross" in Nazareth was heavy, thankfully it was only temporary, as He soon left to minister in other cities. But Mary didn't.

She stayed behind in a hometown and home place filled with hatred for One she loved. While Jesus "went about all Galilee, teaching in their synagogues, and preaching the gospel of the kingdom" (Matt. 4:23), Mary went on about her humble daily rounds in Nazareth, living among children, relatives, friends, and fellow synagogue-goers who greatly misunderstood and sharply rejected her Son, His message, and His works. Every day this long, broad "sword" struck yet another fresh wound in her hurting heart: "And when his [and Mary's] friends heard of it...they said, He is beside himself" (Mark 3:21).

This painful situation was exacerbated by the fact that Mary couldn't answer for Jesus. How could she explain Jesus satisfactorily to her fellow Nazarenes when she didn't fully understand Him herself? How could she give Jesus' siblings answers that she didn't have? We assume she knew at least some, perhaps many, of the messianic scriptures, but surely not well enough to debate theological point and counterpoint with the scholarly and rhetorically polished scribes.[5] Who would have believed *she* was the virgin Isaiah foresaw conceiving and delivering Immanuel (Isa. 7:14)? Not a soul! This preposterous predicament left Mary with three humble options: ponder, pray, and practice. So for three years she recalled and ruminated the frustratingly incomplete facts she knew, prayed for insight (which God later gave), and practiced and perfected her patience. So "his mother kept all these sayings in her heart" (Luke 2:51). Eventually her pain reached its agonizing summit.

Mary's "sword" reached its cruel climax when, during the year's most high-profile event, Passover week, Jesus was shockingly betrayed by one of His original disciples and then publicly and ignominiously tried, mocked, scourged, and crucified. It was her worst nightmare, a horror story come to life. Yet John tells us that when the end came, Mary stood faithfully by the cross: "Now there stood by the cross of Jesus his mother" (John 19:25). There, at Calvary, Mary's figurative wounding terminated with the final physical wound inflicted on her Son. When "one of the soldiers, with a spear, pierced" Jesus' battered, bloodied body (v. 34), God's "sword" of empathetic sorrow pierced Mary's battered, bowed soul for the last time. It was all over then. The Roman soldier withdrew his spear, the heavenly Father sheathed His "sword," and the earthly mother of His Son stopped hurting. Finally, the furious hatred, vicious lies, swirling scandal, religious leaders' opposition, national debate, local anger, family opposition, and public horror ceased.

Mary's healing

"To everything there is a season, and a time to every purpose under the heaven... *a time to heal*" (Eccles. 3:1, 3). Mary's time to heal began immediately after her brutal wounding ended.

Just moments before the Romans pierced Jesus' side on the cross, Jesus ordered John to care for Mary after His departure and asked Mary to cooperate by living in John's home (John 19:25–27). Because of these last-minute arrangements, as well as her personal faith in Jesus, Mary found herself in the Upper Room with Jesus' apostles and other disciples, awaiting the coming of the Holy Spirit: "When they were come in, they went up into an upper room, where abode Peter, and James, and John.... These all continued with one accord in prayer and supplication, with the women, *and Mary, the mother of Jesus*, and with his brethren" (Acts 1:13–14). After Mary received the fullness of the Holy Spirit, the divine Comforter-Teacher, she soon understood the things she had long pondered in her heart. Suddenly the separate pieces of the Christ-knowledge puzzle she had gathered over the last thirty-three years came together, creating a clear image of who her Son really was; why He had suffered, died, and risen; and why she had been "pierced." At last the perplexing nonsense made perfect sense. This Spirit-given insight into the facts she already knew, and the teachings the apostles added, began the mending of her soul-wounds.

The rest of Mary's life was spent in joyful fellowship with her own sons, James and Jude,[6] who were converted shortly after Jesus' resurrection, and with John, in whose home and family she resided. After three cruel years of ceaseless wounding, these God-ordained years of healing were a blessed relief—days of heaven on earth, days filled full of Spirit-illuminated conversation, apostolic fellowship, private and church worship, and fruitful service, as much information Mary shared with John and the other apostles found its way into the first-century oral evangel and our four written biblical Gospels.[7] In the end, Mary felt no pain. Her healing was complete, her wound healed, and her joy full.

But she wasn't alone. Others closely related to God's chosen ones experienced His wounding and healing so that eternal fruit could be borne.

JACOB—WOUNDED AND HEALED

As stated in earlier chapters, Joseph was a very fruitful servant of the Lord: "Joseph is a fruitful bough, even a fruitful bough by a well" (Gen. 49:22). But to produce this fruit, the heavenly Farmer had to wound Joseph—and someone else very near and dear.

Jacob's wounding

With characteristic honesty, the Bible acknowledges, "Israel [Jacob] loved Joseph more than all his children" (Gen. 37:3), because (1) "he was the son of his old age," (2) he was the son of Jacob's most beloved wife, Rachel, and (3) he was a faithful, obedient boy, unlike his often wayward and mischievous brothers. Thus Jacob's heart, his very life, was intertwined with Joseph's.

When Jacob, an old man at the time, saw the staged "evidence" of his most beloved son's reported death, his soul was suddenly and brutally pierced with shock and grief: "And they sent the [blood-stained] coat of many colors…to their father; and said, This have we found: know now whether it be thy son's.... And he recognized it, and said, It is my son's coat; an evil beast hath devoured him; Joseph is without doubt torn in pieces" (vv. 32–33). Though both the patriarchs' physical evidence and inferred conclusion were false, Jacob's psychological suffering was true. Joseph's body had not been torn in pieces, but Jacob's heart had been torn asunder as surely as his robes: "Jacob *tore his clothes*, and put sackcloth upon his loins, and *mourned for his son many days*" (v. 34). Joseph's physical demise was unreal, but Jacob's emotional disintegration was very real, intense, and unrelieved: "His family all tried to comfort him, but he refused to be comforted. 'I will go to my grave mourning for my son,' he would say, and then he would weep" (v. 35, NLT). Like the psychological broadsword that pierced Mary, Jacob's sword pierced him deeply, widely, and for a long time—twenty-two years, to be precise.

Then God faithfully began His healing process.

Jacob's healing

When the worldwide famine struck, Jacob sent his surviving sons to Egypt for food. There, though still unaware of his true identity, they found themselves standing before Joseph, now very Egyptian in appearance, language, and manner, and the prime minister of Egypt.

Divinely and emotionally prompted, Joseph revealed his identity to his stunned brothers and immediately dispatched them to summon his beloved father to Egypt. When Jacob heard their report that Joseph was alive and well, and the *ruler of Egypt*, it was almost more than Jacob's aged body could bear: "[They] told him, saying, Joseph is yet alive, and he is governor over all the land of Egypt. And *Jacob's heart fainted*" (Gen. 45:26). Initially electric, the shock soon became a rejuvenating tonic: "When he [Jacob] saw the [distinctly royal, Egyptian] wagons which Joseph had sent to carry him, *the spirit of Jacob, their father, revived*. And Israel said, It is enough: Joseph my son is yet alive; I will go and see him before I die" (vv. 27–28).

The joyful reunion that followed was as sweet as the previous separation had been bitter. There was no more silence now; Jacob could visit his favorite son any day he wished. There was no more deception now; Jacob knew the truth, and it set him free. There was no more grieving and weeping now; every day Jacob praised and worshiped God for sparing Joseph and restoring their loving family communion. And, like Jacob's wounding, his healing was deep, wide, and long—seventeen years! "Jacob lived in the land of Egypt *seventeen years*" (Gen. 47:28) with the loving, faithful son who had been stripped away from him—when he was *seventeen years* old! It is a fitting end to a famous story.

To make Joseph fruitful, God had to wound not only him but also his father. But the hand that wounded also healed him. And in the end Jacob felt no hurt.

In light of the above, there are some facts we should face and ponder.

If we go on to fruitfulness in Christ, some who are close to us will undoubtedly be hurt. The "sword" that visited Mary and Jacob will visit and "pierce" those who are close to us. Jesus said as much: "Think not that I am come to send peace on earth; I came not to send peace, but a *sword*" (Matt. 10:34). As our loved ones watch us suffer emotionally, they will suffer empathetically. Their season of pain may be deep, wide, and long. When they can't understand us, they'll worry over our decisions. When they can't explain our actions to others, they'll be frustrated. When we're misrepresented, they'll mourn. When we're mocked, they'll moan. When we're demonized, they'll agonize. When our adversaries hold the upper hand, they'll be confused and troubled by the seemingly permanent but passing "triumphing of the wicked" (Job 20:5). When we faithfully hold to our divinely appointed course and work despite the reproach, they'll beg us to turn back—or fear we're hopelessly deluded. And that's not all.

Some close to us will suffer for *opposing* us. They will misjudge us, belittle our faith, and bitterly oppose our faith, work, or ministry.

Jesus again warned that our foes will be among our closest relations: "A man's foes shall be *they of his own household*" (Matt. 10:36). He further warned that some may betray us: "And ye shall be *betrayed... by parents, and brethren, and kinsfolk, and friends*" (Luke 21:16). And some, without natural affection, may even try to harm us physically: "And the brother shall deliver up the brother *to death*, and the father the child; and the children shall rise up against their parents [to have them executed]" (Matt. 10:21). By impenitently pursuing these or other persecutions, our adversarial relations bring the Abrahamic curse on themselves. God promised Abraham, and all his children of faith, "I will... *curse him that curseth thee*" (Gen. 12:3). So God will resist them for resisting us. The more they wound us, the more He wounds them. If they're stubborn, they may systematically self-destruct before our eyes—emotionally, physically, financially, maritally, mentally—almost to the point of death.

But know this. If we will go steadily forward doing our "Father's business," as our Master did, the day will come when the hand that wounded them will also heal them. The sword will at last depart, and a salve come in its stead—a supernatural balm to heal every wound and restore every joy. God will wipe away all tears, fill our mouths with laughter, and restore the years the sword has slain. He did it for Jesus by healing Mary. He did it for Joseph by healing Jacob. He'll do it for us.

When God's time to heal comes, it will be so complete, so wonderful, so "exceedingly, abundantly above" our limited human expectations, that we will forget the sword and its piercing and say with Joseph, "God... hath made me forget" (Gen. 41:51); and, with Isaiah, "The former troubles are forgotten" (Isa. 65:16); and with the Book of Job, "He maketh sore, and bindeth up; he woundeth, and his hands make whole" (Job 5:18). Believe this!

Then, when the Lord's sword gets sharp and His sayings hard, you won't go back.

THINNING THE RANKS

From that time, many of his disciples went back, and walked no
more with him.

—JOHN 6:66

A BOUT A YEAR before the end of Jesus' ministry, a remarkable
and rarely mentioned turn of events occurred. In one day the
steadily swelling ranks of His followers suddenly thinned!

In the sixth chapter of his Gospel, John states, "From that time,
many of his disciples went back, and walked no more with him" (John
6:66). This was not a minor defection but a major rift. Not few but "many"
of Jesus' followers walked away. And they weren't locals or newcomers
but seasoned members of His traveling band of "disciples," people who,
having received or seen Jesus' ministry, had sincerely committed themselves to follow Him, His teachings, and His ways of living, presumably
for the rest of their lives. And once they broke with Him, they never
returned to Him or His faithful followers: "and walked *no more* with
him." Why did they stop going on and abruptly go back? What turned
these devotees into defectors?

The answer is found in the same chapter of John's evangel.

JOHN SIX—THE DISCIPLES AND THE DESERTERS

As Jesus' ministry circuited throughout Galilee, Judea, and beyond, an
ever-increasing number of people began following Him. But this throng
was not homogeneous. There were two general groups of believers, the
committed and the curious, the spiritual and the selfish, seekers of the
Benefactor and seekers of His benefits.

To simplify, we'll call these two groups disciples and deserters.

The disciples

Most of those who followed Jesus' ministry were "disciples" (Greek, *mathētēs*), meaning "learners, pupils, students," or more precisely, students who were "believers and close followers."[1] In the first century Greco-Roman world, "disciples" were usually young men who dedicated their lives to learning, living, and spreading the teachings of a Greek or Roman philosopher or, if they were Jews, a Jewish rabbi. Far more than intellectually curious, these extraordinarily devoted learners were often committed to their masters with monastic abandon. They wanted to study their master's teachings, closely observe his lifestyle, imitate his ways, and obey his counsels until they were transformed into his image.

Such disciples formed the majority of the multitude that followed Jesus from city to city, hearing His words, witnessing His works, and anticipating His kingdom. This company began forming and growing as soon as Jesus' ministry began, being drawn to Him by His teachings and healings. Matthew says as the fame of Jesus' Galilean ministry grew, so did His followers: "And Jesus went about all Galilee, teaching...preaching...and healing...and his fame went throughout.... *And there followed him great multitudes of people*" (Matt. 4:23–25). This was a culturally diverse group, "from Galilee, and from Decapolis, and from Jerusalem, and from Judea, and from beyond the Jordan [east of the Jordan River]" (v. 25). Peter later testified that these volunteer disciples "companied with us all the time that the Lord Jesus went in and out among us, beginning from the baptism of John" (Acts 1:21–22).

Among this larger body of disciples were "the twelve" (John 6:67), the smaller, handpicked circle of Jesus' constant companions and protégés whom He later empowered and commissioned as His special messengers, or "apostles." Also among them were "certain women" (Luke 8:1–2), who, besides being Jesus' student-followers, also provided Him and His apostles with vital financial support: "who ministered unto him of their substance" (v. 3); or, "These women used their own money to help Jesus and his apostles" (NCV).

The apostles, the women, and most of the other disciples in this throng were not fly-by-night types. Having "left all" to follow Jesus (Mark 10:28), they were in His camp for the duration. Sink or swim, win or lose, kingdom or no kingdom, they were set to "be with him" (Mark 3:14).

But many others in this multitude of followers didn't share their total devotion.

The deserters

Among the multitude of Jesus' faithful followers were those who were distinctly less committed.

These were very loyal, but only if conditions were favorable. They followed Him when He miraculously healed the sick: "And a great multitude followed him, because they saw his miracles which he did on those who were diseased" (John 6:2). They followed Him when He multiplied the bread and fish to feed them a sumptuous free banquet by the lakeside (vv. 5–14). They followed Him when He crossed the Sea of Galilee, buzzing with excitement over the report that He had miraculously walked on its roiling waters (vv. 15–24). Healings, feedings, miracles—while these and other benefits were flowing freely from Jesus' fount of blessings, they walked closely to Him. And why not? Life was good and the faith easy.

But when Jesus' sayings became hard, they immediately became offended and began to turn off the One who had turned their heads. On the record, their complaint was, "This is an *hard saying*. Who can hear it?" (John 6:60). Exposing the real, inner lowness of their characters, they gave up their high hopes and deserted the Nazarene, with His free lunches, lectures, and miracles, and returned to the normalcy of their former lives. Thus, in a moment, their great quest was quenched. Why? Jesus' hard sayings.

Let's take a closer look at these hard sayings.

Jesus' Hard Sayings

John 6, and other New Testament passages, help us define Jesus' hard sayings. They were His teachings or statements that were hard to understand, hard to carry out, or hard to accept.

Hard to understand

To ensure clear communication with the masses, whether from the ranks of the literate or illiterate, Jesus typically spoke in simple terms, using very understandable, down-to-earth metaphors in His parables. But some of His statements in John 6 were atypical.

There He spoke mystically, using language His hearers found quite difficult to comprehend. When Jesus claimed to be the "bread of life" (v. 35), His audience accepted this, understanding that just as bread was the staff of their physical life, Jesus was now claiming to be the source and stay of their spiritual life. But when He added that His true followers would "eat" His flesh and "drink" His blood (v. 53), many nonbelieving Jewish bystanders mistakenly assumed He was speaking literally and advocating the abomination of cannibalism. Stunned, they instantly lost interest in this strange rabbi and walked off arguing about His cryptic message: "The Jews, therefore, strove among themselves, saying, How can this man give us his flesh to eat?" (v. 52).[2]

Jesus' more rationalistic disciples also tuned Him out. This Messiah was too far up in the clouds for them. Their natural minds (unredeemed and unaided by the Holy Spirit) couldn't fully grasp His ultra-spiritual talk, since "the natural man receiveth not the things of the Spirit of God" (1 Cor. 2:14). But as many others did, they could have decided to trust this Teacher, whose unique love and power they knew well, beyond the limits of their human reason or patiently ask Him to give them clarifying insight. But they weren't willing to do this. Instead they wrote His teaching off as the ramblings of a fool—"...for they are foolishness unto him" (v. 14)—and protested that He couldn't be understood: "Many, therefore, of his disciples, when they had heard this, said, This is an hard saying, *Who can hear [understand] it?*" (John 6:60). Then they promptly "went back, and walked no more with him" (v. 66). Where did they go?

They went back to their old way of thinking, to relying on human reason alone. Others could "trust the Lord with all thine heart" (Prov. 3:5) if they wanted to, but they would play it safe and trust only so far as they could explain.

Hard to carry out

At other times Jesus said things that were easy to understand but hard to put into practice. Why? The disciples' personal wills got in the way.

Throughout the Gospels we find Jesus making statements that are volitionally volatile, or of explosive impact on the human will. As stated in an earlier chapter, He ordered a young wealthy seeker to give up all his earthly possessions (Luke 18:22–23). He called another man to leave his deathly ill father to "go…and preach the kingdom of God" (Luke 9:60). He taught that if even the *best things* in our natural life—our right eye or right hand, figuratively speaking—hinder our spiritual development, they should be sternly cut off from our lives, however maimed we may look or feel (Matt. 5:29–30). He warned that true Christianity would split some families right down the middle (Matt. 10:34–39; 12:46–50). And He informed His eager students that the way they had embarked on, the way to find and live in ever more of His wondrous life, was not wide but narrow, not easy but hard, and not traveled by many but by few: "*Narrow* is the gate, and *hard* is the way which leadeth unto life, and *few* there be that find it" (Matt. 7:14). Thus He lit a delayed fuse to a bomb set to explode in their unsuspecting human wills.

And it burned, slowly but surely, until it disrupted their hearts, resulting in full surrender—"Yes, Lord, not my will but thine be done. Have your way in my life"—or a return to full selfishness—"No way, Lord. Your terms are too hard. I've tried but can't comply."

Hard to accept

The Lord also spoke to and dealt with His followers in ways they found hard to accept, or hard for their human pride to take. This should not surprise us, coming from the God who openly adores humility and abominates pride. (See Proverbs 6:16–17; Matthew 23:12.)

Jesus not only spoke edifying proverbs, parables, prophecies, and exhortations, but He also issued mortifying rebukes and corrections. He informed James and John they didn't know what spirit they were of, censured the twelve for not trusting Him in a great storm, corrected Judas for calling Mary of Bethany's loving sacrifice of spikenard a "waste," angrily overruled the apostles when they refused to let Him bless little children, sternly warned them when they argued which of them should be "greatest" in His kingdom, and flatly predicted Peter's self-trusting promise to never forsake Him would fail. Ouch! They understood all these hard sayings, but their pride didn't like them one little bit. Yet, by God's grace, they yielded and humbled themselves and went on to learn the profound lesson that "reproofs of instruction are the way of [or to more] life" (Prov. 6:23). They also learned to "despise not…the chastening of the Lord" (Heb. 12:5), realizing His hard sayings were signs of God's love, Fatherhood, and intent to train and use them fruitfully (vv. 6–11).

But the deserters loathed these lessons. They liked Jesus' sermons and miracles but not His mastering. They submitted to His teaching but not His training. They wanted only a remote religious professor, not a hands-on, in-your-face, here's-the-truth-about-you-now-deal-with-it spiritual trainer. Afflicted with ambivalence, their minds said Jesus' corrections and rebukes were right, and their will said they should obey them, but their pride arose and threw the matter out of the court of their souls. So, after a brief period of listening to Jesus' corrections, they rejected them, and Him, and "went back, and walked no more with him."

True to His Word, Jesus made the way very hard and narrow so much that their pride couldn't fit into His kingdom life, no matter how hard they squeezed! It, or they, had to *go*!

Laboring—but for the Wrong Reasons

The disciples who went back did so primarily because they were laboring for the wrong reasons. They labored to seek Jesus, just as the others did, but only to obtain power, provisions, and political gains, not to have more of Him, His soul-nourishing Word, and His reviving Spirit.

They began following Jesus after seeing His healing power manifested: "And a great multitude followed him, *because they saw his miracles* which he did on those who were diseased" (John 6:2). Then, in an astounding feat of miraculous provision, He fed as many as five to twenty thousand[3] of them in the wilderness with only "five barley loaves and two small fishes" (v. 9, see verses 5–14). So impressed were they with this man who could heal the sick and feed the hungry that they immediately were convinced He was "the prophet" (v. 14) Moses said would come, to whom they should give unwavering obedience (Deut. 18:15–18). And their conclusion was right! But then they went too far.

Because Jesus was their great Prophet and Messiah, they reasoned it was therefore God's time[4] to eject the Romans from Israel. And Jesus was just the man to do this. He was their health-care policy, welfare program, plan of prosperity, and system of government incarnate! These nationalistic disciples quickly envisioned Pilate assassinated, Jesus coronated, and themselves empowered! Inspired, they were ready to launch their coup, apparently whether the new "king" was ready or not: "They would come and take him by force, to make him a king" (John 6:15).

When Jesus got wind of this, He quickly took evasive action: "He departed again into a mountain himself alone" (v. 15). It wasn't His Father's time for the kingdom, and He would have nothing to do with a political or military revolt. He knew the Father's plan: He was bound for a cross, not a crown. So that night the twelve launched their boats and crossed the Sea of Galilee (vv. 16–21) to find less politically minded disciples. Jesus rendezvoused with them in the middle of the sea, and they all landed together at Capernaum (v. 21).

When the insurrectionists realized Jesus and His disciples were gone, they labored to find Him: "They also took boats and came to Capernaum, seeking for Jesus" (v. 24). The next day they located Him (v. 25)—but they may have wished they hadn't. He had some hard sayings for them, a rebuke and a correction.

His rebuke informed them that they needed to reprioritize their motives. He acknowledged they sought Him zealously: "Ye seek me..." (v. 26). But He said this was only for worldly needs and desires—healing power, provisions, and political help—not spiritual needs. He singled out their driving desire for provisions: "Ye seek me...because ye did eat of the loaves, and were filled" (v. 26). In correcting them, He urged them to seek ("labor" for) spiritual things first, specifically more of the "bread" of His Word, with the same zeal they had in seeking provisions. They had *labored*, rowing across the northern waters of Lake Galilee, to find Jesus to have more bread and fish for their stomachs. They should now *labor* just as enthusiastically to fill their souls with eternal bread, by studying His Word to build their faith in Him, and knowledge of His will and ways: "Labor not [only] for the food which perisheth, but *[labor] for that food which endureth unto everlasting life*" (v. 27). To induce obedience, He added a promise. If they would labor to have His spiritual bread, He would load them with it: "...which the Son of man shall give unto you" (v. 27).

While their wills and pride were still smarting from this hard saying, He added another, this one hard to understand. They should "eat His flesh" and "drink His blood" if they wanted to have His life in them (John 6:30–59). Taken together, this was too much for many of them. Unwilling to reprioritize their motives, they refused to seek the things of the Word more than the things of the world. They delighted in His benefits but despised His correction. Unwilling to submit to Jesus' authority, they changed their minds about His kingship. So, disillusioned with their "Prophet" and His vision, they deserted.

Here's an interesting fact: *the crowd that so readily deserted Jesus in Capernaum was the same crowd that was so eager to follow Him in rebellion the day before!* Christ's hard sayings paralyzed their self-centered religious zeal. Instead of following Him to war, they forsook Him in peacetime. And suddenly His army of followers shrank.

HIS HARD SAYINGS—ACCIDENTAL OR INTENTIONAL?

Should Jesus have just kept quiet and held His church together by not dealing with their true inner condition? Was His attempt to correct His eager followers a blunder or a master stroke? Did He release these hard sayings at this time accidentally or intentionally?

The latter is surely the case. We know this because Jesus knew His followers' hearts all along. John tells us, "For Jesus knew from the beginning who they were that [truly] believed" (John 6:64). He knew that those who labored to find Him just to obtain miracles, provisions, or political victories would reject His humbling rebukes, invasive corrections, and deeply spiritual teachings. Graciously He healed and fed them anyway. But the time came when He had to faithfully lay the truth on the line and let them make their own crucial life choices. This wasn't the only time He did this.

As stated in chapter 21, when later in His ministry "there went great multitudes with him," Jesus turned to His excited followers and again spoke hard sayings, this time revealing the costly conditions of discipleship (Luke 14:25–33). He knew the spiritual explosion caused by this bombshell of truth would drive away only those who had not the resolve to follow Him all the way. The rest, the true disciples, would stay.

Therefore, He spoke His hard sayings to test His followers and separate the disciples from the deserters. By these penetrating statements His followers' wills were measured, their motives searched, their humility examined, and their true "gods," or dominating loves, exposed. The hard sayings drove them to a choice, and that choice, like a litmus test, made the "disciples indeed" (John 8:31) stand out from the disciples in appearance only. Thus, like Gideon's militia long ago (Judg. 7:1–7), Jesus' spiritual army was reduced to its true soldiers. Here's another interesting fact: *out of all the tens of thousands that gathered to Jesus at the height of His ministry, only 120 faithful souls endured to the end—through the betrayal, mock trial, and cross to the Upper Room* (Acts 1:15). Knowing this beforehand prompted Jesus to not artificially increase the number of His followers and, on at least two occasions, to purposely utter hard sayings to *reduce* them, or thin the ranks.

Jesus didn't want another "mixed multitude" like that which caused Israel so much trouble in the Exodus. If religious people had other ends to serve, He let them go and serve them, knowing that proud, self-serving, or self-indulgent recruits would only weaken the resolve of His good soldiers. He remembered God's words to Gideon: "By the three hundred men who lapped will I save you...*let all the other people go*" (Judg. 7:7). This is why Jesus refused to appeal to those who served Him only for healings, food, prosperity, or political success. His guiding maxim was, "Those who won't go all the way may go away." He wanted permanent, not passing, disciples, faithful Joshuas and Calebs who would follow Him "wholly" (Josh. 14:8). He would invest the wealth of His time, toil, and truth in them—not Achans and Demases.[5]

COMPARING YESTERDAY AND TODAY

How different our attitude is today. Believing that security lies in large numbers, we too often worship multitudes, whether pure or mixed. We dilute Jesus' words, alter His image to fit ours, and market Him to the masses. Anything and everything is said and done to draw people into our organizations with little or no thought for either the faithfulness of our message or the motives of our converts—or our motives.

Yet despite our changes, Jesus hasn't changed. He is still "the same yesterday, and today, and forever" (Heb. 13:8), and His hard sayings still test us and thin our ranks.

Of the many millions today who profess Christ, comparatively few are willing to follow Him all the way. Most professing believers are interested primarily, and in some cases exclusively, in "bread"—the bodily or material benefits He bestows on us presently in this world. At first, they appear truly interested in Jesus and His wondrous words: "They who, when they hear, receive the word with joy" (Luke 8:13). And consciously, they *are* interested in Him and His teachings. But though Jesus knows them thoroughly, they don't know themselves. And when the initial excitement of meeting Jesus and experiencing His sweet, redeeming love and powerful ministry dies down, and they begin sitting under the teaching of His hard sayings and experiencing hard tests, one by one they fall away: "And in time of testing fall away" (v. 13). Like Jesus' original deserters, they stop believing, seeking, worshiping, and fellowshiping, and "go back, and walk no more with him."

Has something like this happened in your church? Has the influx of excited new converts slowed or stopped, and a quiet outflow of back-sliders begun? Are your multitudes fast becoming "minitudes"? Don't be troubled; your Master is at work: "It is I; be not afraid" (John 6:20). The teaching of His hard sayings and the visitation of hard trials are not indiscreet blunders by your leaders and their Lord. They are timely master strokes. Jesus is using them to examine, purge, and divide your "multitude." He's sorting His professing church to find His pure remnant. Paul taught that disruptive troubles and issues, even divisive heresies, must occasionally arise in churches, so that, by taking the right stands, approved disciples may distinguish themselves from disapproved deserters: "For there *must* be also heresies among you, that they who are approved may be made manifest" (1 Cor. 11:19); or, "It is necessary to have differences among you so that it may be clear which of you really have God's approval" (NCV). (See 1 John 2:19.) When this inevitable thin-ning process is over, only divinely called disciples will remain. Why? *The souls God adds don't go back!*

At the Last Supper, Jesus praised the eleven for their lasting loyalty. They had faithfully endured to the end: "Ye are they who have continued with me in my trials" (Luke 22:28). For this outstanding service He rewarded them richly, promising them authority, honor, and blessings in His future kingdom (vv. 29–30). But that wasn't all. In the near term

He promised, and only fifty days later delivered, the greatest reward of all—not free lunches, political power, or material prosperity, but the very treasure of heaven, the full richness of the Holy Spirit! They were the first to receive the *Paraklētos*, who then enabled them to enter into a close, deeply spiritual walk with Jesus, have authority to continue His teaching and healing ministries, and witness the greatest wonder on earth—an extended visitation of God among His people!

In the end, these true disciples were glad they had not gone back.

Summing up, we all recognize God's work when church attendance is on the rise. The Lord is surely present when many press into our places of worship. But this lesson shows us the other side: *He is also at work when many depart.* I would be remiss to not mention exceptions.

Jesus' hard sayings are not the only things that divide churches. When leaders practice sin, defend impenitent sinners, justify oppression, teach heresy, or generally practice anything else that quenches the flow of the Spirit and Word in an assembly, it's time for its faithful disciples to pray hard and respectfully exercise correction, "speaking the truth in love" (Eph. 4:15). If such godly correction is refused, yes, the disciples may need to prayerfully search for new leaders and flocks. In such cases, the Lord is still present, permitting the leadership's divisive sin or folly to test, identify, separate, and regather His overcomers, as mentioned above (1 Cor. 11:19). The immediate supernatural "driver" of the division is, of course, Satan, the thieving wolf or lion who seeks to divide and devour the flock. But he can do "nothing" unless it is "given him from above" (John 3:27). (See John 19:11; Job 1:11–12; 2:4–7.) Thus, whatever Satan devises, and with divine permission initiates, hoping to do evil, God turns, uses, and "causes" to "work together for good" (Rom. 8:28, NAS).

So when our churches are declining in membership, boiling in controversy, or being torn apart by differing beliefs, let's discern that the

Lord is present, thinning the ranks. And let's be content to fellowship with His faithful ones, whether they remain or depart, are reproached or praised, or are many or few. John 6 proves Christ would rather have a loyal microchurch than a megachurch filled with seekers of bread. And when the next revival breaks out, He'll reward us just as surely as He did the eleven. We'll be glad, then, we didn't go back.

And, our faith confirmed, we'll know God's judgments—decisions to bless or punish—are always just. And sure to occur.

Chapter Twenty-Five

SHALL HE FIND THIS BELIEF?

Nevertheless, when the Son of Man cometh, shall he find faith on the earth?

—LUKE 18:8

AMONG JESUS' MANY parables, one stands out from the rest. It is His story of a persistently praying widow and her long, hard quest to receive justice from a very indifferent and "unjust judge" (Luke 18:1–8).

More than an important lesson regarding importunate prayer, this parable is prophetic, revealing something about these last days. Christ alludes to the last days in verse 8: "*When the Son of Man cometh*, shall He find...?" Ever so subtly, yet surely, He implies that conditions similar to those described in the parable will exist "when the son of Man cometh," or when He appears to catch away His people. In their final hour on Earth, Jesus' true disciples—the bride church—though spiritually triumphant, will be rejected and opposed by sinners and backslidden and lukewarm Christians just as the widow was oppressed by her adversary. Like this holy but harried woman, Christ's bride church will seek the justice of deliverance from Him, the heavenly, and seemingly indifferent, Judge of all—and, at last, receive it!

With this in mind, let's examine this parable more closely.

THE PARABLE OF THE PERSISTENT
WIDOW AND THE UNJUST JUDGE

Let's better acquaint ourselves with this story by considering the key word, God's promise to deliver, the widow's persistence, Jesus' conclusion and promise, and His searching question.

The key word

Unquestionably the key word in this parable is *avenge*. It appears four times in this parable's brief eight verses:

> *Avenge* me of mine adversary.
>
> —LUKE 18:3

> I will *avenge* her.
>
> —LUKE 18:5

> And shall not God *avenge* his own elect...
>
> —LUKE 18:7

> He will *avenge* them.
>
> —LUKE 18:8

There are two closely related Greek words used in these four instances, *ekdikeo* and *ekdikesis*. Primarily their meaning is "to vindicate,"[1] or clear from false charges, and "to give justice,"[2] or render a fair verdict as opposed to an unfair one. Secondarily, but just as importantly, they also mean "to punish, to exact vengeance for a crime."[3] What does this tell us?

This language reveals that sometime before she began her persistent pleas for relief, this widow had been falsely accused and grievously wronged by an anonymous adversary. Her good name had been slandered, so she sought vindication; her rights had been violated, so she sought justice. Granting either of these requests would necessitate the punishment of her presumably impenitent adversary. Accordingly, the King James Version translators used the English word *avenge*, which "implies the infliction of deserved or just punishment for wrongs or oppressions."[4]

Such avenging is properly executed by a higher authority. So Jesus didn't describe this injured woman as a vengeful, violent vigilante on the loose but as a humble, probably poor and lawyer-less widow who, rather than take matters into her own hands, repeatedly asked her local higher authority, the judge, to avenge her: "She came unto him, saying, [You, sir, please] *Avenge* me" (Luke 18:3).

Being avenged, therefore, differs from taking revenge. Revenge is personal retaliation motivated by anger arising from the infliction of an unredressed wrong and executed by the wronged party. It seeks not the beauty and relief of justice but the sadistic satisfaction of seeing one's injurer injured. It is gratified, not by painful inequalities being put back into a peaceful balance, but by causing pain to those who have disturbed our peace. Hasty, it is unwilling to wait for due process. Unfair, it doesn't seek to know all the facts. Blind, it doesn't see that innocent people will also be hurt. Ignorant, it doesn't consider the self-regret that always follows impetuous revenge. Jesus, the Prince of Peace, is *not* advocating revenge in this parable. To the contrary, He taught us to "resist not evil" (Matt. 5:39) and inspired the apostolic orders "Recompense to no man evil for evil....Avenge not yourselves" (Rom. 12:17, 19).

Therefore, when hateful, deceived, or spiritually ignorant people oppose or persecute us to stop our faith, lifestyle, or ministry, we must learn to react as this widow—patiently and believingly crying to our Judge, Jesus,[5] to avenge us of our adversaries. We're asking Him to, in His time and way, turn our injustice into justice and vindicate us for His name's sake, which we bear. We're praying He will intervene and do whatever it takes to relieve the oppressive situation, to justly send whatever adversity or discipline is required to convict our adversary of sin and cause him (or her) to repent. Why? So we can be released from oppression to continue working ever more effectively for Him until His kingdom comes in many other lives as it has in ours.

God's promise to deliver

Though not stated in this parable, it is repeatedly said and shown throughout the Bible that, at some point, God must deliver His true servants from their oppressors if they are to serve Him freely and fruitfully in this world. In his Gospel, Luke says God promised this to Abraham's posterity, whom we are by faith: "*That he would grant unto us that we, being delivered out of the hand of our enemies, might serve him* without fear, in holiness and righteousness before him, all the days of our life" (Luke 1:74–75). The apostle Paul asked the Thessalonians to pray for him and his ministry team to receive such deliverances, as needed: "Brethren, pray for us, that the word of the Lord may have free course...that we may be *delivered from unreasonable and wicked men*" (2 Thess. 3:1–2). And in nearly every psalm David decried his enemies' unjust and oppressive actions, prayed for release, and expressed confidence that ultimately God would faithfully and fairly deliver him and other servants of God from all oppressors: "For he shall deliver the needy when he crieth; the poor also, and him that hath no helper" (Ps. 72:12).

The widow's persistence

Like David, Paul, and other believers, the widow in Christ's parable sought justice—but from an unjust judge who "feared not God, neither regarded man" (Luke 18:2). A law unto himself, and true to his name, this unjust justice refused to give the widow her due legal relief and vindication "for a while" (v. 4). He must have been a hardened old cuss to have denied the daily pleas of such a helpless plaintiff without feeling the slightest guilt. (In Jesus' day, widows, especially childless ones, were notoriously poor, neglected, and vulnerable.) Not only was the court's authority on his side, but also its precedents. His cool callousness implies he had dismissed many similarly needy plaintiffs who, when ignored, quietly gave up and walked away without making a fuss.

But not this widow. She persisted. Christ's description implies that every time the judge appeared at the city gates for judgment, she also appeared, fervently and shamelessly petitioning him for help. Finally her relentless insistence broke him down. One day he suddenly yielded and reversed his previous decision, not because of the rule of law, legal ethics, or love of his neighbor, but due to sheer personal irritation and exhaustion. Pure selfishness moved him to act: "Because this widow troubleth *me*, I will avenge her, lest...she weary *me*" (Luke 18:5). The wording of his opinion alone is sufficient evidence to convict him of judicial unfitness. What a pity there weren't judicial conduct boards in his time!

Jesus' conclusion—and promise

In summation, Jesus tells us to consider carefully what this unjust judge said and did: "*Hear* [ponder long and deeply] what the unjust judge saith" (v. 6). First, he finally gave the widow justice. Thus, though long frustrated, she ultimately received satisfaction. Second, the unjust judge responded only because of her persistence, her "continual coming" (v. 5). Thus the Lord teaches us that we too will ultimately receive the satisfaction of justice if we imitate this woman by steadily petitioning God in patient faith until, moved by our "continually coming," He responds.

Then He draws a sharp contrast between God and the unjust judge: "Hear...the unjust judge...*and shall not God* avenge?" (Luke 18:6–7). God is like the judge in the parable in only two points:

1. He is the higher authority whose intervention we seek.
2. He responds to persistent intercession.

In no other point is heaven's Judge like this parable's earthly judge. Consider their distinct differences.

The unjust judge is unfair. God is fair and His decisions perfectly just. The unjust judge is callous. God is compassionate, and His heart yearns to relieve all sufferers, especially His redeemed children, "his own elect" (v. 7). The unjust judge showed no respect for man's law. God honors and keeps His law, the covenant promises and warnings of His Word. The unjust judge was silent to the widow, offering no words of explanation or encouragement during her ordeal. God speaks to us throughout our tests by quickening timely Bible verses to strengthen our faith and hope every time we study His Word. The unjust judge refused to suffer anything unpleasant or burdensome: "lest…she *weary me*." God always suffers with His suffering people, "though he *bear [their sorrow] long with them*" (v. 7). So, Jesus reasons, how much more responsive will God be to our prayers than this judge was to the widow's petitions?

I would paraphrase His conclusion:

> *If even an unjust judge* will avenge his supplicants due to their persistence, shall not *God*, who is just and merciful, *God*, who has promised to deliver, *God*, who has always rescued His people of old, ultimately avenge you, even though He may severely test your faith and patience before doing so?
> —LUKE 18:6–7, AUTHOR'S PARAPHRASE

Or, to put it in Abraham's words, "Shall not the Judge of all the earth do right?" (Gen. 18:25). After drawing His conclusion, Jesus gave us a very precious promise.

Our Promiser spoke not hesitantly but assertively: "I tell [declare, promise] you…" (Luke 18:8). And what He promised was not cloudy but clear—clear as the noonday sun: "*He will avenge* [vindicate, give justice to] them [his elect] speedily" (v. 8). Thus spoken, Jesus' sacred pledge is on the record. Consequently we may be absolutely confident that, sooner or later, Christ, the *just* Judge of all, will give every persistently praying, believing member of His elect body the satisfaction of justice and vindication in every situation in which they have been wronged, maligned, or oppressed. And, He adds, He'll do so "speedily" (v. 8).

Here one question naturally arises: How can the Lord both "bear long with" us as we suffer injustice, pray, and await His help, and also come "speedily," which, in the Greek means, with "swiftness, speed, fleetness, or velocity"?[6] The answer is simple. Like earthly judges, God has an appointed time, place, and manner of executing His sentences. Until that time comes, He suffers long with us as we, like the widow, come continually to Him in believing prayer. But when His time arrives, our Judge, who has long seemed asleep, will awake and move with startling speed. The psalmist Asaph wrote, "Then the Lord awoke as if from sleep...[and] He drove His adversaries backward" (Ps. 78:65–66, NAS). So in the time of testing He bears long, but in the time of judgment He comes speedily.

Jesus' searching question

Arguably the most important statement in this parable is its last. After stating His conclusion, Jesus asked this searching question: "Nevertheless, when the Son of man cometh, *shall he find faith on the earth?* (Luke 18:8). By faith He does not mean our general belief in God—that God exists, the Bible is true, God created the heavens and earth, Jesus is God's Son, etc. Rather He means the faith under consideration in the context, namely, *confidence in the eventual unerring justice of God.* The thought is, "But when I come again to catch away My people, will this belief that God avenges His own elect still be present?" Will Christians still believe that God is not only their Advocate but also their Avenger? Will they still believe He overthrows oppressors to deliver the oppressed, not only in international and national but also in individual conflicts? Will they look to Him confidently for vindication in their personal conflicts? Will they continue to pray and wait for His righteous intervention even after long periods in which He seems indifferent toward them? Or will they believe the lie that God is unjust, unconcerned, and unreliable and, offended, walk away from Him?

Twenty centuries later, Jesus is still searching our hearts for the answer to this question: "Will *this belief* still exist in the days just prior to My appearing?" Or, "When the Son of man cometh," will that generation of Christians be so saturated with lukewarm morality, unbalanced teaching, unbiblical thinking, ignorance of God's character, and doubt in the warnings of His Word that they no longer believe God judges as surely as He saves?

It's a timely question, because that generation is ours.

OUR GENERATION'S "LAODICEANISM"

I wish I could confidently report that our generation is filled with Christians who are spiritually mature, clear-sighted, and blessed with a deep, full knowledge of the Bible and an intimate walk with its Author. But what Jesus foresaw, and what we can now see, won't let me.

Jesus' messages to the seven churches of Asia (Rev. 2–3) are not only historic but also prophetic. They foretell seven successive periods in the Church Age. His last message, addressed to the Laodicean Christians, is an inspired preview of the last period in the Church Age (Rev. 3:14–22). I am convinced we are living in this last period. That our generation of Christians, particularly current popular American Christianity, is indeed "Laodicean" in spirit and practice, is confirmed by our Lord and His language.

In His message to Laodicea, Jesus described not only the Laodiceans but also typical last-days Christians as: materialistically minded, self-deceived, publicly boastful but privately "miserable," spiritually "poor" yet complacent, "blind" in discernment, and "naked," or having their fleshly nature and sins exposed for all to see (v. 17). Most significantly, He says our generation is "lukewarm"—or given to spiritual and moral compromise instead of being faithfully committed to the absolute, timeless truths of God's Word. Alarmingly, He says this lukewarmness makes Him want to "spew" (Lit. "vomit,"[7] NKJV; or "spit," NIV, NLT) us out of His mouth (v. 16)—strong symbolism for rejecting us as unfit for His approval and use. What He foresaw then by the Spirit we can now see all around us in popular American Christianity, if we're humble and honest enough to acknowledge it. The Lord's language also confirms His words.

The word *Laodicean* is a combination of two Greek words: *laos,* which means common "people"; and *dicea,* which means "opinion." This suggests the fuller definition, "ruled by the opinion [or will of the majority] of the people."[8] This describes a *democratic society.*[9] For nearly 250 years, the American republic's democratic "experiment" has survived and grown. As its international influence has increased, particularly during the last half of the twentieth century, democracy has become more popular worldwide, especially in the West. Meanwhile, monarchies and other nondemocratic forms of government have been fading. Simultaneously, post–Revolutionary War American Christianity has gradually risen in international influence and is presently the most influential (though not necessarily best or purest) form of Protestant Christianity in the world. Before the American Revolution, there wasn't a Christian generation that was fully "Laodicean" or democratically ruled. Now there is. Could modern popular American Christianity be the epitome, the very fulfillment, of Jesus' preview of end time Christianity, especially the heavily materialistic, self-centered, morally compromised Christianity that has developed in the post–Second World War era?

Despite their deplorable condition, there was hope for the historic Laodiceans. Jesus offered intimate fellowship with Him, spiritual riches, insight, authority, and other blessings to "any man" (Rev. 3:20) who repented of his lukewarmness and built a close fellowship and overcoming walk with Him (vv. 18–22). Similarly, there is hope today for every Christian who recognizes his (or her) "Laodiceanism" and turns from it—and there will be many who do so, awaking to join the ranks of the emerging remnant (or bride) church focused on preparing for Jesus' appearing despite this unprepared, compromised generation (Matt. 25:5–6). To overcome our personal "Laodiceanism," we must first eliminate the Laodiceans', and our, most prominent fault: spiritual and moral lukewarmness. This results in part from an incomplete understanding of God's character.

Our Generation's Unbalanced Perspective

Generally, our generation suffers such an unbalanced view of God.[10] For decades we have been flooded with talk of God's love. The softer side of the divine nature has been overemphasized, while His firmness has been downplayed or ignored. Much of our teaching, testimony, and public conversation focus on God's grace, kindness, and tenderness, without giving equal discussion to His other essential attributes. This has created a false impression of God, an un-Christlike Christ, in our churches and surrounding societies—who depend on *us*, the "light of the world" (Matt. 5:14), to illuminate for them the true knowledge of God. This soft view of God has created an American Christianity and culture that's permeated with permissiveness. We have forgotten the four pillars of the divine character.

They are God's holiness, love, faithfulness, and righteousness. God is holy, or sinlessly pure. God is love, or full of goodwill and passionate mercy for all His creatures. God is faithful, or utterly reliable to do whatever He says and unfailing in all His responsibilities. And God is righteous, or always upright, fair, and without prejudice in all His decisions and actions. Is our view of Him complete?

Many Christians prefer a selective view of God. We pick the parts of His character we like and overlook the rest. His love and faithfulness are particularly endearing; His righteousness and holiness we can do without—or so we imagine. It's time we exchange our illusions of God for the reality of God and round out our perspective of the Eternal. As surely as "God is faithful" (1 Cor. 10:13), "the LORD is righteous" (Ps. 145:17). As surely as "God is love" (1 John 4:8), our "God is holy" (Ps. 99:9). While we tend to favor God's love over His holiness, Scripture indicates, if anything, a subtle tipping of the scales in the opposite direction.

Two mighty men of God, the prophet Isaiah and the apostle John, beheld God in all His resplendent glory. The lasting impression made on and duly recorded by both was not that of His love but of His holiness. They each testified that angelic beings stand by His throne and ceaselessly praise Him for His holiness: "*Holy, holy, holy* is the LORD of hosts" (Isa. 6:3; see also Revelation 4:8). This is not stated to undermine faith in God's love but to establish the fact that He is first of all holy and therefore uncompromisingly just in all His judgments against sin.

Thankfully, we don't have to choose between God's love and His holiness, or hold one above the other. Both are equally essential pillars of God's innermost being. Oswald Chambers taught, "God and love are synonymous.... Whatever God is, love is. If your conception of love does not agree with justice and judgment, purity and holiness, then your idea of love is wrong."[11] Today, our conception of God's love is unbalanced precisely as Chambers describes.

Sixty years ago you rarely found a Christian who didn't believe that God still executes righteous judgments in this world; now you rarely find one who does. We firmly believe He forgives, blesses, and prospers, yet we draw back when it's asserted that He also disciplines, opposes, and destroys. We're confident He forgives the penitent, but we're unsure He will punish the defiant. Yet His wrath is as dependable as His love and His justice as predictable as His forgiveness. Nahum's declaration is still accurate, and it's a prescription that will cure us: "The LORD...will not at all acquit the wicked" (Nahum 1:3). Why is this medicine necessary?

Many Christians are sick with offense at God over what they consider convicting evidence of His injustice. Jesus predicted this misjudgment of God would cause many to lose their faith in the end times: "Because iniquity shall abound, the love of many shall grow cold" (Matt. 24:12). This evidence is partly the injustice we or our loved ones encounter and partly the gross injustice we see in our society. Too often murderers go unpunished and their victims' rights ignored. Good men are ruined while the ungodly continue prospering. Hypocrites are praised while righteous men are maligned. Where is the God of justice in all this? It suggests God is not unlike but *like* the "unjust judge" of Jesus' parable! But He's not. As Jesus instructs us, He is just "bearing long" with the righteous until His appointed time of judgment—and hearing every cry for justice from every sufferer every day. He also turns and uses their evil sufferings for His good purposes.

For nonbelievers, injustice and adversity are His hand lovingly pressuring (though never forcing) them to call on Jesus so He can save them, not only from worldly injustices but also from their worst oppression—bondage to Satan, sin, and condemnation. If He didn't allow such injustices or adversities, we would never seek a Savior! For Christians, the prime fruit of the Spirit—faith, patience, meekness, self-control, love, peace, joy—are developed in us as our Judge bears long with us. The hotter and longer our trials, the larger and sweeter these fruits grow in our souls. Many of our hottest tests are heated by the reproach of man, and we must learn to take the heat.

"Fear not the reproach of men" (Isa. 51:7). Aware of our culture's deep permissiveness and many Christians' unbalanced perspective, some believers are afraid to confess their faith in a God of righteous judgment lest they be tagged as unloving, mean-spirited, hate-mongers, or demonized. But we must not fear ignorant reproach. The Master of love Himself, Jesus, the compassionate Savior who hung from the cross, declared emphatically that His Father and ours is utterly just and will one day avenge all His suffering servants: "And shall not God avenge his own elect?...*I tell you that he will avenge them speedily*" (Luke 18:7–8). If faith in God's eventual unerring justice is unloving, Jesus is unloving; if it is wrong, He is wrong.

THE APPLICATION OF THE PARABLE

Applying Luke 18:1–8 prophetically, the wronged widow is a type of the righteous remnant of overcoming Christians in these last days. Just as the widow suffered injustice and indignity for a season, so God will permit all true disciples to experience a measure of mistreatment and slander. As the widow prayed persistently, so must we. As she was denied for a while, so our pleas will seem rejected for a season. As she was at last avenged by the unjust judge, so we will be given just deliverance and vindication by Jesus when He appears to translate us to heaven. How? The Rapture will trigger the start of the seven-year tribulation, and our impenitent persecutors will be forced to endure that awesome hour of trouble while we escape (Luke 21:36). But note this.

While we bear long under injustice and pray for deliverance, God will do a deep work of purification and transformation in us. While at first we may find ourselves wanting our detractors to receive their due, as time passes, so will the venom of vengeance in us. As we daily forgive our enemies, forsake anger, refuse malice, pray for our enemies, and do good to them whenever possible, God's grace-implanted love will grow in us. In time we will become fully identified with His attitude toward our adversaries. As God is "not willing that any should perish, but that all should come to repentance" (2 Pet. 3:9), we also will increasingly desire and request not their punishment but their penance, praying earnestly for them to see the light and repent before it's too late. We won't be the only ones to learn these lessons.

The prophetic application of this parable is not limited to Christians in the last days of the Church Age.

It also applies to the Christ-worshiping Jewish remnant and their Gentile converts during the first half of the tribulation (Rev. 7). They too will be a kind of "widow" persecuted by their own adversaries as Israel's final revival, celebrating Jesus as their Messiah, sweeps first the Holy Land and later all nations (Zech. 8:20–23).

It will further apply to the hidden Jewish remnant of the latter half of the tribulation. These Christ-worshiping, Antichrist-rejecting Jews who remain on the earth (after the believing Jewish and Gentile remnant's mid-tribulation translation, Rev. 7:9, 14) will be yet another "widow" murderously harassed and demonically defamed by the worst adversary in history, the Antichrist. Like the widow of Christ's parable, they will "come continually" to Christ, the just Judge, requesting justice. And He will "bear long with them" in their various hiding places throughout the "wilderness" of this spiritually dry, fruitless world (Rev. 12:14–16) until He returns to dramatically avenge them at Armageddon (Rev. 19:11–16).

Ponder this prophetic application for inspiration, but never lose sight of its practical implications in your life today.

When you or your loved ones suffer injustice, don't fret or abandon your faith. God's temporary permission of injustice is not His approval of it. Ugly human injustice will ultimately pass and beautiful divine justice prevail. It must—our Lord has spoken! He will give you closure! Remember the four pillars of His character, and trust in the God of righteous judgment. And practice this parable. Come continually to your just and merciful Judge, Jesus, until speedily—with startling suddenness—He rises to deliver you from the people and forces that seek to destroy you, your faith, and your work. If you give God submission and trust now, He will not only bear long with you but also one day give you justice and vindication, "for them who honor me I will honor" (1 Sam. 2:30).

Here's the last word, straight from the just Judge:

Many are the afflictions of the righteous; but *the* Lord *delivereth him out of them all.*

—Psalms 34:19

NOTES

CHAPTER 1
THE ATTITUDE OF ACCEPTANCE

1. James Strong, *A Concise Dictionary of the Words in the Greek Testament and the Hebrew Bible* (Bellingham, WA: Logos Research Systems, Inc., 2009), s.v. "*ponēros.*"

CHAPTER 2
THE POWER TO ENDURE

1. George Mueller, *Answers to Prayer* (Chicago: Moody Publishers, 2007).
2. As quoted in Mrs. Charles E. Cowman, *Streams in the Desert* (Grand Rapids, MI: Zondervan Publishing, 1965).

CHAPTER 3
MADE STRONG THROUGH ADVERSITY

1. Oswald Chambers, *My Utmost for His Highest: Selections for the Year*, NIV ed. (Westwood, NJ: Barbour and Co., 1993).

CHAPTER 4
TEACHING AND TESTING

1. Jews and Samaritans had long contended over many doctrinal issues, including the proper place of worship. The Jews claimed Jerusalem, while the Samaritans insisted on Mount Gerizim.
2. Elijah successfully invoked fiery judgment on his adversaries only because his life was threatened (2 Kings 1:1–12). Here neither Jesus nor His disciples were threatened, but only insulted.
3. Oswald Chambers, *God's Workmanship* (Hants, UK: Marshall, Morgan and Scott, 1996).
4. Ibid.
5. A. W. Tozer, *The Root of the Righteous* (Camp Hill, PA: Christian Publications, 1955).
6. Dictionary.com, s.v. "graft," http://dictionary.reference.com/browse/grafted (accessed May 25, 2010).
7. Strong, *A Concise Dictionary of the Words in the Greek Testament and the Hebrew Bible*, s.v. "iniquity."
8. James Strong, *The Exhaustive Concordance of the Bible*, electronic ed. (Ontario: Woodside Bible Fellowship), s.v. "iniquity."
9. Strong, *A Concise Dictionary of the Words in the Greek Testament and the Hebrew Bible*, s.v. "*rachab.*"

10. R. L. Thomas, *New American Standard Hebrew-Aramaic and Greek Dictionaries, updated edition* (Anaheim, CA: Foundation Publications, Inc., 1998), s.v. "righteousness."

CHAPTER 5
ANOTHER CHANCE

1. W. A. Elwell and P. W. Comfort, *Tyndale Bible Dictionary* (Wheaton, IL: Tyndale House Publishers, 2001), s.v. "Tartessus."

2. The balance of the Book of Jonah shows that, because Jonah continued to yield to his unmerciful prejudices, he ultimately failed to please God and project His unbiased love to all nations. That said, his second call excellently models our second chances.

3. W. W. Wiersbe, *The Bible Exposition Commentary* (Wheaton, IL: Victor Books, 1996).

CHAPTER 6
GOD IS WATCHING

1. This is an approximation based on chronological information in *The Modern Language Bible, the New Berkeley Version in Modern English* (Grand Rapids, MI: Zondervan Bible Publishers, 1969).

2. A. C. Myers, *The Eerdmans Bible Dictionary* (Grand Rapids, MI: 1987), s.v. "Kiriath-sepher."

3. Thomas, *New American Standard Hebrew-Aramaic and Greek Dictionaries,* updated edition, s.v. "Kiriath-sepher."

4. P. J. Achtemeier, *Harper's Bible Dictionary*, 1st ed. (San Francisco: Harper & Row, 1985), s.v. "Kiriath-sepher."

5. J. F. Walvoord and R. B. Zuck, *The Bible Knowledge Commentary* (Wheaton, IL: Victor Books, 1983), s.v. "Cushan-rishathaim."

6. Myers, *The Eerdmans Bible Dictionary*, s.v. "Cushan-rishathaim."

7. S. Smith and J. Cornwall, *The Exhaustive Dictionary of Bible Names* (North Brunswick, NJ: Bridge-Logos, 1998), s.v. "Cushan-rishathaim."

CHAPTER 7
RISE ABOVE IT!

1. As discussed more fully in chapter 4, "Teaching and Testing."

2. Strong, *The Exhaustive Concordance of the Bible*, s.v. "overwhelmed."

3. The Greek here indicates that the "millstone" is not a small one, hand-turned by a woman, but rather the much larger (Greek) *mylos onikos*, meaning "millstone of [or pulled by] a donkey." —Strong, *A Concise Dictionary of the Words in the Greek Testament and the Hebrew Bible*, s.v. "millstone."

4. This is defined variously as "*little* (small in size), *short* or *younger* (of brief time), *unimportant* (low in status)." —J. Swanson, *Dictionary of Biblical Languages with Semantic Domains: Greek (New Testament)*, electronic ed. (Oak Harbor: Logos Research Systems, Inc., 1997), s.v. "*micros*."

CHAPTER 8
TAKE THE SERPENT BY THE TAIL

1. Some scholars believe this pharaoh to be Ramses II; others, Amenhotep II. — Elwell and Comfort, *Tyndale Bible Dictionary*, s.v. "Pharaoh."

2. J. A. MacMillan, *The Authority of the Intercessor* (Harrisburg, PA: Christian Publications, 1942).

3. "Satan" is derived from the Hebrew word *śāṭān*, the Greek word *Satanas*, and means basically "adversary." —D. R. W. Wood and I. H. Marshall, *New Bible Dictionary*, 3rd ed. (Downers Grove, IL: InterVarsity Press, 1996), s.v. "Satan."

4. Swanson, *Dictionary of Biblical Languages with Semantic Domains: Greek (New Testament)*.

5. The Greek word used for "thorn" is *skolops*, its only usage in the New Testament. *Skolops* means not only "thorn" but also "pointed stake." *The Theological Dictionary of the New Testament* (Abridged) states, "This rare term denotes a 'pointed stake,' such as is used in pits or palisades. Being fastened to such a stake is a form of execution; the reference is to crucifixion." —G. Kittel, G. Friedrich, and G. W. Bromiley, *Theological Dictionary of the New Testament* (Grand Rapids, MI: W. B. Eerdmans, 1995), s.v. "*skolops*."

6. In Galatians 4:12–15, Paul says that when he first preached to the Galatians, they responded graciously to his "trial…in my flesh" and would have "plucked out your own eyes, and…given them to me," if possible. The first time Paul visited Galatia, we have no record of him suffering sickness or eye problems. We do know he was stoned in Lystra (Acts 14:19), yet despite horrific injuries to head and body, he persisted in ministry in the Galatian cities of Lystra and Derbe (vv. 20–22). This we know was a "trial…in my flesh," since his eyes, face, head, and entire body would have been bruised, lacerated, and grotesquely swollen for weeks.

CHAPTER 10
GOD'S SANDING PROCESS

1. For more information about the High Point Market, see http://en.wikipedia.org/wiki/High_Point_Market (accessed 6/9/2010) or http://www.highpointmarket.org/.

2. In this context, Paul compares treasures of precious metal to more common earthly substances of wood and earth, stating that, comparatively speaking, the latter are typically reserved for less honorable uses. Yet both wooden and earthen material, when purified and artfully crafted into fine furniture and stoneware pottery, may also become "vessels to honor."

CHAPTER 11
MERCILESS CRITICISM

1. Satan, "the serpent," will release a similar "flood" of "waters" of reproach against the hidden remnant of believing Israel, or "the woman," in the Great Tribulation, hoping thereby to "sweep" her away (Rev. 12:15). But this flood also shall fail (v. 16).

2. This does not make God responsible for Shimei's harassment, only for using it for His higher purposes, once Shimei chose to pursue it.

3. "Evil" is here taken from the Hebrew *Ra*, meaning "adversity, affliction, bad, calamity, displeasure, distress." —Strong, *A Concise Dictionary of the Words in the Greek Testament and The Hebrew Bible*, s.v. *"Ra."*

CHAPTER 12
REFRESHING SPIRITUALITY

1. Swanson, *Dictionary of Biblical Languages with Semantic Domains: Hebrew (Old Testament)*, s.v. *"yatsa."*

2. Ibid.

3. Abigail had been David's wife for many years at this juncture, and it is very likely they had reflected on the whole Nabal affair and its spiritual lessons many times.

CHAPTER 13
WHEN RELIEF IS ON THE WAY

1. Wiersbe, *The Bible Exposition Commentary*.

2. Again, God's help was "sufficient" to supply all His children's basic needs. Meanwhile, Josephus says many (unconverted) Jews in Judea perished in the severe famine (A.D. 45) for lack of money to buy what little food was available. —Wiersbe, *The Bible Exposition Commentary*.

3. Popularized by the Nazis' rapid-attack method of warfare in the Second World War, "blitzkrieg" is German for *lightning war*. See www.dictionary.com.

4. From the first great persecution spurred by Stephen's murder in A.D. 35, to the present time, A.D. 44. —M. Galli and T. Olsen, (2000). *131 Christians Everyone Should Know* (Nashville, TN: Broadman & Holman Publishers, 2000). Also, *The Modern Language Bible, the New Berkeley Version in Modern English*.

5. The well-informed Bible student will also note that behind Satan's devious plan to spoil David's approaching "relief" was God's more basic and enduring plan of correction. Prompted by unbelief (1 Sam. 27:1), David had departed from God's will in moving to Philistia (vv. 2–6). So now, after David wasted sixteen months in God's permissive will (v. 7), God used Satan's plan and servants to destroy David's self-made, second-best "kingdom" to prompt his repentance and return to full faith in the God who promised him the kingdom of Israel (1 Sam. 30:6–8).

6. Though Psalm 118 cites no author, some scholars feel that this Hallel psalm's Messianic content, phraseology, and allusions to experiences like those David faced (vv. 5, 13, 18, 22–23), point to a likely Davidic authorship. —J. E. Smith, *The Wisdom Literature and Psalms* (Joplin, Mo: College Press Pub. Co., 1996).

7. Biblical examples of this abound, thus reflecting God's delight in those who, in deep trouble, worship confidently *before* His help arrives (1 Sam. 7:9–10; 2 Chron. 20:20–22; John 11:41–42; Acts 16:25–26).

8. Though James (the Just, or the Elder) was the Jerusalem church's president, Peter's shepherdship under Christ was nevertheless overarching. Thus we make the comparison to a senior pastor in modern churches.

9. "Afflicted" is a translation of the Greek *kakopatheō*, "to suffer distress, withstand trouble, endure hardship." —Swanson, *Dictionary of Biblical Languages with Semantic Domains: Greek (New Testament)*, s.v. "afflicted."

CHAPTER 14
"SANS BLESSINGS" SAINTS

1. Dictionary.com, s.v. "sans," http://dictionary.reference.com/browse/sans (accessed October 23, 2010).

2. The "hedge" Satan saw was a supernatural, impassable barrier of guardian angels (Ps. 91:10–12) standing wing to wing around Job and everything dear to him. The same "hedge" surrounds the righteous today and is passed through by the adversary only by direct divine permission for purposes of testing or chastening (Job 1:12; 2:6).

3. The only definite time given is that *following* Job's trial, 140 years (Job 42:16). We don't know how long the first assault lasted (chapter 1), or the second (chapter 2), or Job's lengthy debate with his three friends and Elihu (chapters 3–37). Some scholars conjecture that Job's trials lasted from nine to twelve months; it is evident that no one could endure the agony of a boil-covered body very long.

4. Steeped in Egyptian culture, shepherding would have been detestable to young Moses, because "every shepherd is an abomination to the Egyptians" (Gen. 46:34). The reason for this was twofold: before Joseph's time, Middle and Lower Egypt suffered oppression from a series of kings who were of the *Hyksos*, a tribe of nomadic shepherds; also, the highly cultured Egyptians looked down on the comparatively lawless and uncivilized ways of such nomadic peoples. See J. M. Freeman and H. J. Chadwick, *Manners and Customs of the Bible*, rev. ed. (North Brunswick, NJ: Bridge-Logos Publishers, 1998).

5. Moses' meek silence before his friends-turned-critics, complete dependence on divine justice, and quickness to pray mercy for his offenders are a study in contrasts (Num. 12:1–13, esp. v. 3).

6. The meticulous Bible student will note that Job's complaining (Job 3:1) preceded, and in a sense prompted, his colossal debate with his critics (Job 4:1–31:40). Thus complaining, not self-defense, was the initial breach in Job's wall of spiritual strength. This warns us not to complain when we suffer and calls us to instead offer thanks and praise to God (Acts 16:23–25; 1 Thess. 5:18).

7. While it's not expressly declared, the reference to Job's 140-year extension of life (Job 42:16) implies he resumed his wide and effective ministry (4:3–4); it's unthinkable that God would make His best minister better and then not use him!

8. Why "with persecutions"? First, because those who refuse to sell out for Christ's sake envy and persecute those who do, wanting their reward without their resolve. Second, God wisely uses this to counterbalance the elation of great blessing and keep us sober-minded (2 Cor. 12:7). In every season of our lives, God's plan includes a measure of rejection to keep us close to and relying on Him.

CHAPTER 15
WHERE TO TURN WHEN OTHERS TURN AWAY

1. Saul stood a full head above the average Israelite (1 Sam. 10:23).

2. Some credit Holocaust survivor Corrie ten Boom with this inspirational quip.

CHAPTER 16
TROUBLE IN THE CENTER OF HIS WILL

1. See chapter 8, note #1.

2. As alluded to in Acts 16:37–38, Paul and Silas were Roman citizens and, as such, were never to be punished without a hearing or under any conditions flogged (scourged).

3. Jesus called Satan "the prince of this world" three times (John 12:31; 14:30; 16:11), and Paul called Satan's demonic agents "the rulers of the darkness of this world" (Eph. 6:12); hence, the term "prince of darkness."

4. Besides "light" and "darkness" symbolizing *truth* and *falsehood* regarding God, they also represent *righteousness* and *sin*, respectively (1 John 1:5–7).

5. Light-bearers are Word-loving, Word-living, and Word-ministering disciples of Christ. For Jesus' original and still authoritative instructions to light-bearers in a sin-darkened world, study Matthew 10, especially verses 16–42. The nature of our life and ministry struggles today parallels the experience of the twelve original light-bearers.

6. That "Lot sat in the gate of Sodom" (Gen. 19:1) reveals he held an undisclosed position of authority among the local rulers. Compare Ruth 4:1–2.

7. While zealous Christians may feel and claim Lot was not saved, God's Word undeniably says he was accounted "just" and "righteous" (2 Pet. 2:7–8) and so symbolizes not an unredeemed sinner but an uncommitted Christian.

CHAPTER 17
VICTORY THE HARD WAY

1. That both of these sad chapters describing the prevalence of unchecked, publicly aggressive homosexual rapists bear the same number is significant. God wants us to recognize the similarities. Note in both cases that when sin became this "full," particularly public acquiescence to homosexuality, extinctive judgments soon followed. Ever hopeful of repentance, God is often patient with gross sin but never permissive; ultimately, He will judge it. (See 2 Peter 3:9–10.)

2. Whether due to tribal pride or sympathy with immorality, nevertheless, the Benjamites sinned and deceived themselves by justifying and militarily defending the depraved, criminal, and impenitent sinners of Gibeah (Judg. 20:12–14).

3. See chapter 14, "Sans Blessings Saints."

4. In early Christian history, the term *confessor* was used of a believer who continued to faithfully confess Christ, not the Roman emperor, as their Lord, despite suffering persecution and torture, though not death.

CHAPTER 18
THE PRICE OF FRUITFULNESS

1. The Salvation Army is one of the oldest and finest charitable "branches" on the "mustard tree" of the church. Another outstanding example, more recently founded, is World Challenge, Inc. (David Wilkerson Ministries) and their many compassion minis-

tries in New York, America, and abroad. See http://www.worldchallenge.org/en/missions (accessed July 17, 2010).

2. Walvoord and Zuck, *The Bible Knowledge Commentary*.

3. Hellenists were Greek-speaking Gentiles (or Jews) who lived by the customs and beliefs of Greek culture.

4. This was a league of *ten cities* (Deca-polis) in northeast Galilee, east of the Jordan river, unified by a common Hellenistic culture, coinage, and military. —Wiersbe, *The Bible Exposition Commentary*.

5. C. S. Keener, *The IVP Bible Background Commentary: New Testament* (Downers Grove, IL: InterVarsity Press, 1993).

Chapter 19
We Must Be Courageous

1. *Webster's New World College Dictionary*, fourth edition (Cleveland, OH: Wiley Publishing, 2005), s.v. "courage."

2. We derive this from cowardice's brief definition, "lack of courage." Cowardice is also "shamefully excessive fear of danger, difficulty, or suffering." —*Webster's New World College Dictionary*, s.v. "cowardice."

3. When the Civil War broke out in April 1861, Grant tried to obtain a commission in the U.S. Army, but his request was ignored. A few months later, to get into the action, he accepted a commission with the Illinois Volunteers. Dogged by his past reputation as a heavy drinker, Grant was not commissioned as an officer in the regular U.S. Army until March 1864.

4. Thomas B. Allen, *The Blue and The Gray* (Washington DC: National Geographic Society, 1992).

5. Grant received this distinguished rank, by the authorization of Congress and the appointment of President Andrew Johnson, on July 25, 1866.

6. More than a personal genocidal rage, Haman's monstrous decree of death to all Jews was Satan's veiled attempt to thwart salvation itself. Jesus could not come of the tribe of Judah and live righteously under the law as the perfect sacrifice for sin, as prophesied, if the Jewish people were exterminated five centuries before the "fullness of time" (Gal. 4:4).

7. Strong, *A Concise Dictionary of the Words in the Greek Testament and the Hebrew Bible*, s.v. "*nepilim*."

8. Walvoord and Zuck, *The Bible Knowledge Commentary*.

9. Kittel, Friedrich, and Bromiley, *Theological Dictionary of the New Testament*, s.v. "*endynamoō*."

Chapter 20
God Empowers Those Who Take a Stand

1. Or so the Greek says, "taking refuge," not slowly but "with real haste." — Swanson, *Dictionary of Biblical Languages With Semantic Domains: Greek (New Testament)*, s.v. "fled."

2. Ibid.

3. Though scholars debate the precise chronology of the Assyrian invasions of Palestine during Hezekiah's rule, it appears Hezekiah paid tribute to Sennacherib on one occasion (2 Kings 18:13–16), but not during this second invasion (2 Kings 18:17–19:7; also 2 Chronicles 32:1–15, 30).

4. Second Kings 18:5 states Hezekiah "trusted in the LORD God of Israel; so that after him was none like him [in depth of trust] among all the kings of Judah."

5. "Knowing the necessity of an adequate water supply for a city under siege, Hezekiah had a 1,777-foot (542-meter) tunnel cut through solid rock from the spring of Gihon to the Siloam Pool to bring water into the city and to prevent the Assyrians from gaining access to the spring water outside the city (2 Kgs 20:20; 2 Chr 32:3–4)." —Elwell and Comfort, *Tyndale Bible Dictionary*.

6. For more on this, see chapter 10, "God's Sanding Process," and chapter 12, "Refreshing Spirituality."

7. Oswald Chambers, *Our Brilliant Heritage* (London: Marshall, Morgan, and Scott, 1965).

CHAPTER 21
WHEN THE CLASH COMES

1. Strong, *A Concise Dictionary of the Words in the Greek Testament and the Hebrew Bible*, s.v. "*miseō*."

2. Walvoord and Zuck, *The Bible Knowledge Commentary*.

3. Wiersbe, *The Bible Exposition Commentary*.

4. Charles C. Ryrie, *The Ryrie Study Bible* (Chicago, IL: Moody Press, 1978).

5. *The Modern Language Bible, the New Berkeley Version in Modern English*.

6. The late Walter Beuttler was an exceptionally insightful Assemblies of God instructor for many years at Eastern Bible Institute, Green Lane, Pennsylvania, who, beginning in the mid-twentieth century, also traveled extensively, teaching in many countries.

CHAPTER 22
A MATRIMONIAL MESSAGE

1. Moses' father-in-law, Jethro, is also called Reuel (Exod. 2:18; 3:1).

2. Scripture does not state that Moses became ill, but rabbinic tradition holds this was the manner in which "The LORD...sought to kill him" (Exod. 4:26), unless he complied with God's command to circumcise his second son.

3. That he had apparently circumcised his first son, Gershom, but not his second indicates that Moses' zeal, once hot, had cooled during the latter years of his long waiting period. After forty years of apparent divine indifference, Moses became indifferent, failing to circumcise Eliezer. His dispirited faith and Zipporah's spirited opposition to the rite combined to cause this sin.

4. Smith and Cornwall, *The Exhaustive Dictionary of Bible Names*, s.v. "Zipporah."

5. Only twice in *forty years* of such constant trials did Moses lose his patience with the petulant Israelites (Exod. 32:19–20; Num. 20:10–11)!

6. F. B. Meyer, *Through the Bible Day by Day* (no further publishing information available).

CHAPTER 23
HE WOUNDS AND HE HEALS

1. So the Greek indicates. The word translated "sword" is *rhomphaia*, meaning "a large, broad sword" used in war. —R. L. Thomas, (1998). *New American Standard Hebrew-Aramaic and Greek Dictionaries*, updated edition (Anaheim: Foundation Publications, Inc., 1998), s.v. "sword."

2. His supposed father, Joseph, is last mentioned actively in the account of Jesus' visit to Jerusalem at age twelve (Luke 2:48). The subsequent repeated references to His "mother" alone (Mark 3:31–35; John 19:25–26; Acts 1:14) imply that Joseph, who was much older than Mary, passed sometime between Jesus' twelfth and thirtieth years.

3. Dictionary.com, s.v. "empathy," http://dictionary.reference.com/browse/empathy (accessed October 24, 2010).

4. Myers, *The Eerdmans Bible Dictionary.*

5. When even the learned and respected Nicodemus tried to defend Jesus before his Pharisaic peers, they put him down rapidly and rudely (John 7:50–52).

6. Jesus' half-brothers became leading ministers in the early church. James, to whom Christ personally appeared after His resurrection (1 Cor. 15:7), presided over the Jerusalem church and its councils and wrote the epistle bearing his name (James 1:1); Jude was also a church leader (1 Cor. 9:5) and the inspired writer of the Book of Jude.

7. For instance, information such as the extraordinary circumstances of Jesus' birth (Luke 1:26–56; 2:8–20), dedication (Luke 2:21–38), visit to the temple at age twelve (Luke 2:41–50), and so forth.

CHAPTER 24
THINNING THE RANKS

1. Swanson, *Dictionary of Biblical Languages With Semantic Domains: Greek (New Testament)*, s.v. "disciples."

2. The Romans later continued this literal take on Jesus' figurative description of the Lord's Supper and stirred persecution against early Christians by accusing them of cannibalizing their Founder. Keener, *The IVP Bible Background Commentary.*

3. Only men were included in the biblical count of five thousand. So the real sum, including women and children, was probably closer to fifteen thousand to twenty thousand. —Keener, *The IVP Bible Background Commentary: New Testament.*

4. It would have been, had the Jewish leaders accepted Jesus. But because they had already rejected Him, the kingdom was deferred.

5. Judas was an exception. Jesus did invest His full teaching and counsel in Judas' life, but only because he was necessary to the divine plan.

CHAPTER 25
SHALL HE FIND THIS BELIEF?

1. Strong, *A Concise Dictionary of the Words in the Greek Testament and the Hebrew Bible*, s.v. "ekdikeo."

2. Swanson, *Dictionary of Biblical Languages with Semantic Domains: Greek (New Testament)*, s.v. "ekdikesis."

3. H. Liddell, *A Lexicon: Abridged From Liddell and Scott's Greek-English Lexicon* (Oak Harbor, WA: Logos Research Systems, Inc., 1996).

4. *Webster's New World College Dictionary*, s.v. "avenge."

5. The New Testament emphatically and repeatedly reveals that God the Father has committed all judgment to Jesus. Thus Jesus' Judgeship is as valid as His Saviorship and Lordship. See John 5:22; Acts 10:42; Romans 14:10–12; 2 Thessalonians 1:7–8; 2 Timothy 4:1; James 5:8; Revelation 19:11.

6. Liddell, *A Lexicon: Abridged From Liddell and Scott's Greek-English Lexicon*, s.v. "*tachos.*"

7. Strong, *A Concise Dictionary of the Words in the Greek Testament and the Hebrew Bible*, s.v. "spew."

8. Smith and Cornwall, *The Exhaustive Dictionary of Bible Names*, s.v. "Laodicean."

9. Laodicea had in the past (ca. 133 B.C.) enjoyed the status of a Roman free city. Free cities enjoyed local autonomy and could elect their magistrates, make their own laws, and mint their own coins, all subject to imperial approval.

10. I'm speaking here of the *popular* Christian viewpoint, not the more full-orbed knowledge of God held by serious seekers of God and devoted theologians worldwide. While the latter know God's character more fully, the prevailing popular view of Him is incomplete and distorted.

11. Oswald Chambers, Oswald (1968). *Run Today's Race*. Fort Washington, PA: Christian Literature Crusade, 1968).

CONTACT THE AUTHOR

GREG HINNANT MINISTRIES
P.O. BOX 788
HIGH POINT, NC 27262

TEL. (336) 882-1645
EMAIL: RGHMINISTRIES@AOL.COM
WEB SITE: WWW.GREGHINNANTMINISTRIES.ORG

OTHER BOOKS BY THIS AUTHOR

Walking in His Ways
978-0-88419-758-4

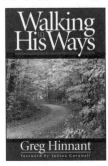

Walking on Water
978-0-88419-875-8

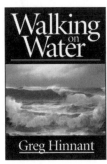

Precious Pearls From the Proverbs
978-1-59185-900-0

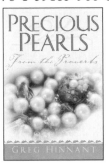

*Word Portraits: Five Illustrations
of the Mature Christian*
978-1-59979-087-9

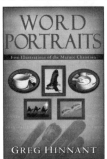

*DanielNotes: An
Inspirational Commentary
on the Book of Daniel*
978-1-59185-169-1

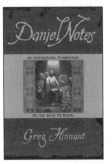

*Gold Tried in the Fire:
Tested Truths for
Trying Times*
978-1-59979-364-1

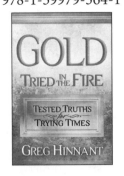

*Key New Testament
Passages on Divorce
and Remarriage*
978-1-931527-49-1

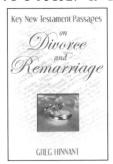